D0897924

WATCH OFFICER'S GUIDE

Twelfth Edition

WATCH OFFICER'S GUIDE

A Handbook for All Deck Watch Officers

Revised by Commander David M. Lee, USN
Lieutenant John M. Brown, USN
Lieutenant Robert Morabito, USN
Lieutenant H. Scott Colenda, USN

NAVAL INSTITUTE PRESS • ANNAPOLIS, MARYLAND

by the United States Naval Institute, Annapolis, Maryland

First edition published in 1911

Twelfth edition published in 1987

Library of Congress Cataloging-in-Publication Data
Watch officer's guide.
  Bibliography: p.
  Includes index.
  1. United States. Navy—Watch duty. 2. United States. Navy—Officers'
handbooks.   I. Lee, David M. (David Michael), 1946–
V133.W37.   1986   359   86-23685
ISBN 0-87021-757-7

Printed in the United States of America

10 9 8 7 6 5 4 3

CONTENTS

Preface   vii

1. Introduction   3
2. The Watch in General   13
3. The Ship's Deck Log   26
4. Communications   48
5. The Watch Underway   66
6. Shiphandling   97
7. Safe Navigation   121
8. Standard Commands   132
9. The Watch Officer in Port   146
10. Safety   172
11. Boats and Vehicles   204
12. Honors and Ceremonies   213
13. Flags, Pennants, and Boat Hails   223

Appendixes
A. Sample Orders   241
B. Beaufort Scale   253
C. Material Conditions of Readiness   255
D. Typical Time Schedule for Getting Underway   257
E. Typical Time Schedule for Entering Port   261

Suggested Reading and References   265
Index   267

PREFACE

"This volume is the result of an endeavor to collect and put into a compact form those details pertaining to deck duty which will be found necessary or convenient to an officer carrying on a watch." This sentence is from the preface to the *Watch Officer's Manual*, by Ensign Charles Emerson Hovey, U.S. Navy, published in January 1911.

In September 1911 Ensign Hovey was killed while leading a landing party against outlaw Moros in the Philippines. He was cited for conspicuous gallantry in action, and in 1919 the destroyer *Hovey* (DD–208) was named in his honor. That old four-piper has gone now, sunk by the Japanese in Lingayen Gulf in 1945, but this volume, which is governed by the objectives set forth by Ensign Hovey, is a lasting memorial to a promising young officer.

Hovey's manual was the first of its kind in the U.S. Navy, although there had long been such guides in the Royal Navy. The second edition, revised and enlarged by Lieutenant Solomon Endel, U.S. Navy, and published in 1917 by the U.S. Naval Institute, was the last to carry Hovey's name. Shortly after World War I the Institute acquired all rights to the book and in 1930, when the extensively revised third edition was produced by Commander W. S. Farber, U.S. Navy, changed its name to *Watch Officer's Guide*. This change was made in order to avoid confusion with manuals published by the navy department.

The purpose of this revision, the twelfth edition, is to provide in a single text a compendium of information that the watch officer must have at his or her fingertips, along with some proven advice on how the job can best be done. A list has been provided of publications that the watch officer must be familiar with. Since a Rules of the Road section could easily become out of date because of rule changes before the next revision of this text is published, such a section is not included in this revision. There can be no substitute for complete knowledge of the rules now in effect. Many changes to doctrine and procedure, as they affect a watch officer today, have been incorporated. This revision has been the work of Commander David M. Lee, U.S. Navy; Lieutenant J. Michael Brown, U.S. Navy; Lieutenant H. Scott Colenda, U.S. Navy; and Lieutenant Robert E. Morabito, U.S. Navy. It is their hope that each copy will become well worn, stained, and dog-eared in serving as a valuable guide to watch officers at sea.

WATCH OFFICER'S GUIDE

1 | INTRODUCTION

An officer in charge of a watch shall be responsible for the proper performance of all duties preşcribed for his watch, and all persons on watch under him shall be subject to his orders.

OpNavInst 3120.32.

The officer of the deck

The officer of the deck (OOD) in a naval ship occupies a unique position. Nowhere in military or civilian life is there a parallel to the range and degree of responsibility that is placed in the hands of the OOD. As direct representative of the captain, he acts with all the authority of command and, next to the captain and the executive officer, is the most important person in the ship. Modern technology has given him sophisticated tools but, at the same time, has added to the scope of his traditional duties and responsibilities. Qualification as officer of the deck is the cornerstone of professional growth for a surface line officer and the most critical milestone of the surface-warfare qualification.

A junior officer must devote every moment he can spare to learning the skills that will enable him to qualify as an officer of the deck and, while he is doing so, he must expect to be closely and critically observed. His mistakes will be corrected on the spot because, in the fast-paced atmosphere of modern fleet operations, there often is no time for lengthy critiques and explanations. As demanding as this learning process may be, its rewards are superbly satisfying. There is no feeling quite like that of standing watch for the first time as a fully qualified officer of the deck underway, knowing that you are in control of the ship. Be that ship a fleet tug or an aircraft carrier, the trust given to the OOD carries with it a time-honored and unique distinction.

Responsibility and authority

The duties, responsibilities, and authority of the officer of the deck are delineated in OpNavInst 3120.32. Standard Organization and Regulations of the U.S. Navy. These regulations have legal status under *Title 10 of the U.S. Code.* They prescribe minimum duties and responsibilities. Factors such as the special mission of a ship, command policy, and guidance for a particular situation, may add to these duties and responsibilities, but may not reduce them. Even more important than the letter of the regulations is the unwritten but traditional requirement that an officer of the deck apply good judgment, intelligence, and initiative to his duties, and exercise fully his authority. This can be difficult. Given the diverse and often complex activities that take place aboard a ship at sea, it is easy for a watch officer unwittingly to allow his authority to be delegated to a subordinate, particularly where specialized operations are concerned. There is nothing wrong with delegating authority, but the OOD must clearly understand that, regardless of how he chooses to carry out his duties, the responsibility for their being carried out is always his. It is good practice, for example, to allow the quartermaster or the junior officer of the deck to take and plot navigational fixes. This does not, however, relieve the OOD of his responsibility for the safe navigation of the ship. "Experts" who perform some of the many tasks required on a watch are always assistants but never surrogates.

Accountability

On the sea there is a tradition older even than the traditions of the country itself and wiser in its age. . . . It is the tradition that with responsibility goes authority and with them both goes accountability.

"Hobson's Choice," *The Wall Street Journal,* 14 May 1952.

Accountability is a very subtle thing that does not even exist in many areas of human endeavor and is often misunderstood. A naval officer is accountable for the outcome of his duties, good or bad. When he accepts designation as officer of the deck, he automatically accepts accountability for everything entrusted to him. Just as the commanding officer is inescapably accountable to his superior for everything that happens aboard his ship, so is the OOD accountable to the commanding officer for everything that happens during his watch. The only exceptions to this accountability are those laid down by law or regulation. As the captain's direct representative, the OOD is the only person on board who can make decisions that affect the safety of the ship and the lives of her people. The captain cannot be on the bridge at all times and, as history has repeatedly demonstrated, the OOD sometimes has to take actions on his own that determine whether he and his shipmates live or die. Accountability is one of the reasons why the officer of the deck holds a unique position. No OOD should ever forget that.

Priorities

There is nothing that indicates which of the watch officer's duties are most important, for the simple reason that they are all equally important. It is necessary, however, to establish priorities, because the OOD can expect to be constantly confronted with the need to decide without delay where he should focus his attention. Training his watch, for example, is always important, yet there will be times when he must forego training in order to carry out other duties. The safety of the ship and fulfillment of her mission always come first and must never be neglected. On the other hand, there will be times when the ship's activities allow the officer of the deck to delegate many of his responsibilities and to become, for a while, a teacher and observer. At such times, allowing the junior officer of the deck to run the watch ought to be a standard procedure for all watch officers. Not only does this procedure give the junior officer self-confidence, but it gives the OOD a chance to step back and observe from a detached position just how well he has done his own job.

Although, theoretically, the officer of the deck is responsible for all the things that go on during his watch, he obviously cannot exercise personal control over them all. If he attempted to do so, he would find himself hopelessly enmeshed in detail, and his attention would probably be drawn away from those aspects of the ship's operation over which he *must* have control.

Making a distinction between what is of direct concern and what is not requires a well-developed sense of judgment, and acquiring that sense is a vital part of a watch officer's training. The OOD should not become involved, for example, in how a petty officer on the fo'c'sle assigns a paint-chipping job to his men. However, if he sees one of those men using a power tool without regard for safety precautions, he must become involved to the extent of ensuring that the situation is corrected immediately. Taking this sort of action can cause conflict. A department head or a senior officer may want to take an action that is in itself proper but will interfere with more important tactical operations being controlled by the watch. Here again, the duty of the OOD is to keep his priorities straight, even if it means referring the matter to the executive officer or the captain for resolution.

Command relationships

The officer of the deck reports directly to the commanding officer for the safe navigation and general operation of the ship; to the executive officer (and command duty officer if appointed) for carrying out the ship's routine; and to the navigator for sightings of navigation landmarks, and for course/speed changes. He may request advice and assistance in the discharge of his duties from any person assigned to the ship for duty.

OpNavInst 3120.32.

The officer of the deck's command relationship with the commanding officer of the ship is clear and fixed. His other command relationships are equally important, but are much less clearly defined. Although the regulations imply that the executive officer has authority over the OOD only on matters pertaining to the ship's routine, in most ships the executive officer is empowered to correct or modify any action taken by the watch officer that he considers to be incorrect. Since the extent of the executive officer's authority is a matter of individual command policy, the OOD must be familiar with the ship's regulations and with standing orders and directives that deal with this subject. The executive officer is second only to the captain as the most senior and experienced surface warfare officer on board. Therefore, his advice and authority should be carefully weighed by the OOD. In addition, the OOD has a responsibility to the executive officer for the complete and accurate execution of the ship's routine. The OOD must keep the executive officer informed of potential changes that may affect the ship's routine, just as he must keep the commanding officer informed of potential changes that may affect the operational picture.

The relationship between the OOD and the engineering officer of the watch (EOOW) must be clearly understood by both officers. All regulations are very specific in stating that the EOOW reports to the OOD. However, each captain must outline in writing his policy regarding any automatic actions by the EOOW. For example, it may be a captain's policy that in the event of an engineering casualty, the EOOW is to take automatically whatever action is required and to keep the OOD informed of the status of the propulsion plant. Another captain may require that the EOOW get the permission of the OOD before altering any propulsion plant condition, regardless of the casualty. Another possibility would be a policy directing automatic actions by the EOOW except under certain conditions when the permission of the OOD is required. The OOD and EOOW must each have a clear understanding of the policy of the captain. It is a good idea for the OOD, upon relieving the watch, to review with the EOOW the ship's policy regarding automatic actions by the EOOW.

In the rapidly changing world of modern warfare, a ship must be capable of the quickest possible reaction to a threat. Often there is not sufficient time to move from a normal underway condition to general quarters with weapons systems ready. In order that weapons-system readiness may be maintained for a long time, the tactical action officer (TAO) concept has evolved. The TAO is a watch officer who not only is a qualified OOD, but also knows weapons systems capabilities as well as potential enemy threat and capabilities. The TAO normally stands his watch in the combat information center (CIC) and has the authority to release the ship's weapons systems.

The relationship between the OOD and the TAO is especially important, because it involves a significant exception to the concept that the OOD is the final decision-maker during his watch. Tactical control of the ship, particularly in the areas of threat-analysis and reaction, belongs to the TAO in the CIC. This officer is normally a department head, and is often senior in rank and experience to the OOD. Because he stands his watch in CIC, he has direct access to sensor information and weapons control and has at his disposal the means to evaluate enemy threats quickly and take immediate action against them. *OpNavInst* 3120.32 and the ship's tactical doctrine may authorize him to direct the OOD in the tactical handling of the ship and, depending on the circumstances and condition of readiness, to fire weapons without permission from the OOD. Even when a TAO watch is set, however, the OOD remains responsible for the safety of the ship. If, in his judgment, a course of action directed by the tactical action officer would put the ship in immediate danger, he may decline to follow it, but he must immediately inform the commanding officer of the situation. Assignment of decision-making responsibilities must be clearly understood by both watch officers at all times. In the fast-paced environment of modern systems, there is not likely to be time to discuss a decision or to debate who should make it.

Specifically, control of the ship may be shifted, by positive command, to the TAO in CIC or, in some cases, to other watch station officers; but the safety of the ship remains the responsibility of the OOD.

A TAO is stationed when the threat requires the ability to react fast or the tactical situation dictates that the ship be capable of assessing and reacting to a rapidly changing environment. The OOD must know the source of the TAO's authority and understand his relationship to the TAO.

The OOD has a unique relationship with the navigator. While on watch the OOD is responsible for the safe navigation of the ship. This is a dual responsibility, shared with the navigator, who is at all times responsible for the safe navigation of the ship. It is quite clear, therefore, that the OOD must understand the navigation plan, the intended track, potential dangers to navigation, and the quality of fix available. The navigator may be authorized by the captain to relieve the OOD if in his judgment the OOD is endangering the ship from a navigation standpoint. Such a policy will be in writing and would only be executed in very rare situations.

Normally, the quartermaster of the watch (QMOW) maintains the navigation picture for the OOD and is the navigator's representative while the navigator is away from the bridge.

Many large ships are organized to provide for the assignment of a command duty officer (CDO) at sea. He is required to keep himself informed as to the tactical situation and the status of equipment, and he must be prepared to assume operational direction of the ship. His position relative to the OOD is similar to that of the executive officer. He may be, and usually is, authorized by the commanding officer to relieve the OOD if necessary. When a ship underway has a CDO assigned, the OOD should make all the reports to him that he would normally make to the executive officer and the commanding officer.

These brief descriptions show that, although the OOD's relationships with other key watch-standers are regulated, there is latitude for each command to supplement, and to some extent modify, the various regulations. This is a prerogative of the commanding officer, whose duty it is to see that his watch organization is the best one possible to meet the needs of the ship. This might mean that in wartime he would order the TAO to direct combat. When a TAO watch does not appear to be necessary, he might decide not to set one, in order to use his people to better advantage. These are command decisions that will, in all cases, be communicated either orally or in writing to the watch officers concerned. It then becomes the duty of the watch officer to make sure that he understands clearly and without any doubt what his position in the organization is.

Characteristics of the officer of the deck

Forehandedness

The watch officer should be ready for any situation that might arise and, for that reason, normal personal and professional qualifications being assumed, the most important faculty for him to cultivate is forehandedness. If he has reason to think that there will be fog while he is on watch, he should check over the fog procedure before taking the deck. If his ship is to take part in fleet exercises, he should arrange to look over the orders before going on watch. If his ship is to enter New York Harbor, for example, he should review the Inland Rules of the Road. If there are to be ceremonies during his watch, he should make himself letter-perfect in the honors required, and put a little extra snap in his own appearance. He must always look ahead, a minute, an hour, or a day, and make it a matter of pride never to be caught unprepared.

If he is wise, he will rehearse mentally the action he would take in the event of a fire, a man overboard, a steering failure, or any other serious casualty. This habit is not difficult to acquire and is certain to pay large dividends. Forehandedness is the mark of the successful man in any capacity.

Vigilance

Next to forehandedness, the most important quality for the officer of the deck is vigilance. In no position more than that of OOD is vigilance essential to safety. The OOD must, of course, observe intelligently all that comes within his vision, both outside and inside the ship, but his vigilance must extend beyond the visible. He should develop vigilance on the part of all others concerned with his watch.

Judgment

A third important quality for the officer of the deck is judgment, which in his position means largely a sense of proportion and of the fitness of things. Watches vary all the way from hours of tenseness when the OOD has his ship and his shipmates in his hands every instant, as in high-speed work at night in a darkened ship, down to the calm of a Sunday afternoon at anchor, when he is just "keeping ship." On a darkened ship, only essentials count and the OOD must key his mind to its keenest pitch. On a quiet Sunday afternoon, it may be that his most important immediate responsibility is to be affable to visitors.

Sixth sense

Most officers who have spent some time at sea have a special sense for what is going on around them. An experienced chief engineer will awaken immediately if the sound of a blower or a pump is not right, just as a good navigator will go to the bridge to check the weather when he feels even the smallest change in the ship's motion. There is nothing magic about this ability and it requires no special talents. It is the product of such officers' experience and of their carefully cultivated habit of close and continuous observation of what is going on around them. To a new officer, so many things seem to be happening at once that concentration on one detail is almost impossible. Yet, as he gains experience and learns more about his profession, things begin to sort themselves out, and before long what seemed like a confusing and impossibly complex environment becomes understandable. At this point the learning process that makes a good watch officer begins. Once the basics of the watch have become second nature, he can turn his attention to developing an ability to observe and evaluate everything that is going on during his watch.

Leadership

The fourth important quality is leadership, which the navy officially defines as "the sum of those qualities of intellect, of human understanding and of moral character that enable a man to inspire and to manage a group of people successfully." Every watch officer should cultivate dignity, forcefulness, confidence, and precision in his manner of standing watch, and should exact similar qualities from his assistants. Striving to avoid any indication of confusion or peevishness and to do his job quietly, he should always act the part of what he really is—next to the captain and the executive officer, the most important person in the ship. *U.S. Navy Regulations, 1920,* said: "while never permitting anyone to perform his duties in a dilatory or perfunctory manner, the officer of the deck should display a spirit of deference to superiors and kindness to inferiors."

Technical knowledge

The OOD, no matter how well endowed with forehandedness, vigilance, judgment, and leadership, must also know the technical aspects of his job, know the relative importance of his many responsibilities, and have experience. This book cannot cover the technical knowledge that the OOD requires, nor can it furnish him with experience; it attempts, however, to indicate these things:

1. The kind of technical knowledge with which a watch officer must be familiar.

2. The relative importance of the watch officer's many responsibilities.

3. The lessons of accumulated experience, so far as they can be reproduced on the printed page.

4. Certain useful information that otherwise might not be readily available when wanted.

2 | THE WATCH IN GENERAL

An officer in charge of a watch shall be responsible for the proper performance of all duties prescribed for his watch, and all persons on watch under him shall be subject to his orders.

He shall remain in charge and at his station until regularly relieved. He shall scrupulously obey all orders and regulations and shall require the same of all persons on watch under him. He shall instruct them as may be necessary in the performance of their duties and shall ensure that they are at their stations, attentive, alert, and ready for duty. He shall endeavor to foresee situations which may arise and shall take such timely and remedial action as may be required.

Before relieving, he shall thoroughly acquaint himself with all matters which he should know for the proper performance of his duties while on watch. He may decline to relieve his predecessor should any circumstance or situation exist which, in his opinion, justifies such action by him, until he has reported the facts to and received orders from the commanding officer or other competent authority.

OpNavInst 3120.32.

Preparation

The more thorough his preparation before going on watch, the more likely is the OOD to perform his duties efficiently.

A newly commissioned officer reporting to his first ship, or an experienced officer ordered to one that is unfamiliar, will be required quickly to learn about the ship, her organization, and the people who run her. He will have to get most of this information for himself, and there are some very helpful references available. *OpNavInst* 3120.32, when supplemented by amplifying instructions for the particular type and class of ship concerned, constitutes the *Standard Ship's Organization and Regulations Manual,* familiarly known by its acronym SORM. At first, the sheer bulk of all this material may seem dismaying, but most of the chapters of the SORM contain material that can be absorbed gradually, as the newly reported officer acquaints himself with the ship's operation. A watch officer should immediately begin making himself thoroughly familiar with his ship's watch organization. The SORM chapter on this subject contains the most important guidance and regulations of the watch and details precisely the duties and responsibilities of, and relationships among, watch-standers. Particular attention must be paid to the italicized sections, because these are regulatory and have the force of law. The sections in bold-face type provide guidance in the organization of the command. There are a number of ship's instructions that detail the specific duties of the various watch-standers, such as sounding-and-security and roving patrol. Since the first duties of a junior officer of the deck are likely to involve checking in some way on the performance of these watch-standers, it is important that he should know what their duties are, especially if the ship has special watch requirements.

Although the organization for damage control on a warship is quite complex, the basics of its organization, including the location of repair lockers, the number and composition of repair parties, and the essential components of installed fire-fighting and drainage systems, should be learned as soon as possible.

Today's fleet operations require a watch officer to be familiar with a wide range of tactical and operational situations on any given watch. It is therefore foolish for an oncoming OOD or TAO to assume the watch after only a ten- or fifteen-minute rundown on "what's happening." Preparation must be longer than that. Operation orders, concepts of operations, and letters of instruction (LOI) should be studied carefully, well before the information is needed, and not in the corner of a darkened bridge on a rough night. Essentially, preparation for the underway watch begins before the ship gets underway. The OOD must participate in pre-exercise briefings and be familiar with the at-sea commander's standing orders. However, the immediate situation must be absorbed and reviewed just prior to the watch. The best place to do this sort of preparation is usually the CIC, where formation disposition, tactical data, and communication plans are all displayed. However, the CIC is not the only place the OOD should stop before relieving the watch. It is a good idea for him to stop by the EOOW and find out the details of plant status as well as any possible extra drills, maintenance, or repairs that are being planned. A tour of topside spaces will give first-hand knowledge of readiness for heavy weather and send a signal to the lookouts that the officer will be in charge for the next watch.

The OOD should be physically prepared, fresh and well rested, before assuming the watch. He should be dressed for the weather conditions and take with him his own equipment—flashlight with red filter, notebook, etc.; he should not expect to borrow them from the officer he is relieving. On a night watch, he should give himself at least twenty minutes to become night-adapted before he even considers being ready to relieve. It is most important to be psychologically prepared. For the four hours or so of his watch, the OOD's mind should be on nothing else, regardless of what concerns he may have. In a fast-moving tactical situation, only a few seconds of inattention can cause him to "lose the bubble," sometimes with disastrous results.

Relieving the watch

Relieving the watch will be a controlled and precise function. Experience has shown that the ability to handle casualties and tactical decisions is significantly reduced during the transition period between watches.

OpNavInst 3120.32.

The actual process of relieving the watch should not be undertaken until the relief is sure that he is familiar with the general situation. It used to be that the oncoming OOD would appear on deck fifteen minutes before the hour, but modern operations at sea usually demand more discussion between the offgoing and the oncoming watch than is possible in the traditional fifteen-minute turnover. Unless the oncoming officer has prepared himself beforehand, the information that the offgoing officer passes to him during the oral turnover will make little sense. He will then be in the unpleasant position of either having to ask for information that he should already have or, even worse, taking over without really understanding what is going on and then spending the rest of the watch trying to catch up.

No matter how thoroughly the relieving officer has prepared himself before reporting ready to relieve, the oral turnover is still important. This is his last chance to clear up anything that may seem vague or confusing to him, and it is the on-watch officer's opportunity to pass on to his relief miscellaneous information that he needs to know. The ship on his bow, for example, might have a tendency to wander into his sector because her radar is down, or there might have been some last-minute changes to the watch team. Perhaps the officer in tactical command (OTC) has a weak transmitter on a tactical circuit and can barely be heard. This is the sort of information the relieving OOD needs if he is to run a smooth and professional watch.

The actual oral turnover should be formal and business-like. The officer coming on duty should step up to the officer he is relieving, salute him, and say, "I am ready to relieve you, sir." The officer being relieved returns the salute and says, "I am ready to be relieved." Aside from setting an example of smartness and military courtesy for the men and observing a time-honored custom of the service, there are very sound reasons for this procedure. The key word is "ready." By declaring himself ready to relieve the watch, the officer is stating that he has made all reasonable preparations, gathered all available information, and needs but an oral turnover to assume his duties. A mumbled "What's the dope?" is not an acceptable substitute. The officer being relieved describes the operational situation. He wants to make sure that he covers everything he knows about other ships in the formation and other contacts. He should outline all known events scheduled to take place during the upcoming watch. He then gives a rundown on the propulsion plant status, highlighting any limitations.

While receiving information about the watch, the incoming OOD has an opportunity to observe what is going on, both on board and outside the ship. When he thoroughly understands the situation, has heard all that his predecessor has to say, and has asked him any questions he thinks necessary, it is his duty to salute again and say, "I relieve you, sir." It must be stressed that this is an obligation and must not be done with a sloppy "O.K., I've got it." The officer being relieved returns the salute and replies with "I stand relieved." Both officers then report to the captain the watch has been relieved.

Declining to relieve the watch

The extract from *OpNavInst* 3120.32 quoted at the beginning of this chapter is quite clear on the subject of declining to relieve the watch. Nevertheless, some junior officers feel that they may be considered timid if they exercise their option and decline to do so. It is an officer's duty to decline to relieve the watch if, for example, the ship is out of position in the formation or a busy watch in port has become confused, with boats astray or out of fuel. Of course, a ship may be out of position for good reason and be headed back for her station, in which case it would be proper to relieve the watch. A meticulous approach to this question is recommended. As an old salt said, "Relieve in haste, repent at leisure." A reputation for being fussy in taking over a watch is not a bad thing to acquire. It will keep the preceding watch officer on his toes, ready to turn over his watch without leaving embarrassing loose ends. It must be remembered that once the relieving officer has said, "I relieve you, sir," the full responsibility of the watch is his. If difficulties arise, he cannot then try to pass the blame back to the officer he relieved. It is usually best not to relieve in the midst of a complex operation. Rather, it is better to stand back and observe the situation and, when it is feasible, step forward to relieve.

Leadership responsibilities

[The officer of the deck will] supervise and conduct on-the-job training for the junior officer of the watch, the junior officer of the deck, and enlisted personnel of the bridge watch.

OpNavInst 3120.32.

In addition to his responsibilities for the operation of the ship, the watch officer has an important role as leader of his watch team. No matter how competent or well prepared he may be, he cannot hope to perform well if he does not take positive control of the watch-standers under him. In all likelihood, some of the people on his watch will be experienced, others inexperienced. Some men will be fully qualified, some will be in the process of qualifying, and some may be standing watch for the first time. Their performance will be no better than the leadership given them by the watch officer. Consciously or unconsciously, they will take their lead from what they see the watch officer doing. He is the center of action and the most visible man on the watch team. His manner must therefore convey an attitude of seriousness, concentration, and self-discipline. He should insist that the key officers and petty officer on his watch continually check, inspect, and train their subordinates, and he should not hesitate to relieve a man on watch who is clearly incompetent or is not trained to perform his job.

The high rate of turnover that most ships experience means that a watch officer can expect the training of new people to be a major and continuing duty. In addition, depending on command policy, he may be authorized to sign off on certain portions of junior officers' surface-warfare personnel qualification standards (PQS). Not only does the training of watch-standers bring about obvious improvements in the readiness of the ship, but it also does a great deal for the morale and enthusiasm of the watch-standers. A watch officer who shows a sincere interest in improving the skills of his men almost always gets a good response and builds a team that he can be proud of. The quality of his watch helps significantly to determine his professional reputation. He must exercise leadership of his team by insisting on high standards of performance and appearance. He should take care that in the relieving process not all his key watch-standers are relieved at once. One other point should be noted: All of the ship's resources are available to the OOD. He must never hesitate to use these resources when he needs them.

Routine

The officer of the deck underway shall . . . carry out the routine of the ship as published in the plan of the day and other ship's directives, keeping the executive officer advised of any changes which may be necessary.

OpNavInst 3120.32.

An intelligently conceived and punctiliously executed routine is essential to good shipboard organization. It is the officer of the deck's job to supervise and closely control the manner in which this routine is carried out. If the plan of the day calls for "turn to" at 1300, he must be sure that, as far as he can determine, the crew does "turn to" at that time. If reveille is scheduled for 0600, he must see that all hands are turned out at that time. If something about the plan of the day does not seem right, he should consult the executive officer, but until the routine is changed, he must see that it is carried out. The plan of the day is a directive. All hands must follow it, whether or not the word is passed over the general announcing system.

The boatswain's mate of the watch, the OOD's most important enlisted assistant, handles much of the detail of carrying out the daily routine. He should be made to feel responsible for the watch routine and for the instruction, behavior, and appearance of the deck watch. It is his duty to see that all stations are manned and that the previous watch has been relieved. Just as the OOD exercises all the attributes of leadership required of a naval officer, the same can be said for the boatswain's mate of the watch and the petty officer of the watch in port. One of the boatswain's mate's major duties is to carry out the plan of the day. He must know what is happening on board ship and must pass the word in accordance with the prescribed routine. The OOD should supervise the boatswain's mate in carrying out the watch routine rather than deal directly with the men on watch. The standard routine is usually written into the ship's organization book and is varied only by specific instructions in the plan of the day. When it seems advisable to change the routine because of unusual and unforeseen circumstances, the OOD must obtain permission for such change from the executive officer or the command duty officer.

Passing the word

[The officer of the deck will] supervise and control the use of the general announcing system; the general, chemical, collision, sonar, and steering casualty alarms; and the whistle in accordance with the orders of the commanding officer, tactical doctrine, and the Rules of the Road.

OpNavInst 3120.32.

In order for the ship's routine to be carried out as planned, the word must be passed. In terms of daily evolutions, few things are more basic, or more abused, than the passing of the word. The amount of control that the watch has over the general announcing system, designated the 1MC, is one of the best indicators of how well the ship is being run and how much attention the watch officer is paying to what is happening in the ship. Except in unusual or urgent situations, the 1MC should not be used as a means of communicating with individuals, nor should it be used as a paging system. The habit of passing the word for individuals (in most cases, simply because it is the easiest way to contact people) is one that is easy to get into and hard to break. Unless watch officers monitor what goes out over the general announcing system, its abuse will very quickly become part of accepted shipboard procedure. Even worse, people will become so accustomed to hearing the 1MC every five minutes that when something really important is passed, no one will listen. By controlling the system, the OOD can not only prevent this from happening but can avert problems in the carrying-out of the ship's routine. If, for example, a ten-hand working party has been called away and fifteen minutes later the quarterdeck is asked to pass the word to "bear a hand in mustering the ten-hand working party," his immediate reaction should be to turn down the request and instead find out why the party was not properly mustered.

When the word is passed, standard phraseology should always be used. This is not only the mark of a smart, seamanlike ship, it is the best way to ensure that the message gets out with maximum clarity and brevity. Standard phraseology (*see* chapter 4) will be found in the *Standard Ship's Organization and Regulations Manual* (SORM), as well as in *Ship Organization and Personnel* and *Naval Terms Dictionary*. A copy of the word to be passed for ship's routine and other standard announcements should be available on the bridge and at the quarterdeck station.

Things to be avoided in passing the word

1. Use of clumsy or redundant language such as "All personnel not actually on watch" and "Now payday is being held on the mess decks at this time."

2. Improper use of circuits. SOPA regulations and port regulations in many foreign ports prohibit the use of topside speakers except in emergencies.

3. Passing word that is not of concern to officers on the officers' circuit.

4. Use of 1MC during church services or ceremonies, except in emergencies.

5. Addressing a long list of people.

6. Use of the phrase "now bear a hand" in any but urgent circumstances.

7. Asking officers or chief petty officers to "lay to." Courtesy demands that they be asked to "please report to. . . ."

8. Pauses, hesitations, and breaks in the course of a message. If the watch is not sure what he is supposed to be saying, the message to be delivered should be written down and read.

Appearance of the watch

The OOD, circumstances permitting, must see that the men on his watch are in clean regulation uniform. He himself sets an example, at all times, for the whole ship. At sea, particularly in bad weather, he should be dressed to keep warm and dry and should see that the men on his watch are similarly protected. In port, when visitors are coming aboard, the maximum of spit and polish is expected; uniforms should be in good condition, shoes polished, and personal appearance should be neat.

The boatswain's mate of the watch should be made responsible for the appearance of the watch, and the OOD should not hesitate to have him send any man who does not come up to standard below to change. Wrinkled, ill-fitting, or dirty uniforms and work shoes are good enough to wear about the deck when a good uniform might get soiled, but are not good enough for a messenger of the watch on the quarterdeck.

Similarly, the appearance of the bridge or quarterdeck should be a matter of interest to the officer of the deck. He should have the boatswain's mate of the watch keep the area clean and tidy. Sweeping the deck, emptying trash buckets and ash trays, and keeping empty coffee cups out of sight are all details that an alert boatswain's mate of the watch attends to.

Conduct on watch

There is need for a certain formality on watch. This does not require pomposity; on the contrary, often a touch of humor is appropriate. But the men on watch must never be permitted to forget that they are on duty and that what they are doing is important. This formality adds to the professionalism of the watch and clearly adds to the reputation of the OOD. It is usually the small things that count most. For example, it is inappropriate for officers on watch to address each other by first names, even if they are roommates. Officers should address crew members by formal title, and crew members on watch should similarly address each other.

A ship is always subject to emergency or disaster; fire, man overboard, or dozens of other events can disrupt the dullest watch. The OOD should make it a practice to run a taut watch and to prevent noisy and idle chatter; he should use common sense and not be arbitrary or harsh in dealing with men.

Relations with the staff

The OOD of a flagship has the additional responsibilities of keeping the embarked staff informed as to what is going on, handling additional boats and vehicles, and, of course, rendering honors.

The staff duty officer is usually the person who should receive special reports. In general, the events and sightings normally reported to the commanding officer should also be reported to the staff duty officer. He bears about the same relation to his admiral or squadron or division commander as an OOD does to his commanding officer.

The flag lieutenant is generally responsible to the admiral for the scheduling of honors and advises the OOD what honors are to take place. In return, the officer of the deck advises the flag lieutenant, as well as the staff duty officer, of unscheduled visits that may require honors.

Staff officers take care to preserve the flagship's unity of command and do not give orders directly to the OOD. Routine requests may be made to the ship's officers, but in matters of any importance the chief of staff usually deals with the commanding officer of the flagship. An OOD will not be inconvenienced by an embarked staff as long as he remembers to consider their needs and to keep them informed.

Turning over the watch

As a watch draws to a close, the OOD is concerned with giving his relief all available information in order to provide the maximum continuity. Both the relieved and relieving officer must make certain that this is done. It may be necessary to make notes, or to keep a check list, but the relieved officer must remember that, even while turning over the watch, he should continue to be alert and on the job. He cannot let the task of turning over the watch distract his attention from maintaining a proper watch. If the OOD feels that the pace of operations makes a relieving of the watch as scheduled inappropriate or even unsafe, he should so inform his relief, and a delay or change in relieving time should be arranged. The oncoming relief must be flexible in this regard.

When the commanding officer is on the bridge underway, the oncoming watch officer should "request permission to relieve the officer of the deck" and the offgoing OOD should report, "I have been properly relieved as officer of the deck by _____."

Knowing the ship

Listed below are some of the basic facts that an officer should begin learning about his ship as soon as he reports on board. The "OOD Underway" part of the surface warfare officer's PQS contains other things that he will be required to know as part of the qualification process. The surface warfare officer's qualification process is designed to lead to various watch officer qualifications, and following the process is the best way to qualify as OOD. However, by going through the following list, a few things at a time, during a quiet watch or in-port duty day, an officer will soon improve his "feel" for his ship and how she operates.

1. Principal dimensions (beam, draft, length, displacement, etc.).

2. Fuel and water capacity, fuel consumption at various speeds, most economical speed.

3. Maximum speed available under different boiler combinations (steam plants).

4. Engine line-up and combination or turbine line-up and combination (gas-turbine and diesel ships).

5. Capabilities and limitations of weapon systems.

6. Capabilities and limitations of sensors.

7. Rudder angles for standard, full, and hard rudder.

8. Steering-engine controls and steering-engine combinations; emergency steering procedures.

9. Location, sound, appearance, and meaning of all alarm systems on the bridge.

10. Location of and normal use for all radio and internal communications stations.

11. Procedures and safety precautions for raising and lowering boats.

12. Preparations needed for underway replenishment.

13. Preparations needed for entering and leaving port.

14. Operation of radar repeaters.

15. Operation of bearing circles, alidades, stadimeters.

16. Publications kept on the bridge, where they are to be found and how they are accounted for.

17. Procedure for manning watch and battle stations.

18. Make-up and check-in requirements for various security watches.

19. Regulations concerning disposal of trash and garbage.

20. Regulations concerning pumping bilges, oil spills, and environmental protection.

21. Characteristics and limitations of aircraft or helicopters carried.

22. Operational, administrative, and task organizations that affect the OOD, and where his ship is in the organization.

23. Required reports to the OOD.

24. Location and use of emergency signals.

25. Precautions to be taken in heavy weather.

26. Basic ship's tactical information, such as turning-circle diameters under various conditions and limitations on acceleration and deceleration.

27. Thumb rules and quick procedures for "measuring the situation." (See Crenshaw, 4th ed., chapter 1, "Seaman's Eye.")

3 | THE SHIP'S DECK LOG

The deck log shall be a complete daily record, by watches, in which shall be described every circumstance and occurrence of importance or interest which concerns the crew and the operation and safety of the ship or which may be of historical value.

OpNavInst 3120.32.

General

The deck log is the official record of a ship's history during her commission. It presents a complete narrative of noteworthy incidents in the life of the ship and her officers and crew. Everything of significance pertaining to the ship's complement, material, operations, or state of readiness is entered in the deck log. It is thus a historical account of a ship's activities and a detailed source of factual data. Watch officers responsible for the maintenance of the log must appreciate the importance of their undertaking. They must ensure that all entries are complete, accurate, clear, concise, and expressed in standard naval phraseology. Taken together, the entries must constitute a true and understandable historical and legal record of the ship.

Until 1974 the deck log was maintained separately from the quartermaster's notebook and consisted of two parts. The first part, the "tabular data" section, was normally kept by the quartermaster of the watch and contained information concerning weather, hydrographic conditions, and the ship's position. The second part consisted of the OOD's remarks; it was prepared in rough form and then transcribed into a smooth form that became the official record and was mailed to the Bureau of Naval Personnel. Although the format and manner of keeping the deck log have changed, its status as an official record has not changed, nor has the OOD's responsibility for keeping a proper and complete log.

In order to maintain information on weather and aerographic and hydrographic conditions, ships are now required to log this information in OpNav form 3144, *Ship's Weather Observation Sheet*. The quartermaster of the watch is responsible for taking hourly readings and entering them on the sheet. However, it is one of the OOD's duties to inspect this record and ensure that it is accurate and complete. This inspection is important because it not only verifies the accuracy of the information, but also can give an excellent indication of trends in the weather, the approach of storms, or an improvement in conditions. Entries in the *Weather Observation Sheet* should be examined with a very critical eye. Quartermasters observing seas from a bridge thirty-five or forty feet above the water have been known to underestimate them by as much as 50 per cent. Close attention to the *Weather Observation Sheet* is especially important when a ship is acting as a weather guard or is steaming independently. In both cases the accuracy of the forecasts sent to the ship by fleet weather activities will depend directly on the accuracy of the observations that the ship sends.

Since the ship's deck log now combines what used to be the second part of the deck log and the old quartermaster's notebook, it must be kept with care. It must be clear enough to stand alone as the official legal record of the ship's activity and significant occurrences of any one day. The entries in the deck log for each day must give so complete an account of the events of that day, from 0000 until 2400, that reference to the previous day's log is not necessary. This is why the entry made by the midwatch must recapitulate the situation existing at midnight. This entry includes the conditions of readiness in force, status of the engineering plant, command organization, course and speed, other units present, and required tactical information.

The deck log, and the magnetic compass record book, the engineering log, and the engineer's bell book, are legal records and can be used as evidence before legal bodies. Consequently, it is important that the remarks be complete and accurate. Erasures in any of these records would bring their validity as evidence into question. The OOD must initia! his corrections of errors in these logs.

Logs are often consulted in the settlement of claims for pensions by persons who claim to have been injured while serving in the armed forces. A complete entry, therefore, must be made in the log concerning every injury, accident, and casualty, including accidents that could later lead to the discovery of injuries to the officers, crew, or passengers on board. This is necessary both to protect the government from false claims and to furnish a record for honest claimants.

The navigator has charge of the preparation of the deck log. Regulations require that he examine the log book to see that it is prepared in accordance with instructions, and call the attention of watch officers to any inaccuracies in or omissions from their entries. He is responsible to the commanding officer for the entries in the log being in proper form; but the OOD is responsible for the entries made during his watch.

All entries must be handwritten and signed with a ball-point pen in black or blue-black ink. The remarks must be legible, and while the junior officer of the deck may write the log, it must be signed by the OOD responsible for the watch.

Deck-log entries

Since the deck log is handwritten, particular care must be taken in the recording of numbers; proper nouns are to be printed; and, where a signature is required, the name is to be printed under the individual's signature. The Bureau of Naval Personnel will return for remedial action logs that are illegible for any reason, including poor penmanship. No lines may be skipped, except between the beginning and end of successive watch entries. Only abbreviations that are generally accepted throughout the navy by reason of long and continued usage may be used in the deck log. The following are some of the most commonly used abbreviations:

UA	Unauthorized absence
CPA	Closest point of approach

OCE	Officer conducting the exercise
OOD	Officer of the deck
OTC	Officer in tactical command
Commands	ComCarGru 16, CinCPacFlt, etc.
R(L)FR	Right (left) full rudder
R(L) 15R	Right (left) 15 degrees rudder
H(R/L)R	Hard (right/left) rudder
R/A	Rudder amidship
MEET HR	Meet her
R(L) 050	Right (left) to course 050°T
AEA ⅓	All engines ahead ⅓
AE STOP	All engines stop
AEA STD	All engines ahead standard
AEA FUL	All engines ahead full
AEA FLK	All engines ahead flank
P(S)EA ⅓	Port (starboard) engine ahead ⅓
P(S)EB ⅓	Port (starboard) engine back ⅓
145 RPM	145 revolutions per minute

The following sample entries are to be used as guides for recording the remarks of a watch. They are not all-inclusive, nor are they to be construed as the only acceptable ones. Any entry that is complete, accurate, and in standard naval phraseology is acceptable.

Midwatch
UNDERWAY

00-04

0000 Steaming in company with Task Group 30.5, composed of CARGRU I, CRUDESGRU III, and DESRON V, plus USS HAROLD E. HOLT (FF 1074) and USS OUELLET (FF 1077), en route from Pearl Harbor, Hawaii, to Guam, M.I., in accordance with CTG 30.5 serial 061. This ship in station 3 in circular screen. Formation course 220°T, speed 15 knots. Formation axis 000°T. SOPA is CTG 30.5 in USS HALSEY (CG 23). OTC is COMCARGRU I in USS CONSTELLATION (CV-64). HALSEY is guide, bearing 320°T, distance 5000 yds. Condition of readiness 3 and material condition YOKE set. Ship darkened (except for running lights).

Note: On succeeding watches the first entry is "Underway as before."

00-04

0000 Moored starboard side to USS PAUL (FF-1080) with standard mooring lines in a nest of three ships. USS SPRUANCE (DD-963) moored outboard of PAUL to starboard. PAUL moored fore and aft to buoys B-5 and B-6, Norfolk, VA.

Ships present: _____, SOPA _____.

Note: For entries concerning "ships present," see "Ships Present," page 46.

00-04

0000 Anchored in Berth B-4, U. S. Naval Operating Base, Trinidad, The West Indies, in 12 fathoms of water, mud bottom, with 60 fathoms of chain to the starboard anchor on the following anchorage bearings: South Point Light 060, etc. Ship in condition of readiness 3, material condition YOKE set and darkened except for anchor lights. Engineering Department on 30-minute notice before getting underway. Heavy weather plan in effect. Anchor detail standing by. Wind 45 knots from 070. Weather reports indicate possibility of winds up to 60 knots before 0400. Ships present: _____, SOPA _____.

00-04

0000 Moored starboard side to Pier 3, Berth 35, U. S. Naval Base, Norfolk, Va., with standard mooring lines doubled. Receiving miscellaneous services from the pier. Ships present include _____, SOPA _____.

00-04

0000 Resting on keel blocks in Dry Dock Number 3, U. S. Naval Shipyard, Bremerton, Wash., receiving miscellaneous services from the dock. Ships present include _____, SOPA _____.

Note: On succeeding watches the first entry is "Moored as before," "Anchored as before," or "Dry-docked as before."

Air Operations

ENTRIES APPLICABLE TO CARRIERS

1000 Flight quarters.

1005 Commenced launching aircraft for (carrier qualification) (refresher operations) (group tactics), etc.

1025 Completed launching aircraft, having launched 40 aircraft.

1030 Commenced recovering aircraft.

1035 Commenced maneuvering while recovering (launching) aircraft (while conducting task group (force) flight operations).

1055 Completed recovering aircraft, having recovered 40 aircraft.

1143 F-4 Bureau No. 12345 of VF-75, pilot LCDR Ben B. BOOMS, USN, 000-00-000, crashed into the sea off the port bow at Latitude 30°50′N, Longitude 150°20′W, and sank in 500 fathoms of water.

1144 USS ARTHUR W. RADFORD (DD-968) and helicopter commenced search for pilot.

1146 Pilot recovered by helicopter and delivered on board USS AMERICA (CV-66). Injuries to pilot: (description).

1215 Secured from flight quarters.

1300 A-4C, Bureau No. 67890 of VA-9, pilot ENS John P. JONES, USNR, 000-00-0001, crashed into barriers numbers 2, 4, and 6, and overturned. Pilot sustained mild abrasion to left forearm and contusions to both legs. Damage to aircraft: (major) (minor) (strike).

1315 CDR A. B. SEA, USN, Commanding Officer, VA-9, departed with 15 aircraft for Oceana, VA, TAD completed.

1330 CDR X. Y. ZEE, USN, Commanding Officer, VA-26, landed aboard with 16 aircraft from NAS, Norfolk, VA, for TAD.

ENTRIES APPLICABLE TO ALL SHIPS

2100 Maneuvering to take plane guard station No. 1R on USS KENNEDY. Lighting measure GREEN in effect.

2110 On station.

2115 Commenced flight operations.

2210 F-4 aircraft crashed into the sea off starboard bow. Maneuvering to recover pilot.

2214 Recovered pilot LTJG Harvey H. GOTZ, USN, 000-00-0002, VF-74. Injuries to pilot: (description).

ENTRIES APPLICABLE TO SHIPS CARRYING HELICOPTERS

1435 Flight quarters.

1455 Launched helicopter. Pilot: LTJG Ray WINGS, USN: Passenger: BMC A. CLEAT, USN.

1505 Recovered helicopter on main deck aft.

1510 Secured from flight quarters.

Loading and Transferring Operations

AIRCRAFT

0800 Commenced hoisting aircraft of VF-21 aboard.

1000 Completed hoisting 25 aircraft of VF-21 aboard.

Note: When all the aircraft of an air wing or group are hoisted aboard at the same time (i.e., during a period of a day), the entry should say "aircraft of VF-21, VA-26, and VAH-20. . . ."

AMMUNITION

1400 Commenced loading (transferring) ammunition.

1600 Completed loading (transferring) ammunition, having received from (transferred to) USS MT. BAKER (AE-34) 400 rounds 5" / 54 cal. illum. projectiles, 250 5" / 54 cal. smokeless, and 250 5" / 54 cal. flashless charges.

Note: For entries regarding expenditure of ammunition, see GUNNERY, under *Drills and Exercises*, below.

Damage

COLLISIONS

1155 USS PONCE (LPD-15), in coming alongside to port, carried away 39 feet of the ship's port lifeline forward, with stanchions, and indented the ship's side to a depth of 4 inches over an area 10 feet long and 4 feet high in the vicinity of frames 46-51. No personnel casualties.

1401 Starboard lifeboat carried away by heavy sea. Boat and all equipment lost. No personnel casualties.

ENGINEERING CASUALTIES

1018 Lost fires in No. 1A boiler due to high water level. Maximum speed available, 18 knots.

1019 Lit fires in No. 1B boiler.

1130 No. 1B boiler on the line. All conditions normal. Maximum speed available, 27 knots.

Drills and Exercises

GENERAL

1000 Exercised at general drills.

ABANDON SHIP

1005 Commenced abandon-ship drill.

1045 Secured from abandon-ship drill.

ALARMS

0800 Tested general, chemical, collision alarms. All conditions normal.

NBC ATTACK

1440 Set material condition ZEBRA and NBC condition WILLIAM.

1450 Set NBC condition CIRCLE WILLIAM.

1500 (Simulated) nuclear (underwater) (air) burst, bearing 045°T, distance 15,000 yards. Maneuvering to avoid base surge and fallout.

1530 Rejoined formation and took station L6 in formation.

COLLISION

1350 Held collision drill.

1354 Material condition ZEBRA set.

1410 Secured from collision drill. Set material condition YOKE.

FIRE AND RESCUE

1100 Held fire drill.

1110 Secured from fire drill.

1300 Called away the fire-and-rescue party.

1305 Fire-and-rescue party embarked in starboard boat and clear of ship.

1330 Fire-and-rescue party returned aboard. Further assistance not required.

GUNNERY

1245 Went to general quarters. Set material condition ZEBRA.

1300 Commenced missile exercise.

1304 Commenced firing. Fired one _____ missile to starboard (port).

1308 Ceased firing.

1320 Set material condition YOKE.

1325 Secured from general quarters. Ammunition expended: 89 rounds 5" / 54 cal. high-explosive projectiles with 89 rounds full-service smokeless (flashless) powder cartridges with no casualties.

Note: For several exercises fired in close succession, the ammunition expended for all may be grouped in one entry. Normally, material condition will be set and batteries secured before securing from general quarters.

Formations

GENERAL

0700 Maneuvering to take station 1 in formation 49, axis 000°T. Guide is USS CALIFORNIA (CGN-36) in station A.

0800 Rotated formation axis to 180°T.

0900 Formation changed from 49 to 52. New formation guide is USS R. K. TURNER (CG-20) in station B.

OFFICER IN TACTICAL COMMAND (OTC)

0900 COMCARGRU 16 embarked in USS NIMITZ (CVN-68) assumed OTC.

1000 Commanding Officer, USS LYNDE McCORMICK (DDG-8), was designated OTC.

Note: All shifts of tactical command should be logged. When the OTC is the commanding officer of the log-writer's ship, the following terminology should be used: "OTC is Commanding

Officer, USS LONG BEACH (CGN-9)." In every case, the command title of the OTC (e.g., COMCARGRU 2) should be used, and not his name and grade. Entry should state in which ship OTC is embarked.

RENDEZVOUS
0800 USS GLOVER (FF-1098) made rendezvous with this ship (the formation) and took designated station (took station in the screen) (took plane-guard station).
2200 Joined rendezvous with TG 70.2 and took designated station number 1 in formation 4R, with guide in USS ARTHUR W. RADFORD (DD-968) bearing 095, distance 2,400 yards, formation axis 000°. OTC is COMCRUDESGRU 2 in USS TRUXTON (CGN-35).

TACTICAL EXERCISES
1000 Commenced division tactical exercises. Steering various courses at various speeds (in area HOTEL) (conforming to maneuvers signaled by COMDESRON 4) (on signals from COMDESRON 4).

ZIGZAGGING AND SINUATING
1300 Commenced zigzagging in accordance with Plan #1A, base course 090°T.
1400 Commenced steering sinuous course, Cam #1, base course 010°T.
1500 Ceased zigzagging and set course 010°T.

Fueling
IN PORT
1000 Commenced fueling at Naval Fuel Depot, Craney Island, draft forward 22′, aft 23′.
1130 Ceased pumping. Received 254,031 gals. of JP-5.

AT SEA
1345 Set the special sea and replenishment detail. Commenced preparations for refueling from USS CAMDEN (AOE-2).

1426 Maneuvering to take station astern USS CAMDEN (AOE-2).
1438 On station.
1442 Commenced approach. Captain (at the conn) (conning).
1453 On station alongside port side of CAMDEN.
1456 First line over.
1510 Received first fuel hose.
1515 Commenced receiving fuel.
1559 Fueling completed. Received 233,198 Gals. of DFM/F-76.
1606 All lines and hoses clear. Maneuvering to clear port side of CAMDEN.
1610 Clear of CAMDEN.
1612 Secured the replenishment detail.

Honors, Ceremonies, and Official Visits
PERSONAL FLAGS
1200 RADM D. D. WAVE, USN, COMCARGRU 3, broke his flag in this ship.
1300 The Honorable _____, Secretary of the Navy, came aboard; broke the flag of the Secretary of the Navy.
1500 The Secretary of the Navy departed; hauled down the flag of SECNAV.
1530 COMPHIBRON 2 shifted his flag from USS COMPASS ISLAND (AG-153) to USS OBSERVATION ISLAND (AG-154).

MANNING THE RAIL
1000 Manned the rail as the President of the United States came aboard for an official visit. Fired 21-gun salute, broke the President's flag at the main trunk.

VISITS
1430 Their Majesties, the King and Queen of _____, made an official call on VADM D. G. FARRAGUT, USN, COMSIXTHFLT, with their official party. Rendered honors and fired a salute of 21 guns.

1530 The royal party departed. Rendered honors and fired a salute of 21 guns.

CALLS

1000 The Commanding Officer left the ship to make an official call on COMCRUDESGRU 4.

1605 RADM V. A. MOSS, USN, COMCRUDESGRU 4, came aboard to return the official call of the Commanding Officer.

Inspections

ADMINISTRATIVE AND MATERIAL

0930 RADM S. DECATUR, USN, COMCRUDESGRU 13, accompanied by members of his staff and inspecting party, came on board and commenced administrative inspection. Broke flag of COMCRUDESGRU 13.

1100 COMCRUDESGRU 13, members of his staff, and inspecting party left the ship. Hauled down flag of COMCRUDESGRU 13.

1110 COMCRUDESGRU 13 broke his flag in USS CALIFORNIA (CGN-36).

LOWER DECK

1315 Commenced captain's inspection of lower decks, holds, and storerooms.

1400 Secured from inspection.

PERSONNEL

0900 Mustered the crew at quarters for captain's inspection (of personnel and upper decks).

Navigation

ANCHORING

1600 Anchored in Area South HOTEL. Berth 44, Hampton Roads, VA, in 4 fathoms of water, mud bottom, with 30 fathoms of chain to the port anchor on the following bearings: Fort Wook 040°T, Middle Ground Light 217°T,

Sewall's Point 072°T. Ships present: _____, SOPA
_____.

CONTACTS

1405 Sighted merchant ship bearing 280°T, distance about 6 miles on approximately parallel course.

1430 Identified merchant ship as SS SEAKAY, U. S. registry, routed independently from Aruba, NWI, to New York, NY.

1441 Passed SS SEAKAY abeam to port, distance about 2 miles.

1620 Obtained unidentified radar contact bearing 090°T, distance 28,800 yards (14 miles).

1629 Unidentified contact tracked and determined to be on course 180°T, speed 15 knots. CPA 042°T, distance 4.2 miles.

1636 Contact identified as USS JESSE L. BROWN (FF-1089) by USS OLIVER HAZARD PERRY (FFG-7).

1715 Obtained sonar contact bearing 172°T, range 2,500 yards.

1717 Contact evaluated as possible submarine. Commenced attacking (tracking) (investigating).

1720 Lost contact.

1721 Contact regained bearing 020°T, range 2,000 yards. Oil slick sighted on that bearing and range. Commenced re-attack.

1724 Sonar reported hearing breaking-up noises.

1725 Contact lost.

Note: Contacts at sea are logged when they will pass in vicinity of logging ship. Although the exact distance is not specified, normally contacts that pass within 3 nautical miles are logged.

DRY-DOCKING

1420 Commercial tug SEAGOOSE came alongside to port. Pilot C. U. FINE came aboard.

1426 U. S. Navy tug YTB-68 came alongside port bow, U. S.

Navy tug YTB-63 came alongside port quarter.
1431 First line to dock starboard bow.
1435 First line to dock port bow.
1440 Bow passed over sill of dock.
1442 Cast off all tugs.
1450 Caisson in place.
1455 Commenced pumping water out of dry dock.
1540 Resting on keel blocks.
1545 Pilot left the ship.
1550 Commenced receiving electrical power and fresh water from the dock.
1630 Inspection of all hull openings completed.

OVERHAUL, CONVERSION, AND INACTIVATION
1635 Commenced undergoing (overhaul) (conversion) (inactivation).
Commenced limited log entries for duration of (overhaul) (conversion) (inactivation).
0850 Inspection of all hull openings completed.
0900 Flooding commenced in dry dock.
0918 All services disconnected from ship.
0920 Inspection of all spaces for watertight integrity completed.
0925 Ship clear of keel blocks.
0930 Handling lines secure on ship.
0935 Pilot C. U. FINE came aboard.
0950 Commenced moving ship clear of dock.
0958 Stern passed over sill.
1005 U. S. Navy tug YTB-63 came alongside port bow, U. S. Navy tug YTB-68 came alongside port quarter.
1009 Bow passed over sill.
Note: Upon termination of overhaul or conversion, deck-log entries must be recorded daily by watches.

ENTERING HARBOR
0551 Passed Ambrose Lightship abeam to port, distance 1,000 yards.

0554 Stationed special sea detail. OOD (conning) (at the conn), captain and navigator on the bridge.

0600 Commenced maneuvering while conforming to Gedney Channel.

0650 Passed lighted buoy No. 12 abeam to starboard.

0705 U. S. Navy tug No. 216 came alongside port quarter. Pilot B. A. WATCHER came aboard and took the conn.

0706 Maneuvering to go alongside the pier.

0715 Moored port side to Berth 3A, U. S. Naval Ammunition Depot, Earle, NJ, with standard mooring lines. Ships present _____, SOPA is COMDESRON 36 in USS MOINESTER (FF-1097).

0720 Pilot left the ship.

MOORING

1006 Moored port side to Standard Oil Dock, Berth 76, Los Angeles Inner Harbor, CA, with standard mooring lines.

1015 Commenced receiving miscellaneous services from the pier.

SIGHTING AIDS TO NAVIGATION

0102 Sighted Cape Henry Light bearing 225°T, distance about 20 miles.

0157 Passed Cape Henry Light abeam to starboard, distance 7.3 miles.

0300 Cape Henry Light passed from view bearing 315°T, distance about 20 miles.

TIDE

0733 Commenced swinging to flood tide, stern to port.

1046 Completed swinging to flood tide, bearing 347°T.

TIME-ZONE CHANGE

0001 Set clocks ahead 1 hour to conform with +3-Zone Time.

GETTING UNDERWAY

0600 Commenced preparations for getting underway. Set material condition YOKE.

0730 Stationed the special sea detail.

0750 Completed all preparations for getting underway. Draft forward 23', aft 23'.

0800 Underway for Norfolk, VA, (for sea), as a unit of Task Group 20.2 in compliance with COMCARGRU 4 serial 063 (CTG 20.2 Op Order 7-73). Maneuvering to clear the anchorage. Captain (conning) (at the conn), navigator on the bridge.

0810 Standing out of Boston Harbor.

0830 OOD was given the conn. Set readiness condition 3, anchor detail on deck. (Secured the special sea detail, set the regular steaming watch.)

0845 Entered international waters.

SEA AND WEATHER

1130 Visibility decreased to one mile due to fog (heavy rain). Commenced sounding fog signals and stationed (extra lookouts) (lookouts in the eyes of the ship). Winds southeast 25 knots. Sea southeast 8 feet and increasing.

1212 Visibility increased to 5 miles. Ceased sounding fog signals.

Note: Commencement and cessation of sounding fog signals must always be entered.

Personnel

ABSENTEES

0800 Mustered the crew (at quarters) (at foul-weather parade) (on stations) (at quarters for captain's inspection). Absentees: (None) (No new absentees) (SA Roscoe BADEGG, USN, 000-00-0000, absent without authority from muster) (FN M. A. WOHL, USN, 000-00-0000, UA since 0700 this date).

Note: There is no legal distinction between absence beyond leave and absence without leave. Both are logged as unauthorized absence, or UA. The initial entry indicating the man's absence suffices until he returns, is declared a deserter, or is otherwise detached from the ship.

0900 A systematic search of the entire ship for SA Roscoe

BADEGG, USN, 000-00-0000, who missed 0800 muster, disclosed that (he was not on board) (he was found to be sleeping in BOSN's Locker Comp. A-301-A).

1000 RECSTA msg 0311600Z reports that BTFN Arch CULPRET, USN, 000-00-0000, UA since 0800, 15 Apr 1979, returned to naval custody and was being held at that station pending disposition of charges.

Note: An entry such as the above shows that an absentee has returned to naval jurisdiction.

RETURN OF ABSENTEES

2200 PN3 Guy ROAMER, USNR, 000-00-0000, (returned aboard) (was delivered on board by the armed services police), having been UA since 0800 this date.

2300 SH3 "C" A. HAZE, USN, 000-00-0000, UA since 0700 this date, was delivered on board under guard from RECSTA, accused of drunk and disorderly conduct at that station. By order of the commanding officer, he was restricted to the limits of the ship pending disposition of the charges.

REPORTS

0800 Sound-and-security watch reported. All conditions normal.

0830 ASROC roving patrol reported all conditions normal.

COURT OF INQUIRY

1000 The court of inquiry, CAPT A. B. SEA, USN, senior member, appointed by COMSURFPAC 1tr serial 2634 of 2 Apr 1979 met in the case of the late BM3 Andrew J. SPIRIT, USN, 000-00-0000.

1030 The court of inquiry in the case of the late BM3 Andrew J. SPIRIT, USN, 000-00-0000, adjourned to meet ashore at the scene of his death.

SPECIAL COURTS-MARTIAL

1000 The special court-martial, CDR Jonathan Q. DOE, USN, senior member, appointed by CO, USS NIMITZ

(CVN-63), 1tr serial 102 of 1 Mar 1979, met in the case of SA Ralph O. WEARY, USN, 000-00-0000.

1200 The special court-martial that met in the case of SA Ralph O. WEARY, USN, 000-00-0000, recessed to meet again at 1300 this date.

Note: A court adjourns if it will not meet again that date, but if it is to meet again on the same date, it recesses. If known, the date and time of next meeting are logged.

SUMMARY COURTS-MARTIAL

0900 The summary court-martial, LT Abel JUSTICE, USN, opened in the case of SA Ralph O. WEARY, USN, 000-00-0000.

1100 The summary court-martial in the case of SA Ralph O. WEARY, USN, 000-00-0000, adjourned to await the action of the convening authority.

DEATHS

0416 GM1 William P. SEA, USN, 000-00-0000, died on board as a result of _____.

DESERTERS

0800 PN3 Guy ROAMER, USNR, 000-00-0000, was this date declared a deserter from this ship, having been UA since 0800 1 May 1979, a period of 30 days.

INJURIES

1035 During drill on the 5″ loading machine, GMSN Ira M. JONAH, USN, 000-00-0000, suffered a compound fracture of the right foot when a drill shell fell on his foot. Injury not due to his own misconduct. Treatment administered by the medical officer. Disposition: placed on the sick list.

Note: In order to protect the government from false claims and to establish a record of facts for honest claimants, it is important that there be an accurate and complete entry, including all pertinent details, of *every* injury, accident, or casualty, however slight, among the officers, crew, visitors, passengers, longshoremen, harbor-workers, or repairmen.

TEMPORARY ADDITIONAL DUTY

1400 Pursuant to COMNAVAIRPAC 1tr serial 104 of 2 Feb 1979, ENS Willy A. BRITE, USN, 000-00-0000, left the ship for TAD with NAS, Barber's Point, Hawaii.

1700 ENS Willy A. BRITE, USN, 000-00-0000, having completed TAD with NAS, Barber's Point, Hawaii, returned aboard and resumed his regular duties.

PASSENGERS

1000 Mr. Delbert Z. Brown, civilian technician, embarked for transportation to Guam, M. I. Authority: CNO 141120Z May.

Note: All passengers should be logged in and out.

PATIENTS

1306 Transferred LT Lawrence A. LEVY, USN, 000-00-0000, to U. S. Naval Hospital, Yokosuka, Japan, for treatment. Diagnosis: _____.

Note: A ship sailing in U. S. continental waters should log a patient's transfer if his absence is expected to exceed thirty days; outside those waters, such a transfer should be logged regardless of how long the absence is expected to last. Diagnosis, if known, should be included.

PERSONAL EFFECTS

1300 Personal effects of the late GM1 William P. SEA, USN, 000-00-0000, were inventoried and forwarded to _____.

SHORE PATROL

1305 Pursuant to orders of the commanding officer, BM1 Marvin A. FORCE, USN, 000-00-0000, in charge of 17 men, left the ship to report to Senior Shore Patrol Officer, Norfolk, VA, for TAD.

0200 The shore patrol detail with BM1 Marvin A. FORCE, USN, 000-00-0000, in charge, returned to the ship, having completed TAD.

LEAVE

1100 COMDESRON 15 hauled down his pennant and departed on 5 days' leave.

1110 The commanding officer departed on 5 days' leave.

0700 The commanding officer returned from 5 days' leave.

Note: Flag officers and unit commanders embarked and commanding officers are the only personnel who must be logged out on leave and in.

Safety

DIVERS

0900 Secured injection pumps in preparation for divers going over side.

0915 Divers in the water for inspection of STBD shaft.

0945 Divers out of the water.

0950 Restored all equipment to normal operation.

MEN ALOFT

0915 Secured all transmitters and rotating antennas in preparation for personnel going aloft.

0920 Men working aloft.

0945 Personnel secured from working aloft.

0950 Restored all conditions to normal operation.

Ship Movements

1100 USS R. K. TURNER (CG-20) got underway and stood out of the harbor.

1130 USS VALDEZ (FF-1096) stood into the harbor and anchored (in Berth D-3) (moored alongside Pier 4).

1300 USS OLIVER HAZARD PERRY (FFG-7) got underway from alongside this ship and anchored in Berth D-8.

1600 USS GLOVER (FF-1098) stood in and moored alongside (to port) (outboard) of USS SIERRA (AD-18).

Ship's Operational Control

0705 Changed operational control to CINCUSNAVEUR, de-
activated TG 85.3, and activated TG 65.4, composed of
DESRON 6 and DESRON 34, en route to Mediterranean
area from Norfolk, VA.

1045 Detached by COMDESRON 62 from TG 65.4 to proceed
independently to San Remo, Italy.

1435 Detached from CTU 58.3.2; changed operational control
to CTU 57.4.3.

Note: For sample entries regarding commencement of operational control and changes thereto, see UNDERWAY, under *Midwatch*, or RENDEZVOUS, under *Formations*, above.

Ships Present

Ships present: USS ENTERPRISE (CVN-65) (COMCARGRU
4 embarked), USS LONG BEACH (CGN-9), USS MT.
BAKER (AE-34), and various units of the U. S. Atlantic
Fleet, and service craft. SOPA is COMCARGRU 4 in
ENTERPRISE (CVN-65).

Ships present: Task Group 63.1 less DESRON 12 plus USS
NIMITZ (CVN-68) and various units of the British and
French navies. SOPA is COMCRUDESGRU 2 (CTG-63.1)
in NIMITZ (CVN-68).

Special Operations

0904 Underway for special operations in accordance with
CINCLANT Patrol Order 110506 7 July 1978. Maneuvering on various courses at various speeds conforming to Hampton Roads channel. Captain (at the conn)
(conning).

1125 Secured the maneuvering watch. Commenced special
operations. Commenced limiting log entries to non-
operational data as directed by the chief of naval
operations.

1840 Ceased special operations in accordance with CIN-
CLANT Patrol Order 110506 7 July 1978. Commenced
operating in accordance with COMSUBRON 1 Transit
Order 2-78.

Notes: 1. Upon termination of special operations, deck-log entries should be recorded daily by watches that adhere to the regular schedule.

2. The preceding entries are applicable only to ships that have been directed by CNO to limit the deck log to non-operational data. All other ships participating in a special type of operation, which may be classified, must make all required log entries, daily by watches, and classify the log accordingly.

Environmental Conditions

In describing significant changes in wind, weather, and atmosphere, terminology similar to that used in the code tables of the *Manual for Ship's Surface Weather Observations* (NAVWEASERVCOMINST 3144.1) should be used:

STATE OF THE SEA

Cross sea
Discolored water
Heavy sea
Heavy swell from the _____.
Heavy ground swell
Heavy rolling sea
Heavy following sea

Light ground swell
Light following sea
Light swell from the _____
Luminous or phosphorescent sea
Rough sea
Short chopping sea

MOTION OF THE SHIP

Pitching deeply and heavily
Pitching moderately
Pitching badly
Pitching easily

Rolling easily
Rolling deeply
Rolling heavily
Rolling quickly
Laboring greatly

4 | COMMUNICATIONS

Communications have been called "the voice of command," and indeed, without good communications every ship and even individual stations within a ship would be isolated. As a basic function of command and control, communications aboard ship are centralized in key control spaces, including the bridge, CIC, and damage-control center. Communications systems in ships range from the most basic, such as voice tube and buzzer, to the most modern and sophisticated satellite, and each system has specific functions and characteristics. If he is properly to exercise the command authority given him, the watch officer must be familiar with his communications systems and be able to use them with facility.

Internal communications

Internal communications have to do with the ship herself and provide the means for informing and directing her company. In their entirety, they are complicated, mastered only by the specialists who are responsible for their maintenance. A relatively small number of circuits and types of equipment relate to the duties of the watch officer, but he should have detailed knowledge of those installed in the area of the bridge and pilot house and in the CIC.

Sound-powered telephone circuits installed in most ships include the following:

  JA   Captain's battle control
  JC   Ordnance control
  JF   Flag officer

1JG Aircraft control
 JL Battle lookouts
2JC Dual-purpose battery control
1JS Sonar control
1JV Maneuvering, docking, catapult control
 JW Ship control, navigation
 JX Radio and signals
 JZ Damage control

The major circuits, such as the JA, JL, and 1JV, are the most commonly used. The watch officer should learn where they go, who mans them, and which station controls which circuit. The proper voice procedure to use on these circuits differs somewhat from voice-radio procedure. The OOD should know both procedures and enforce their use at all times. It may appear unimportant that a great variety of homemade conversation is passed over the sound-powered telephones, but when an emergency arises it will be evident that only trained talkers, using standard phraseology, can get the correct word from station to station. A ship that permits any originality over her telephones is not only incapable of first-rate performance in an emergency but is liable to experience confusion and mistakes during routine operations.

The intercommunication voice (MC) units, or "squawk-boxes," installed in important stations of most ships are normally used to pass urgent information between officers and petty officers at the station or to amplify sound-powered telephone communications. Here again circuit discipline and correct procedure must be enforced by the officer of the deck. In order to avoid confusion and speed up transmissions, the standard sound-powered phone talker's procedure is used on the MC circuits.

A complete list of MC circuits follows:

One-way systems	Purpose
1MC	Battle and general announcements
2MC	Engineers
3MC	Hangar deck

One-way systems	Purpose
4MC	Damage control
5MC	Flight deck
6MC	Boat control
7MC	Submarine control

One-way systems	Purpose
10MC	Docking control
11MC	Turret
16MC	Turret
17MC	Antiaircraft
18MC	Bridge

Two-way systems	Purpose
19MC	Ready room
20MC	Combat information
21MC	Captain's command
22MC	Radio room
23MC	Distribution control
24MC	Flag officer's command
25MC	Wardroom
26MC	Machinery control
27MC	Sonar control
28MC	Aircraft squadron
29MC	Sonar information
30MC	Bomb shop
31MC	Escape trunk

Certain types of ships have a general announcing system instead of the 1MC system and the special station-to-station communications. Regardless of the system, the principles are the same. The OOD must know what communications systems are available to him and who is on the other end. During an emergency there is no time to try to figure it out. Another important responsibility of the OOD is the *management* of the 1MC circuits. It is a good practice to keep topside 1MC speakers off while in port, except in emergencies or for safety announcements, in order to minimize the noise level and to get the attention of the crew when something of vital importance is passed. Officer circuits should be used only when the message applies to wardroom members. This same courtesy should be extended to the crew when, for example, they are sleeping in preparation for a midwatch or relaxing by watching a movie. At such times the applicable speakers should perhaps be turned off. The 1MC should not be used to call every member of the crew to the quarterdeck to take a phone call or meet a visitor. Other internal circuits or the messenger should be used for these tasks. Proper use of the 1MC is the mark of a thinking, professional watch officer.

The 1MC system

The 1MC system is the most important internal communications circuit in the ship and should be the one most closely controlled by the OOD. As mentioned in an earlier chapter, the control that the watch has over its use is one of the best indicators of how well a ship is being run. More important, however, is ensuring that messages, particularly those required by emergencies or critical situations, that are passed over the system are phrased as clearly as possible. Usage and regulations have made it possible to draw up the following list of basic 1MC messages and to standardize the phraseology to be used in passing them. When the word is passed, this phraseology should always be used:

Event	*Pipe*	*Word to be Passed*
Abandon ship (Prepare)	All hands	"All hands prepare to abandon ship. Simulate (carry out) shallow- (deep-) water destruction. Nearest land bears _____ degrees magnetic relative position (port bow) _____ miles designated enemy (friendly)." Repeat word.

Event	Pipe	Word to be Passed
Abandon ship	All hands	"All hands abandon ship. Nearest land bears _____ degrees magnetic relative position (port bow) _____ miles designated enemy (friendly)." Repeat word.
Air bedding	All hands	"All hands air bedding."
Air bedding (Completion)	Pipe down	"Pipe down all aired bedding."
Away the gig	"Long boat call"	"Away the gig, away." If the captain is not going to use his gig, omit the second "away."
Belay the word	Attention	"Belay my last."
Boarding and salvage	All hands	"Away the boarding-and-salvage party." Pass the word twice.
Boat call	Attention	"Away the motor whaleboat."
Casting off	Attention	"Standby to cast off (ship) to port (starboard)."
Carry on	None	"Carry on, carry on."
C.O. arriving or departing	Number of boat gongs depends on rank	"(Title of officer)."
Church call	None	"Divine services are now being held in _____ (space) maintain silence about the decks, knock off all games of chance."
Collision (Standby)	Collision alarm	"Standby for collision, starboard (port) side,

Event	*Pipe*	*Word to be Passed*
		frame _____ (number). All hands close all water-tight doors aft (forward) of frame _____ (number).
Collision	Collision alarm	"Collision, collision, star-board (port) side, frame _____ (number).
Colors (First call)	None	"First call, first call to col-ors." No word is passed for the execution, or for the carry-on whistle only.
	1 Whistle	To execute.
	3 Whistles	To carry on.
Condition III	Attention	"On deck Condition III, watch (one, two, or three).
Eight o'clock reports (In port)	Attention	"On deck all eight o'clock reports."
Eight o'clock reports (Underway)	Attention	"Lay before the mast all eight o'clock reports."
Fire (In port)	Rapid ringing of ship's bell	"Fire, fire, fire, class _____. Fire in compart-ment _____ (number), (compartment name), away the in-port emer-gency detail section _____ (number). Provide from repair _____ (num-ber.") Pass the word twice.
Flight quarters	All hands	"Flight quarters, flight quarters. All hands man your flight-quarters stations for (HIFR) (VERTREP) (land/launch).

Event	Pipe	Word to be Passed
		All hands not involved in flight quarters stand clear."
Securing from flight quarters	All hands	"Secure from flight quarters."
General quarters	General quarters alarm	"General quarters, general quarters. All hands man your battle stations." Pass the word twice.
Hoist boat	Hook on	"Standby to hoist in (out) the whaleboat."
Holiday routine	All hands	"Commence holiday routine."
Inspection (Personnel)	All hands	"Quarters for captain's personnel inspection."
Inspection (Material)	All hands	"Standby all lower (upper) deck spaces for inspection."
Inspection (Berthing and messing)	All hands	"Standby for captain's (XO's) inspection of messing and berthing spaces."
Knock off	Pipe down	"Knock off ship's work."
Late bunks	Attention	"Up all late bunks."
Liberty	All hands	"Liberty call, liberty call. Liberty commences for sections _____ to expire on board at _____."
Mail call	Attention	"Mail call."
Man overboard	None	"Man overboard port (starboard) side." (*Type of Re-*

Event	Pipe	Word to be Passed
		covery) Pass the word twice.
Mast	Attention	"All mast reports, witnesses, and division officers concerned assemble _____ (place)."
Material condition	Attention	"Set material condition Yoke, (Zebra), (X-ray). Duty damage-control petty officer make reports to _____ (place)."
Meals	Pipe down	None.
Mess gear	Long heave around	"Mess gear."
Mistake	Attention	"Belay my last."
Muster of restricted men	Attention	"Muster all restricted men."
Movie call	Attention	"Movie call."
Movie riggers	Attention	"Duty division _____ division sweep-down crew movie area."
Motor whale-boat	Attention	"Away the motor whale-boat."
Officers (unidentified)	Number of boat gongs depends on rank	"(Rank of officer)."
Officer's call	Attention	"Officer's call."
Pay day	All hands	"Pay day for the crew."
Preparation for getting underway	All hands	"Make all preparation for getting underway."

Event	Pipe	Word to be Passed
Prize crew	All hands	"Away the prize crew." Pass the word twice.
Quarters	All hands	"All hands to quarters for muster, instruction, and inspection."
Quarters (Foul weather)	All hands	"All hands to quarters for muster, instruction, and inspection, foul-weather parade."
Quarters (Leaving port)	All hands	"Quarters for leaving port."
Rain squall	Attention	"Haul over all hatch hoods and gun covers."
Readiness reports	Attention	"All department heads make ready for sea reports to the officer of the deck on the bridge."
Receiving alongside	Attention	"Standby to receive (ship) (barge) alongside to port (starboard)."
Relieving the watch	Attention	"Relieve the watch, relieve the watch, relieve the wheel and lookouts, on deck section _____."
Repel boarders	All hands	"All hands repel boarders." Pass the word twice.
Replenishment (Refueling)	Attention	"Go to your stations, all the replenishment (refueling) detail."
Rescue and assistance	Attention	"Away the rescue-and-assistance detail. Muster at _____ (area). Section

Event	*Pipe*	*Word to be Passed*
		_____ provide (do not provide)."
Reveille	All hands	"Reveille, reveille. All hands heave out and trice up. The smoking lamp is lighted in all authorized spaces."
Secure the sea and anchor detail	Pipe down	"Secure the sea and anchor detail."
Secure	Pipe down	"Secure from (event)."
Shifting the watch	Attention	"The officer of the deck is shifting his watch to the quarterdeck (bridge)."
Security alert	None	"Security alert, security alert. Away the security-alert force. All hands stand fast."
Side boys	Attention	"Lay to the quarterdeck the side boys."
Smoking lamp (Lighted)	Attention	"The smoking lamp is lighted in all authorized spaces."
Smoking lamp (Out)	Attention	"The smoking lamp is out throughout the ship while . . ." or "The smoking lamp is out in (space or area) while. . . ."
Special sea detail	All hands	"Go to your stations, all of the special sea detail."
Sweepers (At sea)	Sweepers	"Sweepers, sweepers, man your brooms, give the ship

Event	*Pipe*	*Word to be Passed*
		a clean sweep-down fore and aft, sweep down all lower decks, ladder wells, and passageways. Now, sweepers."
Sweepers (In port)	Sweepers	"Sweepers, sweepers, man your brooms, give the ship a clean sweep-down fore and aft, sweep down all lower decks, ladder wells, and passageways, take all trash to the receptacles provided on the pier."
Taps	None	"Taps, taps, lights out, all hands turn into your bunks. Maintain silence about the decks, the smoking lamp is out in all berthing spaces."
Test alarms	None	"The following is a test of the general, chemical, and collision alarms from the _____ (space)."
Turn to	Turn to	"Turn to continue ship's work" or "Turn to commence ship's work."
Visit and search	All hands	"Away the visit-and-search crew." Pass the word twice.
Working party	All hands	"Now muster a _____ (number) -hand working party (place) with (person in charge)."
Men working aloft	None	"There are men working aloft. Do not rotate, radi-

Event	*Pipe*	*Word to be Passed*
		ate, or energize any electronic equipment while men are working aloft." Pass the word every thirty minutes.
Divers	None	"There are divers working over the side. Do not operate any equipment, rotate screws, cycle rudder (planes or torpedo-tube shutters), take suction from or discharge to the sea, blow or vent any tanks, activate sonar or underwater electrical equipment, open or close any valves, or cycle trash-disposal unit before checking with the diving supervisor (name and rate) or the Officer of the Deck."
Divers (Completed)	None	"Diving operations are completed. Carry on normal and routine work in accordance with previous instructions."
Titivate ship	All hands	"Now titivate ship."

Sound-powered telephone procedures

Standard phraseology and discipline must be maintained over sound-powered telephone circuits. When unofficial conversation is the norm and discipline breaks down, information is lost or, even worse, the wrong information is passed. The discipline of the sound-powered phone circuits is a reflection of the professionalism of the OOD.

When headphones are being worn by phone talkers at both stations, a message can be stated with the call up. For example, if the CIC phone talker has data to pass to the bridge phone talker, the following is passed:

CIC phone talker: "Bridge, combat. Combat reports a contact bearing 040°T, 19,000 yds., on course 330°T, speed 10 knots. CPA is 270°T, 5,000 yds, at time 1045."

The receiving phone talker repeats back the message and answers as follows:

Bridge phone talker: "Bridge, aye. Contact bearing 040°T, 19,000 yds, on course 330°T, speed 10 knots. CPA is 270°T, 5,000 yds, at time 1045."

The repeat-back procedures are critical to insuring that the proper word is received.

Ships' alarm

All ships are equipped with a general alarm, a chemical alarm, and some form of collision alarm. Each of these alarms has a distinctive sound that should be immediately recognizable to all hands. Some ships have, in addition to these universal alarms, special-purpose signals to provide safety or security for critical spaces and situations. Most ships have some sort of alarm system designed to provide a signal on the bridge and quarterdeck station, as well as at local stations, when the temperature in the magazines reaches a certain degree. Non-aviation ships that carry helicopters have an alarm that signals a helicopter crash. Ship's routine usually calls for testing the various alarms on the morning watch and before getting underway. Testing of specialized alarms is normally scheduled as an action of a planned maintenance system (PMS).

Boat gongs and side boys

Most ships sound gongs to indicate the prospective departure of officers' boats and the arrival or departure of visiting officers, unit commanders embarked, and the commanding officer. Some ships use "beeps" on the chemical alarm, rather than gongs, to indicate the arrival or departure of officials. As a boat signal, the gongs are sounded *three* times, ten minutes before the departure of the boat; *twice*, when there are five minutes to go; and *once*, with one minute to go before the boat leaves.

When used to indicate the arrival or departure of an officer, the gongs are sounded in pairs, the same number as the side boys the officer rates, followed by the name of the officer's command or by the word "staff." Gongs, when used this way, are not honors but merely inform those aboard ship of the arrival and departure of senior officers and the departure of crews' boats. In a nest the ships may agree, or the senior CO direct, that such gongs will not be sounded for COs of outboard ships making routine crossings of inboard ships. Officers rate side boys and gongs as follows:

Rank	*Side boys/gongs*
Fleet admiral and vice admiral	Eight
Rear admiral	Six
Captain and commander	Four
Lieutenant commander through ensign	Two

External communications

As a rule, three categories of external communications relate to the watch officer: voice, visual, and record. Each of these modes meets a specific type of communications requirement, and a ship at sea is likely to be using all of them simultaneously to transmit and receive information. With the exception of the visual means, technical control of all communications equipment is the responsibility of the radio watch supervisor or, on larger ships, the communications watch officer. In this regard, the term *technical control* should be clearly understood. The watch supervisor in radio does *not* control what messages are transmitted or received. What he does do is maintain the communications path by monitoring the performance of equipment and placing traffic on a circuit.

Voice communications

To an increasing extent, voice communication is the primary command-and-control tool for the watch officer on the bridge and in CIC. Voice radio-telephone (R/T) is used to pass tactical signals, to report sensor information, and to coordinate operations between units. The use of each R/T circuit is established in the operational commander's communications plan, as are the net control station, if any, and special instructions and procedures for use of the circuit. Depending on their function, R/T circuits may be controlled by operators on the bridge, in CIC, or at other locations. It is extremely important that there be no confusion between CIC and the bridge over who controls, answers, or logs a given circuit, and each watch officer should confirm, as he begins his watch, what the circuit-guarding arrangement is.

Voice radio circuits can be established on almost any frequency, but are most commonly in the high-frequency (HF) band, between 2 and 30 megahertz, or in the ultra-high-frequency (UHF) band, between 225 and 400 megahertz. The former frequencies are usually allocated to long-range circuits for dispersed formations, and the latter are used mainly for short-range, line-of-sight communications. Because of its comparative directionality and short range, transmissions over UHF have the advantage of being difficult for an enemy to detect at long ranges. HF transmissions, on the other hand, can be detected for thousands of miles.

Correct use of the R/T should be one of the first things that a junior watch officer learns. Use of proper procedures and terminology and the ability to authenticate and quickly encode and decode information are basic skills. The competence with which a watch officer handles R/T communications is one of the most visible measures of his professionalism, as well as being one of the best indicators of his ship's operational smartness. From time to time every ship experiences some difficulty with voice communications. The extent to which such difficulties affect operations and the speed with which they are resolved are usually in direct proportion to the watch officer's knowledge of his communications. When it appears that R/T signals are not being heard by other ships, the most common error is for the watch officer or CIC to assume that the equipment is bad and to order that it be shifted or that new gear be put on the line. As often as not, after the new equipment has been patched in, it is found that the problem still exists or that new problems have arisen. At this point both the OOD and the CIC watch officer are ordering new circuit patches, antennas, and equipment, and the radio watch has lost all control of the equipment setup. The problem eventually gets solved, but not without considerable frustration, missed signals, and frayed tempers.

To avoid this sort of confusion, the watch officers in CIC and on the bridge must allow the communicators to do their job. When a circuit suddenly stops working, the chances are that something has been done to make that happen and that only a systematic investigation of all the equipment, remote units, and patching systems can discover the cause. If the watch in radio is allowed to carry out its responsibility for technical control of the circuit, in all likelihood the problem can be found and corrected. If, on the other hand, it is constantly setting up new equipment or changing patches at the insistence of the bridge and CIC, the chances are that, before long, no one will have control of the situation. The watch officer who understands this and has the patience to allow his communicators to do their job has a minimum of trouble.

Two general categories of signals are transmitted over R/T circuits: executive and nonexecutive. Nonexecutive signals are administrative or contain information. Executive signals contain the word "execute" and require an action by the ship. They are subdivided into delayed executive and immediate executive. The delayed executive signals give the OOD time to calculate the required action that will be carried out when the signal is executed. Immediate executive messages require immediate response. The OOD must understand the different categories and what is required of him and his ship.

The use of VHF communications has increased dramatically. The VHF circuits are usually reserved for direct conversations between the OODs of ships to clarify intentions, weather reports, and Coast Guard safety information. With the growth of the use of VHF communications has come a corresponding increase in net traffic. The general channel assignments, as specified by the Vessel Bridge-to-Bridge Radiotelephone Act, are these:

Channel 16   Coast Guard/Emergency use
Channel 13   General bridge-to-bridge traffic

If a conversation of any length is required, the OOD should recommend switching to a channel other than 16 or 13. The Vessel Bridge-to-Bridge Radiotelephone Act is applicable on waters subject to the inland rules. In some cases, the act may apply all the way out to the three-mile limit, depending on where the three-mile lines are located. It requires the OOD or the watch officer of civil vessels of over 300 gross tons (100 gross tons if carrying passengers), towing vessels of over 26 feet, and all dredges and floating platforms, to transmit and confirm on the designated frequency the intentions of his vessel and any other information necessary for the safe navigation of vessels. See U. S. Coast Guard navigation rules for complete details of this act. It is vital that the OOD carefully monitor the VHF circuits for safety information, especially when entering or leaving port. In addition, a log of applicable transmissions is required.

Visual communications

Communications by visual means are the most secure of all but are limited by both distance and visibility. Maximum use should be made of visual communications, especially when a force wants to remain undetected. All officers standing watch on deck should be able to read their own ship's flashing-light call sign and, regardless of what kind of visual watch is being kept, be constantly alert for the signals of other ships. Signal flags should be committed to memory. Learning to recognize all the flags in the flag bag is not difficult and is well worth the effort. Most flag signals are taken from the *Allied Maritime Tactical Signal Book* (ATP-1, Vol. II) or, when a merchant ship is being signaled, from *H.O.102*. The instructions for use at the beginning of these publications must be thoroughly understood in order that the officer may encode and decode signals correctly. Specific signals, even those that are often used, should *not* be memorized, since ATP-1 is subject to change at any time. The practice of breaking or encoding signals from memory can lead to potentially dangerous mistakes. The signals relating to the incidents-at-sea agreement between the United States and the U.S.S.R. are extremely important and should be reviewed whenever there is a possibility that they will be used. It is most important for the OOD to know the ships for which he has visual responsibility. Of particular importance is knowing the difference in meaning between flag hoists at the dip and closed up. When in port, the OOD must be alert for the single flags flying on units moored nearby that could indicate a special evolution such as man aloft, divers in the water, or another ship coming alongside.

Record communications

Most of the nontactical communications sent and received by a ship are handled by radioteletype as record communications. The watch officer on the bridge or in CIC is usually authorized to release various types of messages such as weather reports, bathythermograph reports, or in the case of CIC, certain contact reports. His responsibility as releasing officer is to make sure that these messages are in the correct format and are addressed properly. In addition, it is a good idea occasionally to check the breakdown of coded information in weather and bathythermograph messages to ensure that the information being sent out is correct.

5 | THE WATCH UNDERWAY

The officer of the deck underway is that officer on watch who has been designated by the commanding officer to be in charge of the ship. He is primarily responsible, under the commanding officer, for the safe and proper operation of the ship.

OpNavInst 3120.32.

The position of watch officer underway carries with it unmatched responsibility and authority. When the commanding officer certifies an officer as qualified to be in charge of the underway watch he is displaying a unique degree of personal trust in his judgment, ability, and intelligence. It is a trust that cannot be taken lightly, and one that must be repeatedly justified by performance. Watch-standing at sea is the most important of a junior officer's duties and is the yardstick by which his potential as a surface-warfare officer will be judged. It also offers the finest kind of reward in terms of professional achievement and personal satisfaction. Qualification as a watch officer marks the completion of the first major step toward command at sea and should be the primary goal of every seagoing officer.

Preparing for the watch

Preparation for standing a watch underway does not begin when an officer climbs the ladder to the bridge or CIC. Physical and psychological preparation must begin long before that. The performance of an officer who goes on watch tired, cold, or hungry will be impaired, no matter how capable he may be, and if he is preoccupied with other matters he will not reach that high level of concentration that makes the true professional. The specific way to prepare for a watch is a matter of personal preference, but there are certain things that should become habitual: being dressed properly for the situation, including foul-weather gear if it might be needed; on a cold night, drinking some soup or eating hot food before taking over; and carrying whatever personal equipment will be needed. This last is, again, a matter of personal preference, but should always include a flashlight fitted with a red lens, something to write with, a pad or notebook, and, on a bright day, sunglasses.

Concentration

The ability to concentrate on the job at hand is vital to anyone who performs an exacting task. This is as true of watch officers as it is of surgeons and professional athletes. A watch officer cannot allow himself under any circumstances to be distracted from his duties. No departmental project or personal problem can be allowed to supersede his concentration on the watch. If a watch officer has a personal problem that is serious enough to interfere with his performance, he should discuss the situation with his captain and, if it is necessary, ask to be temporarily taken off the watch bill. Although this kind of action may seem a bit drastic, it is the intelligent thing to do, and the commanding officer, realizing this, will respect the judgment of the officer concerned.

Getting the picture

[The officer of the deck will] keep himself continually informed concerning the tactical situation and geographic factors which may affect the safe navigation of the ship, and take appropriate action to avoid the danger of grounding or collision in accordance with tactical doctrine, the Rules of the Road, and the orders of the commanding officer or other proper authority.

OpNavInst 3120.32.

Information from CIC

Standing a deck watch on a modern warship is far too demanding a task to be undertaken without advance briefing. Usually, the watch officer is expected to brief himself. Therefore, the value of his briefing depends upon whether he knows what questions to ask and what to look for. He should always check in with CIC before he is due on the bridge. The following is a partial list of the kinds of information that he should expect to get from CIC:

1. Formation disposition and location of OTC and guide(s).

2. Ship's condition of readiness; which weapons are manned; the status of weapon systems.

3. What emission-control (EMCON) plan is in effect.

4. Changes in schedule of events, operations order, or task group commander's letter of instruction since his last watch.

5. Which tactical voice circuits are guarded by CIC and which by the bridge. Net-control authority, if assigned, and type of call signs to be used.

6. What recognition and authentication systems are in effect.

7. What intelligence is available on enemy, allied, and other forces.

8. What intelligence-reporting requirements are assigned to his ship.

9. The assignment of surface, air, subsurface, and electronic-warfare reporting within the task group, with particular emphasis on his ship's responsibilities.

10. The status of combat air patrol, electronic-warfare aircraft, and other air assets. His own ship's control duties, if any.

11. His own ship's scheduled flight operations, helicopter or fixed-wing.

Information from the TAO and the CIC watch officer

No attempt will be made here to discuss in detail the duties of the tactical action officer, but the OOD should have a precise understanding of the command relationship between himself and the TAO. Before assuming the watch, he should discuss with the TAO any modification to the standard relationships prescribed by *OpNavInst* 3120.32. The ten or fifteen minutes that the OOD takes in planning with the TAO for the upcoming watch will do a great deal toward ensuring a smooth, well-coordinated watch. When a CIC watch officer, rather than a TAO, is assigned, the same procedure should be used, even though the command relationship differs.

Information from other control centers

Depending on the mission of the ship, other watch stations of importance to the OOD may be manned. In a frigate engaged in antisubmarine warfare (ASW), for example, the watch in sonar control is as important as those on the bridge and in CIC. Therefore, before going on watch, the OOD should be familiar with the status and duties of other watch stations. In the case of a ship with an ASW mission, he should be aware of environmental conditions, the active and passive equipment in use and the mode of its operation, and the recommended action to be taken by him if contact is gained. Similarly, in a ship whose primary mission is flight operations, he must understand the capabilities and limitations of the aircraft that will be operating, and be aware of the carrier's maneuvering restrictions and the type of missions to be expected on his watch. As noted earlier, the watch officer should stop by the engineering control station and discuss with the EOOW the status of the propulsion plant and any training, preventive maintenance, or corrective maintenance that the engineers would like to conduct, operations permitting. A tour of topside spaces will quickly prepare the oncoming OOD for heavy weather. A walk-through of other watch stations will demonstrate to the watchstanders the interest of the OOD and remind them that he is in charge.

On the bridge

When the watch officer is satisfied that he has all the information he needs from CIC and other watch stations, it is time to begin the turnover process on the bridge. If it is a night watch, he should take the time, before and during the relieving process, to adapt his vision to the darkness. The safety of the ship at night may depend on his ability—and that of the lookouts—to see in the dark. This is called dark adaptation. Owls and other nocturnal creatures have acute night vision, because, although they are essentially color-blind and can see neither detail nor distant objects, their eyes are very sensitive to motion. Man, having evolved as basically diurnal in nature, has developed eyes that see color and distant objects in daylight. He can see at night, but he can see much better if he understands the physiology of the human eye.

All vision depends on light-sensitive nerve endings in the retina of the eye, called rods and cones, which transmit to the brain an impression of the image formed on the retina by the lens of the eye. The cones, in the center, are color-sensitive. The rods, in a circle around the cones, detect variations in light intensity, but are highly sensitive to motion. So at night, when there is no color to see, the cones tend to make spots in front of the eyes if a fixed point is stared at too long, but a look out of the corners of the eyes forces the motion-sensitive rods to take over. They won't tell the color of a ship ahead, but they may enable an observer to see that she is moving and thus avoid running into her.

Daylight, in which the rods furnish color perception, is composed of all the colors in the spectrum. The cones are active only in the lower, red range of the spectrum: thus dim red lights have little adverse effect on night vision. It is possible to work on a bridge or in a pilot house so lighted, then move out to the bridge wing and be able to see perfectly.

Exposure to a white light at night greatly reduces vision. A carelessly used flashlight, an open hatch, or even the flare of a match, may so reduce the conning officer's perception that he fails to see a small craft or other object in the water.

Good night vision depends on a slow, roving gaze that systematically covers the field of vision in a simple geometric pattern. Dim objects, almost invisible if looked at directly, will be picked up. If something is sighted and then lost, it is a mistake to concentrate on where it should be. The thing to do is move the eyes all around the spot in a circle. If something was seen and it is moving, the rods in the eyes will find it again.

The effect of bright sunlight on the eyes lasts long after the sun goes down. Men exposed to strong sunlight during the day can see only half as well as others at night; they should wear dark sunglasses topside on bright days. The amount of light by which the eyes perceive motion at sea on a clear, star-lit night is only 1/150,000,000 that of bright sunlight; they need all the help they can get.

The OOD's first few minutes on the bridge is a good time for him to begin getting the "feel" of the watch. If it is at night, he should stand clear of all personnel on watch while his eyes become adapted. Once he feels comfortable, he should start his watch by reading carefully the captain's night orders.

The night-order book

Night orders are a statement in writing of how the captain wants his ship to be run when he is not on the bridge. They are divided into two parts: standing orders, which express the commanding officer's policy and directions under *all* circumstances, and orders for dealing with the situation for each day (see appendix A). The officer of the deck should study and thoroughly understand the standing orders before he assumes his first watch on the bridge of a ship, and he should review them at least monthly and after any long period in port. The second part of the night orders contains a summary of tactical, navigational, and readiness information. Additional information and guidance are added by the captain and the navigator in the narrative sections of the orders. The night orders are signed each night by the navigator and the captain, and the information they contain may not be changed without the permission of the captain. They are also signed by the OOD and JOOD on a watch-to-watch basis. When ships are steaming in company, night intentions are often signaled by the OTC, screen commander, or other unit commander. These night intentions should be studied with the same care as the night orders, since they are in a broader sense the "night orders" of the commander.

The oral turnover

The final and most important phase of relieving the watch is the oral turnover. At this time the officer taking over must obtain or verify all the information he will need to stand his watch, making sure that he understands exactly what is expected. The following is a list of the minimum information that he should obtain during the turnover process.

Navigational information

1. Position of the ship, how and when determined, and fix accuracy.

2. Course and speed; engine rpm required to keep station or maintain required speed of advance (SOA).

3. Method of plotting the ship's position to be used (radar, omega, dead reckoning, etc.) and frequency with which fixes are to be taken.

4. Time and position of expected radar or visual landfall, if any.

5. Aids to navigation in sight or expected; times and positions of expected sightings.

6. Depth of water.

7. Planned changes of course and speed.

8. Possible hazards to navigation.

9. Weather and hydrographic conditions, including winds, currents, barometer trends, and any unusual weather that may be expected.

Tactical information

In addition to the information already obtained from CIC, the following points should be reviewed:

1. The ship's station, location of the guide, and visual identification of the guide.

2. If in a line or multiple-line formation, the prescribed order, distance interval, and sequence numbers.

3. Zigzag or evasive steering plan in effect.

4. Base course, signaled speed, base speed, stationing speed, and maximum speed expected to be required during the watch.

5. Amount and frequency of course and speed changes required to remain in station or in sector, and effects of weather on station-keeping.

6. Expected changes in formation or dispositions, attachments and detachments, and rendezvous information.

7. Maneuvering peculiarities and limitations of other ships in the formation, and approach limits for ships unable to maneuver freely.

8. Lighting and deceptive measures in force.

9. OTC's emergency instructions.

10. Status of all contacts.

Readiness information

1. Status of engineering plant. Speed limitation, equipment on the line, generator and boiler lineup. Casualties to equipment or machinery that affect the speed or maneuverability of the ship.

2. Expected times of light-off or securing of main propulsion (boilers, gas turbines, etc.).

3. Readiness and material conditions set. Expected changes to existing conditions.

4. Status of lookouts, watches, and special details, if set.

5. Status of the watch relief.

6. Unexecuted orders, signals, or evolutions.

7. Changes to scheduled evolution, watch assignments, and watch-standing personnel.

8. Officer having the conn.

9. Location of the captain and flag or unit commanders embarked.

10. Staff duty officer and staff watches assigned, if applicable.

Relieving the watch

Once he is satisfied that he has all the information he needs to stand the watch and has a grasp of the current situation, the oncoming duty officer is ready to relieve the watch. Although the relieving should certainly not be done hastily, it is discourteous to drag it out unnecessarily with questions about minutiae. The relief should be ready to take over about fifteen minutes before the hour. However, no matter how well prepared the new watch may be, it is never wise to take over during an evolution or maneuver.

Relieving a watch is, as stated earlier, a formal process. By saying "I relieve you, sir," the new OOD is announcing to the watch that he has formally accepted responsibility for the watch. Use of any other terminology can leave the matter in doubt. As soon as he has relieved, the OOD should inform the watch of that fact by announcing clearly, "This is _____. I have the deck (and, if so, the conn)." The helmsman and lee helmsman will acknowledge this by calling out, "Aye, aye, sir" and repeating the course steered, magnetic heading, engine order, and rpm rung up. This procedure should always be followed when a new watch comes on duty. It is the proper way to begin.

Organizing the watch

When the entire watch has been relieved, the OOD should check its organization to make sure that it is set up to his satisfaction. Probably the first thing that he will find is that a number of the people on watch with him are undergoing watch qualification and instruction. Supervising the training of these men is an important duty for the OOD and his watch leaders. The boatswain's mate of the watch has specific duties in regard to training the watch, as do the other senior petty officers in the section, and they should be made to take an active part in the training of new men. It is part of the OOD's duty to see that the personnel who are under instruction are indeed being instructed, and not merely "broken in" by non-rated men who happen to have been aboard for a longer time. The latter type of instruction is a sure way to perpetuate bad habits and a generally casual attitude toward qualification.

Training of the watch is generally considered to apply primarily to the lookouts, helmsmen, lee helmsmen, and phone-talkers, on the assumption that such key watch-standers as the quartermaster and the boatswain's mate of the watch are already qualified and need no further instruction. This assumption, however, is not always valid. In many ships, senior boatswain's mates are not on the watch bill, and they assign junior-rated men or promising strikers as boatswain's mates of the watch (BMOW) underway. Although there is nothing inherently wrong with this, it often leads to a nonrated boatswain striker's being in charge of a watch composed of his peers. In this case, unless he is a very strong leader, he may have difficulty setting and enforcing standards on the watch, and the watch officer will be deprived of his most important watch leader, trainer, and supervisor.

A watch officer who finds himself in this situation will have to either train the man to acceptable standards or, if that fails, relieve him in favor of a qualified BMOW. If the situation is serious, the best long-term solution is to take the matter up with the senior watch officer. The BMOW is the most important member of a watch team and should be able to perform to the required standards. If he cannot, it will be almost impossible to train the rest of the watch.

A similar situation often obtains with the quartermaster of the watch (QMOW). The duties assigned to him by *OpNavInst* 3120.32 are wide-ranging and require considerable knowledge as well as completion of an extensive formal PQS program. His responsibilities in the areas of log-keeping, weather observation, and navigational assistance to the OOD affect not only the operation of the watch but a number of other areas such as the accuracy of weather forecasts sent to the ship, the credibility of the deck log and, in some circumstances, the safe navigation of the ship.

A quartermaster's ability to do his job properly is something that the OOD must verify to his own satisfaction by reading the weather data recorded, checking the accuracy of the navigational plot, and closely examining log entries. He may find, for example, that a wind whose velocity and direction have been constant for some time suddenly shifts and shows a radical change in speed when the watch is relieved. Some watch-standers are so oblivious to conditions that they will walk onto the lee wing of the bridge in a gale, record a low wind speed, and think nothing of it. When sent to a weather facility for analysis, inaccurate data can result in a ship's receiving an inaccurate forecast and, consequently, being in considerable danger. Quartermasters should be trained to observe, to use common sense, and if in doubt to call the navigator.

When the OOD has a general idea of the qualifications of his watch, he can decide how and in what areas to train them for the next four hours. If the ship is steaming independently and there are no other ships or hazards in the area, emergency steering drills and procedures should always be carried out. The process of shifting steering units and steering control from station to station and making the required reports is not very difficult, but it must be understood thoroughly by all watch-standers, and the best way to understand it is to do it. Knowing the location and use of alarms, backup systems, and special lights is also an important training requirement, particularly on night watches. This kind of training should be pushed as hard as the tactical situation permits. It will pay big dividends, not only in terms of watch proficiency but also in the satisfaction and pride of the watch-standers. Most people enjoy knowing that they are doing something well and will appreciate the OOD's making the effort to help them to qualify.

Every watch-station qualification is governed by a formal personal qualifications standard (PQS). Checking the PQS status of each of the watch-standers and taking the opportunity to sign off PQS items is a superb way of conducting on-watch training. The watch-standers will feel a sense of accomplishment in seeing actual progress towards a goal, and the OOD will be "qualifying his watch-standers," not just "breaking them in." Innovative ideas on training that meet with the captain's permission will prevent dullness and the development of slothful habits and will help ensure that the team is alert.

Junior officers of the deck (JOODs) should be made to play an important role in training the watch, even in areas where they are not well qualified. With proper supervision by the OOD, they will learn by teaching others.

The conn

To conn means to control, or direct by rudder angles and engine-order telegraph, the movements of a ship. *The conn* means the station of the conning officer. The OOD may have both the deck and the conn, but it is customary for the commanding officer to take the conn when an intricate or dangerous maneuver is to be performed. It is also customary for the OOD to assist in such maneuvers by checking on how the members of the bridge watch are performing their duties and keeping a watchful eye on the entire maneuver in order to inform the commanding officer of any potential danger that might escape his notice. Likewise, when the officer of the deck has the conn during a delicate maneuver or in restricted waters, it is customary for the commanding officer to be on the bridge, watching the overall picture. In effect, then, there is a two-person system in which one person has the conn, giving all orders to the wheel and the engines, and another person assists and advises.

Directing the movements of a modern warship at high speed and in close proximity to other ships is a job that requires intense concentration and the ability to keep ahead of a dynamic tactical situation. At night or when a number of ships are maneuvering simultaneously, it takes only a minute or two of distraction for a conning officer to become so disoriented that he places his ship in danger. For this reason, the officer who has the conn must be able to concentrate all his attention on the job at hand, free from distractions and conflicting duties. During maneuvers the officer at the conn should not have to concern himself with getting the word passed, signing sounding-and-security logs, or becoming involved in any of the other duties of running the watch. When the OOD is at the conn, he should delegate these duties to his JOOD, and similarly, when he gives the conn to his JOOD, he should assume responsibility for carrying out the routine of the watch. Firm enforcement of the policy of not allowing the conning officer to be distracted goes a long way toward reducing the possibility of confusion in tight situations.

Although there is no official set of rules about the conn, the following principles have been accepted by experienced seagoing naval officers.

1. One and only one person can give steering and engine orders at any one time.

2. The identity of the person giving these orders must be known to the people on the bridge.

3. The OOD may delegate the conn to another officer, but he retains responsibility for the ship's safety.

4. The commanding officer may take over the deck or the conn. When the CO takes over the deck, the OOD has no technical responsibility for the direction of the ship's movements, except as specifically detailed by the commanding officer. But when the commanding officer takes over the conn, the OOD carries out all the duties assigned to him by regulations and assists and advises the commanding officer.

5. In taking the conn from the OOD, the captain should do so in such a manner that all personnel of the bridge watch are notified of the fact. If he takes over because emergency action is required, however, the issuing of a direct steering or engine order constitutes his legal assumption of responsibility for directing the ship's movements. When he takes the conn in this manner, the commanding officer retains that responsibility until he formally turns the conn over to another person.

6. Every commanding officer establishes a procedure for letting it be known beyond any doubt that he has assumed direct control of the ship and thereby relieved the conning officer of all responsibility for such control. The procedure for delegating control of the ship to a conning officer must be equally positive. These transfers of control are usually made known by the announcement "This is _____. I have the conn." All bridge personnel, but especially the helmsman and lee helmsman, must acknowledge their receipt of the information with the words "Aye, aye, sir." It is also customary for the helmsman and the lee helmsman to respond by sounding off the course being steered, the magnetic-compass course, and the speed and rpm indicated on the ship-control console.

The officer of the deck has no problem to solve if the above principles are observed at all times in his ship. But even the best of commanding officers is a fallible human being and may, while concentrating on the vital matters at hand, neglect to follow the recommended procedure in taking over or relinquishing the conn. Under these circumstances, it is up to the OOD to clarify the situation with a polite, "Do you have the conn, sir?" or "I have the conn, sir." Then he must see that important persons on the bridge know who has the conn.

When the OOD does not have the conn, he should assist the officer who does. One of the most important ways of doing this is by making sure that the conning officer's orders are *understood and acted upon correctly* by the helmsman and other bridge personnel and that the conning officer knows that his orders are being executed. The OOD may take station where he can best assist the conning officer in maintaining a lookout.

Combat information center

In modern naval operations the combat information center (CIC) and the bridge function as separate facets of a tactical team. Their roles vary according to the type of operations the ship is carrying out, but they are never independent of one another. Since the position of tactical action officer (TAO) came into being, CIC and the bridge have become even more interdependent, and no officer who stands a watch in either of these control stations should attempt to "go it alone."

It used to be the function of CIC to collect, evaluate, display, and disseminate information pertaining to the control of the ship. In today's warships, however, the function of evaluating has been expanded to include, in some situations, actual control of the ship, its sensors, and its weapon systems. Traditionally, the commanding officer's general-quarters station was the bridge. Nowadays, he often exercises control from CIC, since the information available to help him in his decision-making simply cannot be presented on the bridge. This arrangement in no way lessens the importance of the OOD as the officer responsible for the safety and proper operation of the ship. It does, however, require him to possess a broad and intimate knowledge of how CIC operates and what its capabilities and limitations are. The OOD must also know at all times what his command relationship with the TAO is. Confusion on this point leads, at best, to poor coordination between the bridge and CIC, and, at worst, to disaster. It is for this reason that the pre-watch briefing mentioned earlier in the chapter is so important.

Although it is equipped with a variety of sensors, evaluating devices, and data-processing equipment, CIC does have certain limitations. The array of equipment in the modern CIC is so impressive, and sometimes overwhelming, that it is easy to forget this fact. Compared with the capabilities of a million-dollar radar, the eyes of a simple lookout may seem to be very unimpressive sensors. Yet there are times when the only reliable source of information is that lookout, and the usefulness of the entire complex of systems and sensors depends on the accuracy of the information that he can provide. Regardless of how sophisticated a CIC may be or how well trained its watch team, it sometimes happens, especially when maneuvering at close quarters is involved, that the information furnished to the bridge by CIC is incomplete or inaccurate. This is where the OOD's judgment and confidence in his own abilities become important. He must always be aware that he is not only a user of the information provided by CIC, but a major contributor, evaluator, and verifier of the tactical picture. When CIC proposes a course of action that is wrong, it is probably because coordination with the bridge has somehow broken down. It is the responsibility of the OOD to set the situation straight and, when there is time, go over the event with the CIC watch officer or TAO to find out what went wrong. What he should *not* do in this kind of situation is engage in argument with the CIC watch while the situation is deteriorating.

Under most normal steaming conditions, the main channels of routine communication between the bridge and CIC are sound-powered telephone circuits. This means that no matter the quality and quantity of information available for exchange between the two stations, its usefulness depends on the ability of the few individuals, usually nonrated and often nondesignated, who man the circuits. The performance of the telephone-talkers, particularly those on the bridge, can be a major source of conflict and misunderstanding. The bridge talker is often a nonrated man from a deck division who has very little idea of what goes on in CIC and less understanding of the terms, acronyms, and figures that are passed to him. If he makes a mistake he probably will not even know he has done so until he is reprimanded by the OOD or, even worse, ridiculed by the CIC telephone-talker at the other end of the line. When this occurs, it is entirely possible that he will become frustrated, get frightened, or, if the pressure is great, freeze up completely, usually just when he is needed most.

There is an easy way for the OOD to prevent this from happening. He should make the bridge telephone-talker aware of the importance of his job and give him enough familiarization with CIC to enable him to have some understanding of the meaning of the information that is entrusted to him to communicate. On a quiet watch, when no demanding evolutions are expected, talkers can be rotated into CIC for basic indoctrination on radarscopes, contact reporting, and simple procedures. At the same time, it is a good idea to man the bridge telephones and, if possible, one of the lookout stations with CIC watch-standers. It will be an education for both parties, and probably a welcome change from routine duties. For special evolutions, the OOD should not hesitate to put a more senior man on the phones, calling him if necessary to the bridge for the watch. The same applies to bridge and engineering control stations. The OOD should always remember that the entire resources of the ship are at his disposal to get the job done, and he should not hesitate to use any of them if necessary.

In summary, the most important thing to remember about bridge-CIC relations is that both watch centers are part of the same ship-control team and that they share the responsibility for providing the captain, the OOD, and the TAO with the best possible support of the ship's mission.

Aircraft carrier flight operations

In an aircraft carrier, the OOD meets situations not encountered in other types of ships. Flight operations themselves greatly complicate the routine of a ship. Her very size makes the efficient administration of a carrier difficult, unless she is skillfully organized. In large carriers the OOD is supported by a junior (assistant) officer of the deck as well as a junior officer of the watch. The latter frequently handles routine matters underway, such as passing the word, mast reports, and dumping trash. The JOOD handles tactical circuits and relays information between the commanding officer and the OOD, who is, of course, in overall charge and usually has the conn.

When an aircraft carrier is operating with lifeguard destroyers, the officer of the deck has a special responsibility to keep those destroyers informed of the progress of flight operations, unexpected changes in course and speed, and modifications to lighting measures. The lighting and shape of an aircraft carrier make it extremely difficult for another ship to determine visually her aspect, her direction of turn, and her distance. Therefore, the watch officers on the lifeguard destroyers rely heavily on the carrier's OOD to tell them *immediately* of any course and speed changes. The importance of this coordination between carriers and destroyers has been underscored by tragic accidents and loss of life at sea.

It is essential for surface line officers who stand deck watches on carriers to become familiar with the aspects of their duties that concern aircraft. These include the following:

1. Aircraft turnups and jet blasts, and the required safety precautions.

2. Operation of aircraft elevators and hangar-bay doors.

3. Operation of helicopters.

4. Cooperation between the weapons department and the air department in the matter of respotting aircraft and boats.

5. Special need for smoking discipline during fueling and defueling of airplanes, helicopters, and so forth.

6. The use of rescue destroyers and helicopters in plane crashes, and the need to keep them informed.

7. Restrictions on blowing tubes (never during launching and recovery or when soot may blow over the flight deck).

8. Wind and weather information needed before flight operations.

9. Limiting and optimum wind velocity and direction over the deck, and the time needed to accelerate to desired speeds.

10. Messing of air group and air department personnel before, after, and during flight operations.

11. Need to inform the air department when high winds are expected so that aircraft may be secured.

Helicopter operations

The use of helicopters in antisubmarine warfare, amphibious operations, vertical replenishment (VERTREP), and various other logistic and tactical roles continues to increase. Most warships now either carry a helicopter or are configured so that they can operate the helicopters of other ships. An officer of the deck should be familiar with helicopter operations in general, and should have a thorough knowledge of the helicopter-operating capabilities (levels and classes of certification) of his own ship. If his ship carries a helicopter, he should also have a basic knowledge of its limitations, special operating requirements, and operational parameters.

Wind is always a critical factor when helicopters are being operated. Each type of ship and each type of helicopter must operate within certain wind "envelopes" in order safely to spread rotors, start engines, engage rotors, and launch and recover. Relative wind directions and velocities that constitute given envelopes for both day and night operating conditions are graphically displayed in NWP-42. These tables should always be at hand on the bridge and, no matter how often helicopters are operated, should always be consulted before a rotor engagement, launch, or recovery is approved. Only in cases of extreme emergency should helicopters be operated "outside the envelope."

Ship's roll and pitch also affect helicopter operations. Each helicopter has a specified "envelope," or limitations on permissible wind and roll and pitch, for both day and night operations. It is the responsibility of the OOD to adjust his course and speed not only to provide acceptable wind across the deck but also to minimize roll and pitch. As with all special evolutions, it is a good idea to keep a checklist handy for use during flight operations, to help ensure that these critical conditions are provided.

Shipboard procedures

All officers of the deck should be conversant with their own ship's bills and procedures for operating, fueling, and receiving helicopters. One of the best ways to begin acquiring this information on ships that have a helicopter detachment embarked, is to talk to the pilots and deck crewmen. They will be glad to give the OOD all the information he needs and will appreciate his interest, since their lives might well depend on how thoroughly he understands their problems and requirements.

Before any helicopter operations can be undertaken, a number of preparations must be made. The OOD is responsible for seeing that all the required things are done and that the ship is ready to carry out the evolution safely, smartly, and on time. The sequence of events in preparing for and conducting helicopter operations is usually as follows:

1. Pilots and crew are briefed on the mission, weather, expected ship's movement, fields to which they might be diverted, communications, and emergency procedures. It is not necessary for the OOD to know all these things, but he should have access to them through CIC.

2. Before flight quarters is called away, the helicopter should be brought out on deck and preflighted. During this stage of the evolution, the OOD and the helicopter flight crew must maintain close liaison, especially when the helicopter is being rolled out of the hangar and is under less control than at any other time. During this phase, ship's motion should be minimized and hard turns that may cause the ship to heel should be avoided.

3. When the preliminary checks have been completed, flight quarters should be called away and a foreign object damage (FOD) walkdown should be done in the flight-deck

area. The flight-operations area should be roped off and all hands periodically warned to stand clear of it. The smoking lamp should be extinguished in the area of flight operations.

4. After the detail has been manned and communications have been checked, the helicopter may be given permission to start engines. At this point the OOD should have a reasonably good idea of what the flight course will be and should ensure that the ship will be able to maneuver for launch as necessary.

5. When the pilot reports that he is ready to engage rotors, the ship is maneuvered as necessary to get within the engagement envelope, and the OOD gives permission to engage. Final radio communications checks are made.

6. When the helicopter is completely ready, the pilot requests a "green deck" for launch. At this time the ship should come to flight course, and the pilot should be informed of relative wind direction and velocity, altimeter setting, and ship's pitch and roll. The deck crew then pull out tie-down chains and wheel chocks, and launch the helicopter. When the helicopter is well clear of the ship and the pilot has reported operations normal, flight quarters are usually secured and the ship returns to base course until it is time to recover.

Conditions of readiness

Depending on the tactical situation, the OTC usually assigns ready helicopters to such missions as search and rescue (SAR), lifeguard, and ASW, and specifies a given readiness status, which can be any one of the following:

Ready 5: Ready for launch five minutes from signal. All preflight checks complete, pilots in aircraft, and engines warmed and ready to launch. Crew at flight quarters.

Ready 15: Aircraft spotted, rotors spread, and most preflight checks complete. Pilots in flight gear and on call. Flight quarters not set.

Ready 30: Aircraft ready to launch within thirty minutes. All daily preflight checks complete. Depending on limitations of ship, aircraft may or may not be spotted. Crew not at flight quarters.

Each readiness condition has advantages and disadvantages. Ready 5 provides the fastest reaction time but, because of crew fatigue resulting from the ship and aircraft being constantly ready for launch, cannot be maintained for long. Ready 15 does not provide as rapid a reaction time and is contingent upon the crew's ability to get to flight quarters on short notice. However, it has the advantage of requiring fewer people to be on station for a long period of time and can be maintained for days.

Emergencies

The OOD on a ship that operates with helicopters should be familiar with basic procedures for both in-flight and on-deck emergencies, since one of the first things that an aircraft in trouble will attempt to do is land on deck. He should be prepared to recover aircraft on very short notice and, if the situation dictates, without flight quarters' being fully manned. The time the pilot has in which to land safely may be so short that the risk of recovering him without a full flight-deck crew is justified. This is essentially the pilot's decision, and if he considers this kind of action necessary it is probably because his life depends on it.

In the case of on-deck emergencies such as crashes or fires, the OOD may have to decide, after the crew is safe, whether to attempt to save the helicopter or to jettison it in order to avoid danger to the ship. He should plan in advance how to handle such a situation, know what equipment is available to assist in an emergency, and have a good idea of what kind of situation would justify its use. For example, fin stabilizers, with which some ships are equipped, contain a device that induces a large roll of the ship, a capability that could be extremely useful in getting a burning aircraft over the side. An OOD should also be very familiar with procedures for lost communications or aircraft-in-the-water accidents or both.

Submarine operations

The duties of OOD of a surfaced submarine differ from those in a surface ship in several ways. First of all, a submarine is extremely vulnerable when she is involved in a collision. The OOD must keep this fact in mind and never allow the submarine to get into a situation where there is appreciable risk of collision. He must always be alert for the presence of other vessels, because the silhouette a submarine presents to another ship is deceptive. This is true both night and day, but particularly at night, because the lights of a submarine, which may not conform to the rules of the road, are grouped so closely that she gives the appearance of a fishing boat or a very small ship. There is a tendency, then, for vessels approaching a surfaced submarine at night to be unconcerned. Similarly, a submarine tends to present a small "pip" on radar, which also leads to her classification by approaching ships as a small vessel.

The OOD of a submarine must be cognizant of the status of "rig for dive" at all times. When a submarine is underway at sea she should be ready to dive at any time. Once she has been reported "rigged for dive," permission to alter the status of that rig or to do anything that might interfere with diving must be obtained from the commanding officer.

Because a submarine is extremely low in the water, certain safety precautions must be followed at all times at sea. Some of these are as follows:

1. No one should be allowed on the main deck without the commanding officer's permission. Save in exceptional circumstances, all personnel going to the main deck must use life jackets and safety lines.

2. In rough seas the OOD and lookouts should wear safety belts and have life lines secured to a part of the ship that would not be carried away by a boarding sea.

3. In rough seas the OOD should shut the conning-tower or upper-bridge hatch to prevent flooding.

4. In a following sea the OOD should be alert to the danger of water's being taken into the ship through the air-induction system. In submarines equipped with dual induction systems, the main air-induction system should be shut and the snorkel system used to get air into the ship.

When a submarine submerges, the OOD becomes the diving officer, and the conning officer takes over the functions of the OOD.

The duties and responsibilities of the OOD on a surfaced nuclear-powered submarine are not a great deal different from those on a conventional submarine. Nuclear submarines spend so little time on the surface, however, that bridge personnel may forget what those duties and responsibilities are. Following a prolonged period of submergence, the OOD should review the standing instructions and orders covering surface watch-standing and should brief his watch section as necessary.

Search and rescue

The armed services and the coast guard maintain jointly an almost worldwide search-and-rescue (SAR) organization that uses existing commands, bases, and facilities to search for and rescue people involved in air, surface, and subsurface accidents. There are three SAR areas: the Inland Region, whose designated commander is the chief of staff of the U. S. Air Force; the Maritime Region, whose commander is the commandant of the U. S. Coast Guard; and the Overseas Region, whose commander is a designated unified commander. The commander of the unit that arrives first at the scene of a disaster is known as the on-scene commander. When an accident occurs, certain radio frequencies are specified for the use of those involved in SAR operations, and a carefully planned procedure is followed.

Detailed information concerning the SAR organization and its procedures can be found in most fleet instructions and operation orders. The SAR folder on the bridge and in CIC contains the *National Search and Rescue Manual* (NWP-37) and pertinent SAR directives from current operation orders.

The officer of the deck should be familiar with these directives, should know the radio frequencies to be used, the rescue procedures, and special signals made by ships and aircraft in distress.

Replenishment at sea

Replenishment at sea (RAS) involves the transfer of fuel, stores, mail, ammunition, and, sometimes, people from one ship to another while both are underway. Most replenishments are scheduled, but an "RAS of opportunity" can be ordered whenever circumstances warrant it. RAS requires special skills and maneuvering, with which all officers must be familiar, since they are likely to be involved in the evolution either as OOD or as conning officer. This is especially true on destroyers and other small ships, not only because of the large number of people involved in the evolution but also because it is likely to occur often. When RAS is scheduled, the OOD should do the following things:

1. Review *Replenishment at Sea* (NWP-14) for details of the entire procedure. Check *Knight's Modern Seamanship* for a description of the equipment used. Refer to chapter 6 of this text for a brief discussion of shiphandling involved, and to chapters 10 and 11 for safety precautions to be observed.

2. Notify the heads of the departments concerned as soon as practicable.

3. Order that information as to the time of the operation and the stations to be manned be passed over the 1MC circuit.

4. Supervise the use of prescribed signals while the ship is approaching and alongside the replenishing ship.

5. Assist the conning officer in relaying orders to the helmsman, operator of the engine-order telegraph, and rpm indicator.

6. Notify the engineering officer of the watch as far in advance as possible so that he can make whatever changes are necessary in the status of the plant, viz., light off extra boilers, place extra generators on standby, and, if refueling is scheduled, shift his fuel load.

7. Study the characteristics and replenishment arrangements of the ship alongside of which his ship will be going. Set stadimeters to the correct masthead height for the units he will be working with.

8. Check to see that communications equipment available includes radio, flashing light, electric megaphones, and sound-powered telephones, flags, paddles, and wands. During the actual operation, the use of radio between delivery and receiving ships normally is confined to emergencies. Electric megaphones are used during the approach and until telephone lines are connected. Thereafter they comprise the main standby method of communicating.

Heavy weather

One of the attributes of a good naval officer and seaman is weather wisdom. He should know what weather is expected and be prepared to meet its effects on shipboard operations.

When heavy seas and winds of high intensity are anticipated, the OOD must take the following precautions:

1. Have the word passed over all circuits "Prepare ship for heavy weather."

2. Designate divisions to rig inboard life lines on weather decks.

3. Pass, as appropriate, the word "Close all hatches on main deck forward," "Close all topside hatches forward (or aft) of frame _____," "Close all topside hatches, doors, and ports on starboard (port) side." Pass the word for personnel to remain clear of the weather decks as necessary for safety.

4. Require personnel who are assigned to work topside in heavy weather to wear life jackets and safety lines. Men engaged in this exposed work should wear warm jackets.

Hurricanes and typhoons

Cyclonic storms, known as hurricanes in the Atlantic and typhoons in the Pacific, can have devastating effects on even the largest ships. Warnings of such storms and conditions of readiness are as follows:

Condition Four: The path of the cyclone has been fairly well established, and its trend threatens destructive winds of the force indicated within seventy-two hours. Preliminary precautions should be taken.

Condition Three: The cyclone continues to approach and destructive winds of the force indicated are possible within forty-eight hours. Appropriate action to protect people and property should be taken.

Condition Two: Destructive winds of the force indicated are anticipated within twenty-four hours. Such additional action as is required to permit the setting of an appropriate state of readiness on short notice should be taken.

Condition One: Destructive winds of the force indicated are anticipated within twelve hours. Action to minimize injury to people and damage to property should be taken.

Although an OOD is not likely to have to face a cyclone without plenty of company on the bridge, he should know the following procedures:

1. He should determine from the official warnings the bearing, distance, and track of the storm. If there are no official warnings, he should make his own calculations. From this information, plans can be made to avoid the dangerous semicircle of the storm. Proximity to shoal water must be considered.

   a. If the ship is near a storm and no warnings have been received, the bearing of the storm should be determined by the direction from which swells are arriving and by adding 115° to the direction from which observed true wind is blowing.

   b. If the wind gradually hauls to the right (clockwise), the ship is in the dangerous semicircle, i.e., the right side of the hurricane in relation to storm track. If it hauls to the left (counterclockwise), the ship is in the safe, or navigable, semicircle.

   c. If the wind remains steady in direction and increases in speed and the barometer continues to fall, the ship is directly in the path of the storm.

2. Radar should be used to detect cloud masses and track their direction of movement

3. No attempt should be made to outrun or cross the "t" of a hurricane; to do so usually means trouble from the front-running swells of the hurricane, which build rapidly in size as

the center approaches. These swells can cut down ship speed by several knots, whereas the hurricane keeps on at its own appointed pace—or speeds up.

4. If sea-surface temperature charts are available and maneuvering plans permit, the areas of warmest water should be avoided. Hurricanes moving at, say, 10 knots or less, like warm water as a path. Warm water has little influence on storms moving at 16 knots or more.

5. If the ship is caught in the hurricane circulation, even the fringes of it, these are the steps to take:

a. If she is dead ahead of the center of the hurricane, bring the wind on her starboard quarter (160° relative) and make best speed on this course. This is the quickest way to get her from the center and put her in the safe semicircle.

b. If she is in the safe, or navigable, semicircle, bring the wind on her starboard quarter (130° relative) and make best speed.

c. If she is in the dangerous semicircle, bring the wind on her starboard bow (45° relative) and make as much headway as possible.

d. If necessary to heave to, do so head to sea.

6. Proximity to land must be taken into account in maneuvering. An evasive course that carries the ship close to shore is dangerous, particularly if she is in the sector of the storm that has onshore winds.

Damage-control settings

The OOD's responsibility for effective damage-control and watertight-integrity procedures during the period of his watch is an important one. An OOD should have completed the personnel qualification standards (PQS) for damage control and should know the exact location and capabilities of all major and secondary damage-control systems in his ship. He must check to see that the proper damage-control condition is set and that exceptions to that condition are reported and entered in the damage-control closure logbook. When the sounding-and-security watch reports to the bridge "All secure" and presents his readings, the OOD should examine them carefully before he initials them. Changes in water depth in spaces or a requirement to pump spaces frequently ought to be given close scrutiny, particularly in heavy weather when the ship may be making water because hatches or other deck openings have not been properly secured.

While opening and closing of doors and hatches may seem dull and routine, they are matters of great importance to the safety of the ship and the lives of the crew. A ship might go along for years and not suffer from having her watertight integrity neglected, but a sudden grounding or collision may result in disaster. Even half a ship will stay afloat and permit the rescue of many men if her watertight integrity has been maintained. The OOD must always be cognizant of the need to combat carelessness and to make sure that the proper closure setting is maintained.

Material casualties

The OOD must ensure, within, of course, the limits of his capabilities, that all machinery and electronic gear is operable. This means that he must exercise foresight in testing equipment such as winches, radar, and voice circuits that may be used in the immediate future. In addition, the OOD should make certain that the cognizant officer is notified of any material casualties that occur. He must know what effect a given casualty will have, and make necessary reports to the OTC, as well as intraship reports. For example, he should report an important electronics failure to the electronics officer as well as to the captain and admiral (if embarked), and obtain an estimate of repair time.

It should be remembered that the OOD's interest is in how a casualty affects the performance, maneuverability, or safety of the ship, and *not* in how the repairs are to be made, who is to do them, or how long they take. An OOD who badgers the people on the scene of a casualty not only makes no contribution but often adds to the problem and impedes its correction.

Binoculars

The officer of the deck should know how to adjust, clean, and use binoculars. He should know his own focus and inter-pupillary setting. He should also instruct his lookouts and other personnel in the care and use of the glasses. Careless handling, especially dropping, can soon make a pair of glasses unfit for use. The men should be taught to use the neck strap and to keep the glasses in their case when they are not in use. Nothing is more unseamanlike and just plain wasteful of public funds than leaving binoculars adrift. The top of a chart table may seem like safe stowage, but when the ship takes a roll, the user is faced with the embarrassment of having to lean over and pick up a pair of useless glasses. Binocular lenses should be cleaned only with lens paper.

Refuse disposal and pollution control

The Oil Pollution Act of 1961 and the Federal Water Pollution Control Act (P.L. 91-224) establish standards for the control of oil-discharge, waste-disposal, and dumping. These and other federal regulations also establish a timetable for the elimination of unprocessed waste from ships. In general, recently enacted laws have considerably tightened the requirements for disposal of waste, trash, and oily water and have strengthened existing controls. They can be summarized as follows:

Sewage disposal

As of 1 April 1981, all ships are required to be equipped with collection, holding, and transfer tanks (CHTs) capable of holding waste, transferring it ashore, or dumping it at sea beyond the contiguous zone, which is twelve miles from the coastline.

Garbage

Garbage may not be thrown overboard within the navigable waters of the United States and the contiguous zone. In foreign waters it is a matter of courtesy to use the same standards as are used in the United States.

Oil and oily water

Oil may not be deliberately pumped into the ocean. Bilge-pumping is not permitted within fifty miles of the coastline. Caution should be exercised to prevent the spillage of oil.

Solid waste

Solid waste, trash, and refuse may not be discharged at sea within fifty miles of any shore.

Besides the environmental dangers associated with the discharge of oil and refuse at sea, there are operational considerations. Even in midocean trash should never be dumped over the side unless it is rigged to sink, and under no circumstances should trash be dumped during flight operations, because of the danger of creating FOD. Dumping should not be permitted during ASW operations, because solid material could return false echoes. It should also be obvious that the long slick left by a ship pumping oily bilges at sea would assist enemy forces in finding her. When concealment is desired, bilges should be pumped only at night, or when the sea is rough enough to break up the slick.

Reports to the commanding officer

[The officer of the deck shall] make all required reports to the commanding officer. When a command duty officer is specified for the watch, make the same reports to the command duty officer.

OpNavInst 3120.32.

Policy on reports to the commanding officer, as supplemented by his standing orders and standing night orders, requires exact compliance. As unimportant as some of the reports may appear to be, they all contain information that, for one reason or another, the commanding officer needs. Exceptions or changes to what is to be reported can be made only by the captain, not by the OOD. As unkind as it may seem to awaken a tired commanding officer, it is much worse to have to call him to the bridge unprepared when the ship is already in danger. Reports should be concise and specific and should include the OOD's proposed course of action. For example, the OOD may report a contact in this manner: "Captain, this is the OOD. I am presently on a course of 276 degrees at a speed of 12 KTS. I have a contact broad on my starboard bow at 9,000 yards. She has a target angle of 330 degrees R. Her present CPA is off the port bow at 1000 yards. My intention is to alter course 30 degrees to starboard in order to open the CPA to 4,000 yards off my port beam." If a certain format or sequence is prescribed by the captain for reporting certain information, such as surface contacts, it must be adhered to exactly. No commanding officer enjoys being awakened at night to hear a rambling discourse or a collection of disjointed information.

In cases of doubt, it is always the wisest course to call the captain. There is no need to be concerned about waking him; he is accustomed to interrupted sleep when underway at night and will gain peace of mind and reassurance from his OOD's conscientious attention to duty. Some people can acknowledge a message without being really awake. Therefore, the OOD should make certain that important messages are actually understood. If possible, such messages should be delivered by the OOD in person, rather than by messenger.

6 | SHIPHANDLING

The commanding officer of a ship shall afford frequent opportunities to the executive officer, and to other officers of the ship, as practicable to improve their skill in shiphandling.

Navy Regulations, 1973, Article 0728.

The OOD may expect to handle the ship in keeping station, in making turns in formation for changes of course, and on other occasions when no great risk is involved. If his commanding officer is so disposed, the OOD may even handle the ship when she is going alongside a wharf, a pier, or another ship. In any event, the OOD must prepare himself by study and observation to handle his ship. It has happened that junior officers have had to take their ships to sea because of an emergency created by weather or enemy action.

This book is not a textbook on shiphandling. However, this chapter outlines some of the important things about it that an OOD should know. Further study in such standard reference books as R. S. Crenshaw's *Naval Shiphandling* is recommended. That book discusses the basic principles of shiphandling and special problems in handling various types of ships.

Definitions

Pivot point. The pivot point is the point of rotation within a ship as she makes a turn. It is generally about one-third the length of the ship from the bow and fairly close to the bridge (when the ship is going ahead).

Turning circle. The turning circle is the path described by a ship when she turns. It varies according to amounts of rudder and speeds used.

Advance. For any turn, the advance is the distance gained in the direction of the original course from the time the rudder is put over until the ship is on the new course.

Transfer. For any turn, the transfer is the distance gained in a direction perpendicular to that of the original course from the time the rudder is put over until the ship is on the new course.

Tactical diameter. For any amount of constant rudder angle, the tactical diameter is the distance made good in a direction perpendicular to that of the original course line from the time the rudder is put over until the ship is on a reverse heading. It is the transfer for a turn of 180 degrees.

Standard rudder. Standard rudder is the angle of rudder that, under normal conditions, gives the ship standard tactical diameter.

Full rudder. Full rudder is a prescribed angle of rudder, usually a safe distance—5 degrees—short of the stops, that gives the ship reduced tactical diameter.

Acceleration and deceleration rates. Acceleration and deceleration rates are the rates at which a ship picks up or loses headway after a change of speed.

General principles

An officer who desires to become an efficient shiphandler should be aware of certain general principles and their specific application to his ship. Examples of these principles follow:

Effect of the wind upon turning. Most ships, particularly those with high bows, turn slowly into the wind when going ahead, and rapidly when turning away from it. Conversely, they turn rapidly into the wind when backing. The effect on a particular ship can be estimated by comparing the "sail area" forward of the pivot point with that abaft the pivot point. A ship whose "sail area" is greater forward has the above tendencies. One with greater "sail area" aft has the opposite tendencies; this is particularly true of aircraft carriers. The term *sail area* means those surfaces of the hull and superstructure above the waterline against which the wind can exert force.

Effect of speed upon turning. With constant rudder angle, at speeds appreciably above steerageway, any increase in speed makes the turning circle larger. This is because the inertia of the ship tends to keep her going in the original direction of motion. The amount by which the turning circle increases varies from ship to ship and is most noticeable when ships of different types are operating together. Since the guide is usually a large ship and uses the same amount of rudder or standard rudder for all speeds, it is necessary to know what rudder for the ship involved will match the turning circle of the guide for the speed at which any turn is made.

At speeds approaching bare steerageway, a decrease in speed results in a larger turning circle. This is because the rudder acting against the inertia of the ship has less effect and tends to keep the ship moving in a straight line. For a turn at low speeds, therefore, more rudder is needed. The minimum speed at which a ship will still have steerageway should be known.

Effect of shallow water. The less space there is between the ship's hull and the bottom, the less freely can the screw currents flow and act upon the hull and rudder. When that space is very small, the ship may be sluggish or erratic in answering the rudder, a great deal of power is wasted, and the speed through the water is less than that indicated by the propeller revolutions. Additionally, high speed in shallow water may create an effect known as "squatting": the bow rides upon the bow wave and the stern sits deeper in the water.

Time lag in response to orders. There is a noticeable lag between the time an order is given to the wheel or engines and the time the effect of the response is felt. For example, in order to have the rudder go over at the same spot as that of the ship ahead, so that the turn is made in her wake, the order to turn must be given when the kick of the preceding ship's rudder is near the bridge of the following ship.

Backing power available. In steam ships, backing power may be considerably less than the power for going ahead, for two reasons: Because a backing turbine has fewer impeller blades, it produces less power, and propellers are less efficient when turning astern. "Back one-third" and "Back two-thirds" normally call for one-third and two-thirds, respectively, of the power available for backing. The turns for "Ahead one-third" and "Ahead two-thirds" are based upon one-third and two-thirds, respectively, of standard speed. There is no "back standard" speed. "Ahead one-third (two-thirds)" and "Back one-third (two-thirds)" probably do not have quite equal effect. Consequently, besides twisting when one engine is backing and the other going ahead (both at one-third or two-thirds), a ship can be expected to pick up a slight amount of way in the direction of the stronger force. In a gas turbine ship with controllable-pitch propellers, however, backing power is considerably enhanced, since it is the pitch of the propeller blade that determines the direction of the turbine force. The force generated by the turbine in this instance remains nearly constant.

Factors that affect acceleration and deceleration. The manner in which ships gain and lose headway, carry their way, and respond to changes of engine speed varies with the size of the ship, her propulsion system, her underwater lines, the condition of her bottom, the wind, and the state of the sea. A clean-bottomed, heavy ship, or a ship with fine lines, tends to hold her way. A foul-bottomed, heavy ship, or a ship with full lines, tends to pick up headway slowly in response to changes of engine speed; and gas-turbine ships are more responsive to speed changes than are steam ships.

Factors that affect turning. An officer of the deck should know not only how to make a normal turn but how to turn his ship in the shortest time and in the shortest possible space. A ship turns in the *shortest time* by going ahead with full power and her rudder hard over just short of the stops. The procedure for turning a ship in the *shortest possible space* depends upon the ship herself and, sometimes, upon wind conditions.

A ship with twin rudders and screws is the easiest and probably the quickest to turn, and is the least affected by wind conditions: her rudders should simply be put over full in the direction of the desired turn and kept there. "Ahead two-thirds" on the outboard engine and "Back two-thirds" on the inboard engine should be rung up. The speed of the inboard engine can be adjusted to keep the ship from going ahead or astern as she turns on her heel.

A ship with a single rudder and twin screws is slightly more difficult to turn in a short space. If the screws are set well off from the centerline and if the turn is not adversely affected to any degree by the wind, the turn can be made by going ahead on the outboard engine and backing on the inboard engine. When the wind does adversely affect the turn, or when the screws are not sufficiently offset for a good, powerful couple, motion ahead and astern may be necessary to supplement the effect of the rudder. As a general rule, when a ship is going ahead with steerageway, her rudder should be put over in the direction of the desired turn; when a ship is going astern with steerageway, her rudder should be in the opposite direction; when a ship has no way on or less than steerageway, her rudder should be amidships. The amount of way on and the position of the rudder should be carefully watched. Some ships with large single rudders show a tendency somewhat similar to that of a twin-rudder ship, that is, to answer to the effect of an ahead-turning screw on the rudders even when they have a small amount of sternway. The OOD must know the characteristics of his own ship in this regard.

A ship with a single screw is the most difficult to turn in a short space. Most ships of this type have right-handed propellers and need to have some way on. Therefore, to turn them in a short space, headway and sternway have to be alternated. Whenever the engine is going ahead, the rudder should be thrown in the direction of the desired turn. Knowing when to shift the rudder after starting the engines backing is a matter of knowing the ship. It should usually be done shortly after the ship loses headway and then kept there until the engine is put ahead.

Handling in formation

Handling a ship in company with others requires a sound knowledge of the effective tactical instructions and a thorough understanding of the relative motion of ships. Information on the first essential is found in ATP-1, Volumes I and II. Every officer standing deck watches at sea should be so familiar with these important directives that he can find at once the proper guidance for any circumstance that may arise involving the movements of his ship. The opening chapters of both these volumes are particularly important, since they provide the basic concepts and definitions upon which all subsequent instructions are based.

The second essential for efficient shiphandling in formation, an understanding of relative motion, can be attained by study and by practice in working problems on a maneuvering board. *Dutton's Navigation and Piloting* describes maneuvering boards and their uses. Many naval schools provide excellent courses in relative movement, but any officer can learn the subject by a moderate amount of study and much practice. It is recommended that a student officer solve problems both with his own ship at center and with the guide at center. The former method is almost always used in CIC; the latter is often useful on the bridge, particularly for a vessel in the screen. Thorough knowledge of the definitions and general principles cited at the beginning of this chapter provides a sense of timing.

An important by-product of skill in using the maneuvering board is the ability to visualize problems and to solve them mentally. For a complicated evolution, such as taking a new and distant station in a formation, a mental solution would, of course, be only approximate and would be subject to modification by CIC or by a junior OOD who actually worked out the problem. Nevertheless, a mental solution permits an instant change of course and speed, which expedites the maneuver, demonstrates a ship's smartness, and gets her "on the way." For simple problems, such as gaining 10 degrees in bearing on the guide while maintaining distance, a mental solution is sufficient, since it is subject to confirmation by periodic bearings and ranges.

Developing a good "seaman's eye" should be one of a shiphandler's most important goals. Although some people have more natural ability than others in this regard, a true seaman's eye is developed only by experience, practice, and close observation of every maneuver. A shiphandler should learn to visualize and hold in his mind a picture of what is happening during a maneuver. He should practice correlating what he sees from the bridge wing with what the bird's-eye view of the surface-search radar shows him. Perfection of this skill not only sharpens his eye but also gives him a reliable means of checking the maneuvering-board solution against what he actually sees.

When a tactical signal for maneuvering is executed, the shiphandler should be able to come to the required speed immediately and, even if he does not have a complete maneuvering-board solution, put his rudder over and head in roughly the right direction. Course corrections made en route to station do not cause any major problems; being the only ship to remain on the old course and speed does.

Maneuvering signals in formation are likely to require simultaneous action by a number of ships. It is a shiphandler's responsibility, in addition to getting to his new station, to avoid interfering with or embarrassing other units and to make his own movements and intentions clearly understood. He should make it a habit always to have an "escape route" when he is maneuvering with other ships, and to know in advance what he would do and in which direction he would turn if he suddenly had to avoid more than one ship at a time. A common failing among inexperienced shiphandlers is to forget that there are ships behind them. This must not be allowed to happen. A ship that is a thousand yards on another ship's quarter and on a parallel course can become a major problem if the other ship is forced to cross her bow in order to avoid a third ship.

Operating in formation with aircraft carriers places additional responsiblity on the OOD. Most carriers establish a "box" around themselves—an area that other ships must avoid. The box prescribes the "3 : 2 : 1 rule": other ships must never be closer than 3,000 yards off the carrier's bow, 2,000 yards off her beam, and 1,000 yards astern. Not only does a carrier's size impose maneuvering limitations on her, but she is likely to be restricted in the amount of rudder-induced heel she can permit if aircraft are spotted on her deck. A ship that is forward of an aircraft carrier should never turn toward her except in an emergency. If it is absolutely necessary to do so, she should indicate her intentions to the carrier.

Close station-keeping

The mental process, discussed above, of visualizing simple problems in relative motion and solving them correctly is the key to proficient station-keeping in close formation. Although ships do not now steam in close formation as often as formerly, proficiency in this area is still an important requirement demanded by most type commanders. Surface ships still must be able to steam in column, or in line of bearing, at standard distance, and in circular formation darkened at night and at high speed. Steaming in close column, which is largely a matter of speed adjustment, demands a keen appreciation of speed and how a ship carries her way.

The stadimeter is an essential instrument for ships in close formation. Every watch officer should be familiar with its use and know its capabilities and limitations. At close ranges, it is more accurate than most radars, and it is particularly helpful in providing quick and accurate information as to whether distance is opening, closing, or being held steady.

Distance reports should state whether distance is "closing," "opening," or "steady." The terms *increasing* and *decreasing* should not be used, because there is a chance of confusion with reports concerning bearings.

It may not be possible to take stadimeter readings on dark nights when there is not enough light, when the ship is too close for radar ranges, or when radar silence is imposed. At those times, binoculars can be used to obtain a fair estimate of distance if during the day, when the exact distance to a ship can be measured, the amount of the binocular field that she fills has been noted. It takes much practice to become proficient in this use of the binoculars, but it is worth it. See R. S. Crenshaw's *Naval Shiphandling.*

The first ship in a column, or the guide ship, should make every effort to ensure good steering and steady speed. The OOD should see that the proper revolutions are being made. The OOD on the ship astern will appreciate such efforts.

The keeping of proper distance between ships in column depends largely on the OOD's ability to detect early indications of opening or closing motion and to make proper speed adjustments to counteract that motion. In this regard, he should remember that when a ship is following in the wake of another, she requires a few more revolutions than she would in still water to make good the same speed as the ship ahead; this is because she has to overcome the wake turbulence or "kick" of the preceding ship. An erratic helmsman who takes the ship in and out of the wake of the ship ahead complicates the problem of speed adjustment. Therefore, the helmsman should be watched closely. Speed should be corrected with care; it must be remembered that there is a time lag before the effect of change is felt. If this time lag is not allowed for, there is a danger of correcting twice for the same error. That results in a need for a correction, probably larger, in the opposite direction, and once such surging starts, it is hard to stop it. An OOD would be well advised to study the time lag of his ship intently until he gets to know it. The effect of one correction should be carefully observed before another correction is applied. Excessive use of the rudder acts as a brake. Therefore, the steering should always be corrected before the speed is increased.

In general, it is safer for a ship in column to be inside, rather than outside, the prescribed distance; it is easier to drop back than to close up. An OOD ought to know the allowable tolerances and keep within them, because it is also easy to hit the ship ahead if she slows without his noticing it. He should remember the fellow next astern, and keep his own course and speed as steady as possible. The reputation of being a good ship to follow is a difficult one to earn, but it is worth trying for.

The OOD must always keep in mind his ship's number in the column and to which side he is to sheer out in an emergency. This is the same side as that of his position when in column open order, and it follows the standard pattern—odd-numbered ships to starboard, even-numbered ships to port. When for any reason he finds himself getting uncomfortably close to the ship ahead, the thing to do is to ease his bow out very slightly on the side to which he would sheer out in an emergency.

Course changes for a formation in column may be made in two ways: by individual ships turning together, or by wheeling, that is, changing course in succession, following the ship ahead.

When change of course is made by turning together, the rudder must be put over the proper amount promptly on the execution of the signal. The OOD must inform the helmsman of the new course and see that he does not swing past it or use an excessive amount of rudder in meeting the swing. Either of these errors by the helmsman will cause the ship to end up behind bearing in the line of bearing resulting from the maneuver. The OOD should keep the nearest ship toward which the turn is being made under constant visual observation. He should check the bearing of the guide as the turn progresses, with a view to detecting promptly any tendency to gain or lose bearing.

In practice, ships do not maintain perfect position, particularly when making frequent simultaneous turns, and the OOD must know how to adjust a turn to improve his position. This knowledge comes mostly from experience in visualizing the situation and in looking ahead. Of course, any such adjustments must consider adjacent ships on both sides.

Assuming that a ship has turned properly, the one following her will turn in the same water. The knuckle of the first ship's wake should be slightly on the second ship's bow, in the direction of the turn. Slick water inboard of the wake is caused by the stern of the ship sliding in the turn; the inboard edge of the slick marks the path of the ship's bow, the outboard edge, that of her stern.

Conning should be done from the wing of the bridge, from which the ship ahead and the one astern, if any, can be seen. Knowing exactly when to start a turn takes experience, but the OOD usually orders the rudder put over when the knuckle is abreast the bridge. If the turn is correctly timed, the bow of his ship will follow around at the inboard edge of the slick.

If the turn is made late, the ship will go outside the proper turning circle, and the wake of the ship ahead may tend to hold her there. If this happens, the OOD should not swing beyond the new course but remain steadied parallel to the column on the new course. When the ship next astern has completed her wheel, he should gradually regain station; it is almost always necessary to increase speed to regain station.

If the turn is made too early, the ship will go inside the proper turning circle. A slight easing of the rudder will correct this, but speed will probably have to be reduced in order to avoid coming dangerously close to the ship ahead. A common error in such a situation is to ease the rudder too much, with the result that the ship crosses the wake ahead and is outside, after all.

The danger in turns lies in a large change of course being started when a ship is too close to the ship ahead. The choice then is between making a large rudder angle to stay inside the turn, while slowing, stopping, or backing, and easing the rudder and going outside. It is safer to continue the turn inside; hesitation before easing the rudder to go outside may cause the ship to forge ahead while her bow is still inside the stern of the ship ahead, and she will be in danger of collision.

A ship astern of one that turns too soon or too late should not attempt to follow her but should turn correctly in the wake of the guide. If she is slightly out of position when a turn is ordered, she can maneuver to correct: if she is behind station, she can cut the corner; if too close, she can turn a bit late, with full rudder.

At night or in fog, it may not be possible to see the knuckle. If the OOD keeps track of the elapsed time after the signal to execute, he can, on the basis of speed and distance from the guide, determine when the point of turn has been reached. He can do this by utilizing the "three-minute rule," which states that in three minutes a ship travels as many hundreds of yards as the number of knots she is making. That is, a ship doing 15 knots travels 1500 yards in three minutes. Therefore, a ship that is 1000 yards astern of the guide at a speed of 15 knots turns two minutes after the guide executes her turn. This is an invaluable shiphandling tool, worth committing to memory.

Line of bearing

In line of bearing, station-keeping is somewhat complicated, since both distance and bearing are involved. In this situation a thorough understanding of the relative motion of ships is very helpful. When his ship is in close formation, the OOD rarely has time to plot bearings and distances and obtain a solution. He has to visualize the problem and then change course and speed properly and promptly as soon as he detects a deviation from the correct bearing and distance.

He can quickly determine whether he is ahead or behind bearing by lining up his alidade on the prescribed bearing of the guide and then sighting through it. If his line of sight falls ahead of the guide, he is ahead; if astern, he is behind.

When ships are in line abreast, a speed that is greater or less than that of the guide causes a bearing to be advanced or retarded, with negligible variation in range. A slight change of course toward or away from the guide causes a closing or opening of range, with a slight loss of bearing. A small temporary increase of speed, normally only a few turns, can be used when desirable, to counteract this small bearing change.

When the line of bearing is a column, a speed differential causes a closing or opening of distance. A change of course causes a change of bearing, with a very slight opening of distance. A small temporary increase of speed can be used when desirable, to counteract this small change in range.

For lines of bearing between these two extremes—line abreast and column—the effects of a course or speed differential are a little more complex. A combination of changing course and speed is usually required in order to maintain station.

When simultaneous turns are made in line of bearing, it is important to watch the ship toward which the turn is made for a sign that she might be turning in the wrong direction.

Station-keeping in formation

Handling a ship in the main body of a circular formation is slightly easier than handling a ship in close formation, because the distance between ships is usually greater. However, since station has to be kept on a definite bearing from the guide, and at a definite distance, the problems of station-keeping are similar to those in line of bearing. The only additional determination to be made is what the range and bearing from the guide should be when a ship is moving to a new station. CIC can be of great assistance to the OOD in these matters.

In order to determine his range and bearing from the guide, the OOD must be familiar with the system for plotting formations by means of using polar coordinates. Once he has plotted the formation, he can easily pick the range and bearing of the guide off the plot. A continuous plot of the formation should be kept so that ordered changes can be quickly translated into terms of new range and bearing from the guide.

It should be borne in mind that the guide is not always at the center of a formation, and that as soon as a signal has been executed, the guide is automatically on station, regardless of where she might be. This situation sometimes results in the center of the formation moving around the guide, and when it does, it causes the other ships to move a like amount in the same direction.

For any maneuver, when required range and bearing from the guide have been determined from a plot, actual range and bearing from the guide should be worked out. These figures can be used to determine the course and speed required to bring the ship to her proper station. Except when a ship is ordered to a new station, a change of formation axis and a change in the formation itself are the only maneuvers that change either her range or her bearing, or both, in relation to the guide.

Screening

Handling a ship in a screen is quite similar to handling a ship in the main body of a circular formation. Station-keeping procedures are the same. Determining range and bearing is, however, more complex, because the distance from the guide is greater. The OOD of a destroyer-type ship must be familiar with the maneuvering rules that govern screening ships, as well as with the rules that govern maneuvers in the various types of formations.

A continuous, up-to-the-minute plot of the entire formation should be kept, just as for a circular formation, so that any ordered change can be quickly translated into terms of a new range and bearing from the guide.

In order to keep the plot of the screen, the OOD must know where the center of the screen is and the direction of its axis. He must be able to distinguish the signals that cause the screen center and to shift those that do not. And he must know how to determine the amount and direction of such a shift and how to allow for it in his maneuver, whether or not a reorientation of the screen is required.

An OOD must know under what conditions a screen axis changes without a specific signal, and how to determine its new direction in such cases. He should make every effort to start for his new station promptly. A little forehandedness will help him to do this. After each maneuver he should start anticipating the next one. He should check his plot and then determine the minimum change of formation course in each direction that would cause a reorientation requiring him to change station. And when it is appropriate, he should determine the minimum change of course that would require his initial turn to be made in the direction opposite to that of the course change. With these figures firmly in mind, he can quickly translate a signal into action and start the initial turn before the final solution has been worked out.

In working solutions he must be sure to use the course and speed for the guide that he will actually be following while en route to his station. This policy is particularly applicable when he starts for his station before the signal that changes the guide's course or speed or both has been executed.

There are two final points to be made about screening. The first is that station-keeping should be *exact*, with the OOD ensuring that the ship is at all times where it is supposed to be. If the screen plan requires the ship to patrol a sector as opposed to maintaining a continuous, exact range and bearing from the guide, then the patrolling courses and speeds should be controlled exactly. Then the OOD can afford to devote more time to other matters, perhaps delegating, under supervision, the duty of station-keeping to the junior officer of the watch.

The second point is that when a screen is being reoriented or its station is being changed, the OOD must keep an alert watch over the whole formation, using his own eyes to the maximum extent. Others can work out maneuvering-board solutions to check his quick calculations; his primary job under many conditions is that of chief safety officer.

Range to the guide

When his ship is steaming in formation, the OOD must always know the range to the guide. However, to provide himself with this information, he should not put such a burden on the surface-search radar operator in CIC that the operator is forced to keep his radar on short scale and concentrate on giving range-to-the-guide information to the deck. At night or in low visibility, when the surface-search radar must be used for detecting and tracking ships that may pose a threat of collision, this practice can be dangerous. The OOD should use a stadimeter whenever possible; he can use it at night, in good visibility, with running lights as targets. The bridge radar too can be used for checking on CIC and freeing it from the necessity of supplying continuous ranges.

Man overboard

The first requirement in case of a man overboard is prompt action. An alert OOD will see that the men in his watch know what their duties are in such an emergency, and he will be prepared, depending on weather and operating conditions, rapidly to carry out the following:

1. Put the rudder over to the same side as the man went over, in order to kick the stern away from him.

2. Throw over the side immediately a life ring with a strobe light and a smoke float or "rescue ball" to mark the spot as closely as possible.

3. Tell the JOOD, lookout, or anyone available to point at the man, if he is in sight, and continue pointing at him until he is alongside the ship.

4. Have the word passed twice: "Man overboard, port (starboard) side."

5. Sound six or more short blasts on the ship's whistle, and make appropriate visual signals as specified in *Allied Maritime Tactical Instructions and Procedures* (ATP-1, Volume I): "By day hoist OSCAR and at night (in peacetime) display two pulsating red lights or fire one white rocket (Very light)."

6. Notify CIC so that it can provide continual ranges and bearings to the man.

7. Notify ships in company and the OTC.

8. Inform the commanding officer, executive officer, and flag duty officer, if appropriate.

9. Establish communication with the deck recovery detail.

10. Keep the deck recovery detail informed as to whether the recovery is to be made from the port or the starboard side of the ship.

11. Have life raft or other life-saving equipment released immediately. Use searchlights if the situation dictates.

As soon as the word "man overboard" has been passed, CIC should automatically mark the spot, shift the dead-reckoning tracer (DRT) to the scale of 200 yards to the inch, and begin passing ranges and bearing to the bridge.

A helicopter provides the quickest rescue, with the advantage that it can pick up a man who is unable to help himself. If a helicopter is not available, a small boat may be used.

There are a number of methods of recovering a man overboard (see diagrams and descriptions following). The four most often used are the Anderson turn, which is the fastest but requires skillful shiphandling; the Williamson turn, for night or low visibility; the racetrack turn, for fastest recovery when a ship is proceeding at high speed in clear weather; and the Y-backing, for ships with large turning circles and great backing power, proceeding at slow speeds. Very large ships often use a small boat to recover a man from the water. Small vessels also use a boat when the sea is very rough and there is little chance of getting the ship close alongside the man. Under any conditions, the OOD should see to it that swimmers with life jackets and tending lines are ready to go into the water.

Regardless of which recovery method is used, the same basic principles apply. Full rudder should be used to swing the stern away from the man. If the shaft on the side toward the man can be stopped before he reaches the screws, it should be. If it cannot be done, which is likely, the recovery should be continued without any attempt to stop the screws.

Man-overboard maneuvering for naval vessels involved in tactical evolutions can be found in ATP-1, Volume I, chapter 5. Of specific importance are the instructions for column formation. In this situation, the ship that loses the man takes action to avoid him, as do the others, odd-numbered ships in the column clearing to starboard and even-numbered ships clearing to port. The ship in the best position to recover the man does so, and keeps the other vessels informed of her actions.

The man should be recovered in the shortest possible time. Large ships usually use the Williamson method. Small ships, in good weather, use the racetrack method. At night or in low visibility, the Williamson turn, though not the fastest recovery method, must be used to bring the ship back along her track. No matter what method is used, the desired final position is beam to the wind slightly to windward of the man,

METHODS OF RECOVERING A MAN OVERBOARD

Method and Primary Conditions for Use	Diagram Ship on course 090. Numbers refer to the explanation.	Explanation	Analysis	
			Advantages	Disadvantages
Anderson Turn Used by ships that have considerable power available and relatively tight turning characteristics.		1. Put the rudder over full to the side from which the man fell. Stop the inboard engine. 2. When clear of the man, go ahead full on the outboard engine only. Continue using full rudder. 3. When about two-thirds of the way around, back the inboard engine 2/3 or full. Order all engines stopped when the man is within about 15° of the bow, then ease the rudder and back the engines as required to attain the proper final position. 4. Many variations of this method are used, differing primarily in respect to the use of one or both engines and the time when they are stopped and backed to return to the man. The variation used should reflect individual ship's characteristics, sea conditions, personal preferences, etc.	Speed	Requires proficiency in shiphandling, because the approach to the man is not straightaway. Often impossible for a single-propeller ship.
Williamson Turn Used in low visibility, because it makes good the original track. Used when it is believed that a man fell overboard some time previously and he is not in sight.		1. Put the rudder over full to the side from which the man fell. Stop the inboard engine. 2. When clear of the man, go ahead full on all engines. Continue using full rudder. 3. When heading is 60° beyond the original course, shift the rudder without having steadied on a course. 60° is proper for many ships. However, the exact amount must be determined through trial and error. 4. Come to the reciprocal of the original course, using full rudder. 5. Use the engines and rudder to attain the proper final position (ship upwind of the man and dead in the water with the man alongside, well forward of the propellers).	Simplicity. Makes good the original track.	Slowness. Takes the ship relatively far from the man, when sight of him may be lost.

Method and Primary Conditions for Use	Diagram Ship on course 090. Numbers refer to the explanation.	Explanation	Analysis Advantages	Disadvantages
Racetrack turn (Two 180° Turns) Used in good visibility when a straight final-approach leg is desired.		A variation of the one-turn method that provides a desirable straight final approach to the man. 1. Put the rudder over full in the direction corresponding to the side from which the man fell. Stop the inboard engine. 2. When clear of the man, go ahead full on all engines. Continue using full rudder to turn to the reciprocal of the original course. 3. Steady for a distance that will give the desired run for a final straight approach. 4. Use full rudder to turn to the man. 5. Use the engines and rudder to attain the proper final position (ship upwind of the man and dead in the water with the man alongside, well forward of the propellers).	Straight final-approach leg facilitates a calculable approach. Ship will return to the man if he is lost from sight. Reasonably fast. Effective when wind was from abeam on original course.	Slower than one-turn methods.
Y-Backing Used by submarines because of their low height of eye.		1. Put the rudder over full to the side from which the man fell. Stop the inboard engine. 2. When clear of the man, back the engines with full power, using opposite rudder. 3. Go ahead. Use the engines and rudder to attain the proper final position (ship upwind of the man and dead in the water with the man alongside, well forward of the propellers).	The ship remains comparatively close to the man.	Most ships back into the wind or seas, causing poor control.

Method and Primary Conditions for Use	Diagram *Ship on course 090. Numbers refer to the explanation.*	Explanation	Analysis	
			Advantages	*Disadvantages*
Delayed Turn Used when word is received that a man fell overboard, is in sight, and is clear astern of the ship.		1. Put the rudder over full to the side from which the man fell. Go ahead full on all engines. 2. Ahead towards the man. 3. Use the engines and rudder to attain the proper final position (ship upwind of the man and dead in the water with the man alongside, well forward of the propellers).	Fastest method when man is in sight and already clear astern of the ship. Provides a straight run in the critical final phase. Effective when wind was from ahead or astern of ship on original course.	Does not ensure return to the man. Requires good visibility. Takes the ship farther from the man than other methods.
Boat Recovery Used by ships that do not have maneuverability to make a good approach to the man. Used when the ship is dead in the water and the man is close aboard but not alongside. Can be used in conjunction with any of the methods shown above.		1. Put the rudder over full to the side from which the man fell. Stop the inboard engine. 2. When the man is clear, back all engines full almost to stop the ship. Use rudder to the side of the ready lifeboat to provide a slick in which the boat can be lowered. Stop the engines while the ship still has very slight headway to permit better control of the boat and to keep it out of the propeller wash.	Simple. The ship remains close to the man. Does not require that a particular final position be attained.	The man must be in sight. Sea and weather conditions must be satisfactory for small-boat operations.

with all way off. When in this position, the ship provides a lee for the man, and since she will make more leeway than he will, she will drift toward him rather than away from him. It is important that the man be kept *forward* of the main condenser injection intakes, particularly if there is a possibility that he still has a parachute attached; a parachute can clog the intakes, which are ordinarily aft of the midships section, on either side. In her final position, the ship should have the man just off her leeward bow.

Replenishment at sea

The navy's ability to project sea power over long ocean distances depends on its ability to sustain itself at sea for long periods without land-based support. It is the mission of the Mobile Logistics Support Force (MLSF) to provide this support with fuel, stores, provisions, and ammunition. In addition to the naval vessels that constitute the MLSF, certain ships of the Military Sealift Command (MSC) have been designated to provide underway logistic support.

Replenishment at sea (RAS) is the most commonly encountered evolution, and the manner in which it is executed is one of the basic yardsticks by which a ship's performance is measured. It presents one of the most challenging, exciting, and satisfying opportunities for shiphandling that a watch officer will be given. It can teach him more about seamanship and shiphandling than almost any other evolution. Standard doctrine for RAS is outlined in *Replenishment at Sea* (NWP-14), which also contains a tabulation of the locations and functions of the replenishment stations on all MLSF ships. ATP-16 provides the same kind of information for NATO's replenishment ships.

To begin an RAS, a replenishment ship comes to a steady course and speed, which are usually dictated by wind and seas or, if the weather is calm, by the course desired to be made good by the formation. The receiving ship takes station astern of the delivering ship and waits for her to signal her readiness to replenish.

Weather conditions permitting, the normal speed of the

guide ship is between 10 and 15 knots. Speeds less than 8 knots are not advisable because they reduce rudder effect. At speeds greater than 15 knots, venturi effect (the pressure differential created around the hull of a moving ship) dictates the need for a greater lateral separation. See R. S. Crenshaw's *Naval Shiphandling* for a detailed description of how to bring a ship alongside a delivery ship.

The delivery ship indicates preparations in progress to receive a ship alongside by flying "Romeo" at the dip on her rigged side. The receiving ship replies that she is ready to come alongside by flying "Romeo" at the dip on her rigged side. When the delivery ship is ready for the approach, she hoists "Romeo" close up. The receiving ship hoists "Romeo" close up and increases speed by 3 to 10 knots over signaled underway-replenishment (UNREP) speed. She slows down so as to be moving at replenishment speed when in position. When the ships are in proper relative position, transfer rigs are passed and hooked up; when the first line is secured, both ships haul down "Romeo." They both fly "Bravo" if fuel or ammunition is being transferred.

Fifteen minutes before the receiving ship expects to complete replenishment, her OOD orders "Prep" hoisted at the dip to notify the next ship scheduled to replenish. On completion of the replenishment, all nets, slings, lines, and hoses are returned to the delivery ship.

Just before disengaging, the receiving ship hoists "Prep" close up, and when the last line is clear hauls it down. When the side has been cleared, the conning officer increases speed by 5 to 10 knots, depending on ship type, and clears ahead, gradually changing course outboard. Propeller wash caused by radical changes in speed and course is likely to have a bad effect on the steering of the delivery ship, and a dangerous situation might develop if a ship is on her other side.

The most important tasks of the OOD during an UNREP are the coordination of the multitude of preparations and the management of the bridge team while the ship's focus (and the captain's) is on the UNREP itself. The OOD must have the crew on station on time, but should avoid wasting the crew's time with needless waiting on station. Two hundred men waiting thirty minutes on station are a hundred man-hours that could be better spent. Coordination with the weapons officer and the executive officer and watching the progress of other ships conducting UNREP at the same time will help the OOD to call the right time. During the UNREP itself the OOD must make sure that critical functions such as navigation and communication are being correctly carried out. Of utmost importance is a plan for what to do upon completion of the UNREP. He should be extra alert for hints of ship-control problems in the areas of steering, propulsion, and senior performance. Looking ahead and anticipating possibilities are just as important as technical knowledge.

Pilots

A pilot is merely an advisor to the commanding officer. His presence on board shall not relieve the commanding officer or any of his subordinates from their responsibility for the proper performance of the duties with which they may be charged concerning the navigation and handling of the ship.

Navy Regulations, Article 0754.

Only in the following special circumstances does the presence of a pilot, even if he has the conn, relieve the commanding officer of any of his responsibility for the safety of the ship: when a ship is entering a dry dock; when a ship is traversing the Panama Canal with a licensed canal pilot on board; and when a ship is required by the harbormaster to move within a harbor while not under her own propulsion, using only tugs (dead stick). When a pilot is taken on board, the OOD should be sure that the bridge watch understands who has the conn and whose orders to the engine and the helm should be obeyed. Most pilots are accustomed to handling merchant ships, and frequently their commands to the helm and engines differ from standard naval commands. When this is the case, the commanding officer should direct the OOD to relay the pilot's orders to the helm, using proper naval terminology.

If possible, the pilot should be advised of the differences in power and speed between his orders and the OOD's. When he orders "ahead dead slow," for example, the OOD rings up a one-third bell and advises the pilot how many knots the bell was for. As long as the captain, the pilot, and the OOD know how much power is being asked for, differences in terminology can be overcome. The same holds true for orders to the helm. Although pilots usually give orders in degrees of rudder, they often call for "hard rudder," which on most naval vessels is used only in emergencies. The proper procedure in this case is to call on the helmsman for "full rudder," because this is the naval term for what the pilot means.

Most pilots are superb seamen and shiphandlers and the best of them are only too pleased to share their knowledge. Often the commanding officer leaves the conn with the OOD and asks the pilot to act as an adviser to the OOD for the purpose of training. An OOD who is fortunate enough to be in this situation should take the opportunity to learn all he can.

Occasionally, especially in out-of-the-way places, a ship finds herself with a pilot who does not understand her characteristics or who simply does not come up to professional standards. In a case such as that, the captain will normally take the conn himself, and either modify the pilot's instructions or politely ignore them. Under these circumstances, the OOD must pay particular attention to what the helmsman and lee helmsman are doing, because they can easily be confused as to which orders they should follow.

7 | SAFE NAVIGATION

The commanding officer is responsible for the safe navigation of his ship or aircraft, except as prescribed otherwise in these regulations for ships at a naval shipyard or station, in drydock, or in the Panama Canal. In time of war, or during exercises simulating war, the provisions of this article pertaining to the use of lights and electronic devices may be modified by competent authority.

The commanding officer of a ship and, as appropriate, of an aircraft shall:

Keep himself informed of the error of all compasses and other devices available as aids to navigation.

Insure that efficient devices for fixing the ship's position and for ascertaining the depth of water are employed when underway on soundings, entering or leaving port, or upon approaching an anchorage, shoal, or rock, whether or not a pilot is on board. If circumstances warrant, he shall reduce speed to the extent necessary to permit these devices to be operated efficiently and accurately.

Observe every precaution prescribed by law to prevent collisions and other accidents on the high seas, inland waters, or in the air.

When underway in restricted waters or close inshore, and unless unusual circumstances prevent, steam at a speed which will not endanger other ships or craft, or property close to the shore.

Take special care that the lights required by law to prevent collisions at sea, in port, or in the air are kept in order and burning in all weathers from sunset to sunrise, and require that means for promptly relighting or replacing such lights are available.

Navy Regulations, Article 0755.

The officer of the deck shall keep himself informed concerning the tactical situation and geographic factors which may affect the safe navigation of the ship, and take appropriate action to avoid the danger of grounding or collision in accordance with tactical doctrine, the Rules of the Road, and the orders of the Commanding Officer or other appropriate authority.

OpNavInst 3120.32.

Young officers are inclined to look upon accidents at sea as events that are as inescapable as being struck by lightning. On the contrary, collisions and groundings are almost always avoidable. They can usually be avoided by the intelligent application of the fundamental principles of good seamanship combined with the exercise of good judgment and common sense.

Collisions

Analyses of collisions frequently show that one or more of the following mistakes was made:

1. Failure to realize in time that there was a risk of collision.

2. Failure to take timely avoiding action.

3. Failure of a darkened ship to turn on running lights in the emergency.

4. Failure to notify the commanding officer of a potentially dangerous situation.

5. Failure to check for steady bearing in a closing situation until too late.

6. Reliance on CIC and consequent failure to make a common-sense evaluation of the situation on the bridge.

7. Poor judgment in evaluating the effects of wind and tide.

8. Failure to understand the tactical characteristics of the ship.

9. Injudicious use of the power available in the ship.

10. Bridge and CIC radars both on long-range setting, thereby making the detection of close-in targets difficult; or bridge and CIC radars both on short-range setting, causing a failure to detect distant targets on a collision course until very close in.

11. Failure of bridge personnel to keep sharp visual lookout.

12. Failure of CIC and the bridge to ensure that the conning officer understood tactical signals.

13. Making a radical change in course without informing ships in the vicinity.

14. Failure to use whistle signals.

15. Failure to make the required checks between gyro and magnetic compasses.

16. Failure of a ship in formation to broadcast a warning by voice radio when contacts are seen to be merging.

17. Failure of the bridge and CIC to check each other's maneuvering-board solutions.

18. Deck watch officers' lack of familiarity with the rules of the road and with accepted procedures for preventing collisions.

19. Failure to execute tactical signals correctly.

Most of these mistakes are elementary. It does not seem likely that able, intelligent officers would make them, yet these simple mistakes are made with discouraging frequency. It does not require genius to stand a proficient deck watch; but it does require vigilance, alertness, a highly developed sense of responsibility, and good judgment.

Most of these mistakes are discussed farther along in this book; the others need little elaboration. The timely use of navigational lights in uncertain or dangerous maneuvering situations is proper, even under simulated or actual battle conditions. It should be evident in these days of radar that the lights could yield only incidental information to an enemy who might be nearby. Running-light switch panels should be kept set up, and bridge personnel should be drilled in turning them on quickly.

Frequent compass checks of the bearings of all closing ships are absolutely essential. They are the best and most important means of preventing collisions at sea. In low visibility, bearings should be checked by radar. Unless two ships are on parallel, opening courses, a steady bearing with decreasing range means that collision is imminent. Even a slowly changing bearing is warning of a dangerous situation. *Action must be taken.* This means notifying the captain if time permits, changing course, or stopping and backing.

Groundings

Like collisions, groundings are generally attributable to human error. Most of the common errors listed below involve duties that are the responsibility of the navigator but of which the OOD should be cognizant:

1. Laying down the ship's intended track too close to known shoal water, or over water too shallow for the ship's draft.

2. Lack of foresight in failure to plot danger and turn bearings on the chart ahead of time.

3. Reliance on radar navigation alone.

4. Failure of the OOD to notify the captain and the navigator as soon as he doubts safety of position.

5. Improper application of known gyro erroı.

6. Failure to use visible aids to navigation.

7. Failure to have available the latest *Notice to Mariners* concerning temporary dislocation of aids to navigation.

8. Failure to use effectively a dead-reckoning plot.

9. Failure to fix position by distance run between successive bearings when only one landmark was identified.

10. Failure to stop and assess the situation or take emergency action when doubt of safe position first arose.

11. Failure to use fathometer and line of soundings.

12. Failure to account for set and drift and apply the proper correction to the course to be steered.

13. Wrong identification of lights and other fixed aids to navigation.

14. Failure to adjust course as necessary to remain on the dead-reckoning track.

15. Failure to take fixes frequently enough.

16. Too much reliance on nonfixed aids to navigation, such as buoys.

Again, most of the errors that result in groundings are violations of the basic principles of navigation, and, as in collisions, the inescapable conclusion is that disaster results from carelessness and lack of good judgment rather than lack of knowledge. All too often the temptation to take a chance, to slop through the watch instead of expending energy in doing the job correctly, is not resisted. It does not take a master mariner to slow, stop, change course, or notify the captain and navigator whenever the ship's position is in doubt.

Checking the gyro should be the concern of the OOD. A range or a sun azimuth can often be used, or a bearing of Polaris can be taken. The old reliable check against the magnetic compass, which *OpNavInst* 3120.32, Article 422, requires, should not be done in a perfunctory manner. Gyro compasses can suddenly develop large errors, and the only way to detect them quickly is to be aware at all times of the relationship between the gyro and the magnetic compasses. The quartermaster of the watch logs the readings of both in his compass record book. He should be impressed with the importance of this routine chore. When a gyro error has been detected and measured, it must be applied to the course to be steered *in the right direction*. An OOD who does not trust his memory on this point should refer to *Dutton's Navigation and Piloting*, which is available in every chart house.

Radar navigation

Radar has become internationally accepted as the primary means of fixing a ship's position. Properly used, it permits ships to navigate safely at greater distances from land and under worse weather conditions than is possible with traditional visual methods. The danger is that it is so easy to navigate by radar that a false sense of security, a precursor to disaster, is likely to be created.

The OOD's responsibility for safe navigation is in no way lessened by the fact that CIC or the quartermaster is navigating by radar. The clear radar pictures that some topography provides can be deceptive; radar sometimes yields fixes that look accurate, but are in fact miles wide of the ship's position. This is especially so in areas where the shoreline is low and sandy and the terrain behind it rises gradually. Furthermore, the clarity of a radar picture can change as a ship's position changes, and a feature that stands out clearly from one angle may begin to "break up" or disappear altogether when seen from another angle. If this happens when a ship is approaching a turn bearing and no dead-reckoning plot or other navigational tools have been used, she can easily lose her bearings and get into trouble.

When radar is being used to navigate in close or restricted waters, it should be cross-checked with whatever other aid to navigation is available. The bridge and CIC should always lay out the same track, take fixes at the same time, and constantly compare fixes. In this way, differences in the ship's position can be discovered and action taken before it is too late. The importance of the relationship between CIC and the bridge can never be overstressed, especially in regard to safe navigation.

Dead-reckoning plot

In the days before electronics, when good fixes were rare, hard to get, and highly valued, the dead-reckoning (DR) plot was one of a navigator's most important aids. It still is.

When a ship's actual position is in doubt, a DR plot (modified, if necessary, by known factors, such as current) is the best estimate of that position. A good navigator has either the actual or the DR position of his ship instantly available at all times. The mechanics of navigating—the accumulation of fixes that show where the ship has been—is of secondary importance. A navigator's primary duty is to know *where his ship is going,* not where she has been. For this purpose, a DR plot is invaluable and must always be maintained on the chart in use. A mechanical means of keeping, but not of advancing, this plot is the dead-reckoning tracer (DRT), a sometimes-neglected instrument. It should always be set up when a ship is operating on soundings, and its setting should be made to conform with actual fixes. Moreover, the DR must always be laid out to reflect the measured or estimated set and drift. This will require the OOD and the navigation team to remain aware of where their ship is actually going, not merely where they have directed her to go.

The navigator and the officer of the deck

In addition to those duties prescribed by regulation for the head of a department, he (the navigator) will be responsible, under the commanding officer, for the safe navigation and piloting of the ship. He will receive all orders relating to his navigational duties directly from the commanding officer and will make all reports in connection therewith to the commanding officer. . . . The duties of the navigator will include advising the commanding officer and the officer of the deck as to the ship's movements; and if the ship is running into danger the safe course to be steered.

OpNavInst 3120.32.

The navigator and the OOD share responsibility for knowing the navigational situation of a ship. When the navigator is on the bridge, he is usually doing the actual navigation and making recommendations to the OOD as to changes in course and speed in order to make good a track or to keep the ship out of danger. Nevertheless, the OOD has the responsibility, in the words of the regulation, to "take appropriate action" to ensure the safety of the ship. When the navigator and the OOD do not agree on the course of action to be taken, the navigator may, if he has been authorized in writing to do so, relieve the OOD. He must, however, immediately inform the commanding officer that he has done so. This very rare situation is not likely to develop if both the navigator and the OOD understand and are paying attention to the navigation of the ship. It is likely to arise if the OOD is taking little interest in the navigation simply because the navigator or one of his assistants is on the bridge and doing the navigating. The navigator's position as the authoritative adviser on the safe navigation of the ship does not relieve the OOD of any of his responsibility.

Additionally, because of the navigator's unique responsibility for safe navigation at all times, the OOD should keep him informed of anything that may be pertinent. The OOD should never hesitate to consult the navigator, day or night, with questions about safe navigation.

When a ship is in formation, the OOD routinely makes the course and speed changes that are dictated by the tactical situation and are not directly related to the safe navigation of the ship. The OOD should nevertheless inform the navigator of any such changes other than minor alterations necessary to maintain station. He should also ensure that the dead-reckoning plot is revised to reflect any course and speed changes (except for station-keeping) that are held for more than five minutes. This should be done even when a ship changes station. In a large formation, a ship's change of station from one side to the other can have a significant effect on her geographical position.

Fog and low visibility

Radar has made possible the most complicated maneuvering and piloting under all conditions of visibility. However, its assistance does not reduce in any way the duties and responsibilities of a commanding officer. Extensive use of radar has led many inexperienced officers to think they can neglect the older and more reliable means of safeguarding a ship. Radar is an *aid* against disaster, not a *guarantee*. Regardless of the state of visibility, either the OOD or the JOOD should be *outside* the pilot house, using his binoculars and listening for fog signals. "Radarscope fixation" must be avoided. Aviators are taught to constantly scan their instruments and check the air around them. They are warned never to become fixed on one instrument for too long a time. The OOD should develop the same habits. Rather than anchor himself at a radar repeater or at the centerline pelorus, he should be constantly on the move, checking both bridge wings and the area astern of the ship and periodically scanning the radar repeaters.

An officer of the deck must understand the capabilities and limitations of his radars. He should know how to operate all the remote-control gear, who are responsible for the maintenance of the radars, and how to reach them in a hurry. He should have the radars warmed up and checked before dark, when fog descends, and when it begins to rain or snow.

It is important to use surface-search radar in poor visibility. At night and when visibility is low, radar repeaters on the bridge and in CIC should be on different ranges. Surface-search radars should be kept energized when a ship is underway (but not necessarily emitting when operating under an EMCON condition) and they should be checked and calibrated at intervals. Keeping all radar repeaters, both in CIC and on the bridge, on the same range is dangerous, because it can lead to concentration on the immediate area at the expense of detecting contacts in the distance, or vice versa. It should be noted that the courts have held the failure of a government vessel to make use of radar while underway in low visibility to have contributed directly to a collision. This philosophy appears in Rule 2 of the *International Regulations for Preventing Collisions at Sea*, as revised in 1983, which states:

Nothing in these rules shall exonerate any vessel, or the owner, master or crew thereof, from the consequences of any neglect to comply with these rules or of the neglect of any precaution which may be required by the ordinary practice of seamen, or by the special circumstances of the case.

Lookouts

Every vessel shall at all times maintain a proper lookout by sight and hearing as well as by all available means appropriate in the prevailing circumstances and conditions so as to make a full appraisal of the situation and the risk of collision.

International Regulations for Preventing Collisions at Sea, 1983, Rule 5.

International Regulations for Preventing Collisions at Sea, 1983, commonly known as the rules of the road, specifies clearly that a lookout must be both looking and listening. This is an important point, since many lookouts are not aware that, even under normal steaming conditions, they have a responsibility to maintain a watch by "sight and sound." In low visibility the duty of the lookout to report what he hears is especially important; he should be provided with a telephone-talker, so that he himself can concentrate on listening for fog signals. A lookout who is wearing phones when he is charged with listening for signals is *not* standing a proper watch.

Lookouts should not be trained by casual instruction from their peers or by a so-called break-in watch. They should be included in a formal qualification program that comprises training in reporting procedures, recognition and identification, and the use of sound-powered telephones. A lookout should be encouraged to report everything he sees, even floating material of any kind, and his reports should always be acknowledged. If they are not acknowledged he might begin to think that his efforts are wasted and not report anything. Lookouts should be rotated as frequently as possible, at least hourly. When the weather is bad they should be the first members of the watch to be issued foul-weather gear, and they should be relieved as often as necessary. In extremely cold or windy weather, a lookout's efficiency drops to almost zero after he has been on duty for half an hour.

Psychological factors

During World War II, Fleet Admiral Chester W. Nimitz, in a letter to the Pacific Fleet, stressed the impact that psychological factors can have on safe navigation:

There are certain psychological factors which have fully as much to do with safety at sea as any of the more strictly technical ones. A large proportion of the disasters in tactics and maneuvers comes from concentrating too much on one objective or urgency, at the cost of not being sufficiently alert for others. Thus, absorption with enemy craft already under fire has led to being torpedoed by others not looked for or not given attention; while preoccupation with navigation, with carrying out the particular job in hand, or with avoiding some particular vessel or hazard, has resulted in collision with ships to whose presence we were temporarily oblivious. There is no rule that can cover this except the ancient one that eternal vigilance is the price of safety, no matter what the immediate distractions.

No officer, whatever his rank and experience, should flatter himself that he is immune to the inexplicable lapses in judgment, calculation, and memory, or to the slips of the tongue in giving orders, which throughout seagoing history have so often brought disaster to men of the highest reputation and ability. Where a mistake in maneuvering or navigating can spell calamity, an officer shows rashness and conceit, rather than admirable self-confidence, in not checking his plan with someone else before starting it, *if time permits*. This is not yielding to another's judgment; it is merely making sure that one's own has not "blown a fuse" somewhere, as the best mental and mechanical equipment in the world has sometimes done.

8 | STANDARD COMMANDS

[The orders of an officer in charge of a watch] shall be issued in the customary phraseology of the service.

OpNavInst 3120.32.

Nowhere in the navy are terminology and phraseology as important as they are in commands given by the conning officer to the helmsman or the engines. Because misunderstanding or ambiguity can so quickly lead to disaster, there must be no possibility of a command's being misunderstood, and there need be no confusion if official terminology and phraseology are used. Short cuts or individual variations are to be discouraged; all the enlisted men who man the ship-control instruments should become accustomed to receiving their commands in the same form.

Manner of giving commands

Commands should be given in a clear voice, loud enough to be heard, and the tone should be positive and incisive.

The word *helm* should not be used in any command relating to the operation of the rudder. Commands to the helmsman are given in a logical sequence. The first word is *right* or *left*, which indicates the direction in which the helmsman is to put the wheel over. The second word indicates how far he is to put it over, e.g, "Right *standard* rudder." The purpose of giving a command in this manner is to ensure quick and accurate compliance by the helmsman, who starts turning his wheel instantly upon hearing "right" or "left" and, by the time the amount of rudder has been specified, he can bring the rudder-angle indicator to rest on the exact number of degrees.

Similarly, in a command given via the engine-order telegraph, familiarly called the lee helm, the first term, *port (starboard) engine* or *all engines* indicates to the operator which handles or knobs he must prepare to move. The next word, *ahead* or *back*, tells him in which direction he is to move them. The last part of the command, *one-third*, *full*, etc., gives the amount of the speed change and tells him where to stop his instrument. Standard commands to the engines are these:

1. "All engines ahead one-third (two-thirds, standard, full, flank)" or "All engines back one-third (two-thirds, full)."

2. "Starboard (port) engine, ahead one-third (two-thirds, standard, full)" or "Starboard (port) engine, back one-third (two-thirds, full)."

In an emergency, normal acceleration and deceleration tables are sometimes abandoned and orders are given for the ship to go ahead or back with all available power as quickly as possible. In such instances the proper command is "All engines ahead (back), emergency." The operator should then ring up "ahead flank" (or "back full") three or more times in rapid succession.

The exact number of revolutions to be made on each engine should be indicated to the engine room by the revolution indicator. If the number of revolutions desired is not the exact number for the speed ordered, the number of revolutions desired must be specified: "*Indicate* one one seven revolutions." The word *revolutions* should always be included in this order to prevent any possible confusion with orders concerning course or bearings. When increasing or decreasing revolutions by small increments, the exact number of revolutions desired should also be stated: for instance, "Indicate one one seven revolutions," rather than "Up two" or "Take off three."

When practicable, the *number of revolutions desired* should be ordered, rather than the *speed desired*. This would not be practical if, for instance, the OOD were on the wing of the bridge, unable to see or remember the revolutions required, and felt that he should not move. In such a situation he should order, *"Indicate turns for __ knots"* and require a report of the turns rung up, as well as a repetition of the command. The turns-per-knot table should be memorized as soon as possible.

One-third speed and two-thirds speed are one-third and two-thirds of the prescribed standard speed. The revolutions for these speeds are the number of revolutions per minute required to achieve those fractions of standard speed. Full speed and flank speed are greater than standard speed. They are usually based on fractional increments of standard speed. The rpm for these speeds are also those actually required to achieve them. When small adjustments in speed are desired, the only command usually necessary is the one ordering the change in revolutions. However, when one orders revolutions that will result in a speed within a different increment, that increment should also be rung up on the engine-order telegraph.

It is important that all commands be repeated loudly and clearly by the helmsman or lee helmsman just as they were given by the officer at the conn. This practice serves as a check on the officer who originated the command and provides an opportunity for correction of any slip of the tongue, such as "left" when "right" was meant.

It is equally important to require the man at the helm or lee helm to report when he has complied with the command. The conning officer must acknowledge this final report with a "Very well."

Steering commands to the helm

When a specific amount of rudder is desired:
    Command: Right full rudder (or right standard rudder).
    Reply: Right full (standard) rudder, aye, sir.
    Report: Rudder is right full (standard), sir.

When the rudder order is given in degrees:
    Command: Left ten degrees rudder.
    Reply: Left ten degrees rudder, aye, sir.
    Report: Rudder is left ten degrees, sir.

When the helmsman is to steady on a specific course:

Command: Steady on course _____.

Reply: Steady on course _____, aye, sir.

Report: Steady on course _____, sir. Checking _____ magnetic.

When maximum possible rudder is required:

Command: Hard right rudder.

Reply: Hard right rudder, aye, sir.

Report: Rudder is hard right, sir.

Note: The danger in using hard rudder lies in the possibility of jamming the rudder into the stops. For this reason it is rarely used except in emergencies. If hard rudder is chosen in a nonemergency situation, the conning officer may reduce the possibility of jamming the rudder by first ordering full rudder and then increasing the rudder to hard, allowing the helmsman more control of the rudder's movement.

When it is desired to increase the amount of rudder:

Command: Increase your rudder to _____ (right full, ten degrees, etc.).

Reply: Increase your rudder to _____, sir.

Report: Rudder is _____ (right full, right ten degrees, etc.).

When it is desired to decrease the amount of rudder:

Command: Ease your rudder to left _____ (standard, left ten degrees, etc.).

Reply: Ease your rudder to left _____, sir.

Report: Rudder is left _____ (standard, left ten degrees, etc.).

When the rudder is increased or decreased while the ship is turning to an ordered course:

Command: Right standard rudder, steady on course 270.

Reply: Right standard rudder, steady on course 270, aye, sir.

Command: Increase your rudder to right full, steady on course 270.

Note: When the rudder is increased or decreased, the conning officer must restate the desired course.

Reply: Increase your rudder to right full, steady on course 270, aye, sir.
Report: Rudder is right full, coming to course 270, sir.

When course change is less than ten degrees:
Command: Come right, steer course _____.
Reply: Come right, steer course _____, aye, sir.
Report: Steady course _____, checking course _____ magnetic, sir.

When the rudder angle is to be reduced to zero:
Command: Rudder amidships.
Reply: Rudder amidships, aye, sir.
Report: Rudder is amidships, sir.

When it is desired to steer the course that the ship is on at the instant the command is given:
Command: Steady as you go.
Reply: Steady as you go, course _____, sir.
Report: Steady on course _____, sir. Checking course.

Note: Injudicious use of this order could cause momentary loss of control over the ship's swing if the helmsman is required to use a large rudder angle to carry out the order. To prevent this, the order should be preceded by "Rudder amidships." This of course requires anticipation on the conning officer's part to ensure a correct heading. In this situation the conning officer should always maintain positive control of the rudder.

When it is desired to stop the swing of the ship without steadying on any specific course:
Command: Meet her.
Reply: Meet her, aye, sir.

Note: Immediately after the reply is given, the conning officer must order a course to be steered.

Command: Steady on course _____.
Reply: Steady on course _____, aye, sir.
Report: Steady on course _____, sir. Checking course _____.

When equal and *opposite* rudder is desired relative to that previously ordered:
Command: Shift your rudder.
Reply: Shift your rudder, aye, sir.
Report: Rudder is _____ (at an angle equal but opposite to that previously ordered).

When it is desired to determine the heading of the ship at any specific moment:
Command: Mark your head.
Report: Head is _____ (exact heading at that moment), sir.

Note: If the helmsman appears to be steering properly but the ship is not on her correct heading, the conning officer should use this command to compare the helmsman's compass repeater with other repeaters on the bridge.

When the helmsman appears to be steering badly or is continually allowing the ship to drift from the ordered course:
Command: Mind your helm.
Reply: Mind my helm, aye, sir.

Note: No report necessary.

When the ship is in a situation where minor deviation from an ordered course may be permitted to one side but none may be permitted to the other side (e.g., when alongside another ship for refueling):
Command: Steer nothing to the left (right) of course _____.
Reply: Steer nothing to the left (right) of course _____, aye, sir.

Note: No report necessary.

Whenever he orders a course change, the conning officer should perform the following activities:

1. Check the side to which he intends to turn to make sure that it is safe to turn in that direction.

2. Ensure that the number of degrees of rudder ordered does not exceed the amount of course change. If, for example, a twelve-degree course change is desired, the rudder angle ordered should be less than twelve degrees. If possible, it should be given in a multiple of five degrees. In the example given, it would be no more than ten degrees.

3. The ship's speed determines how quickly her head will swing. At very low speeds, a large angle of rudder may be required to bring about a course change; at very high speeds, a large rudder angle may cause her to swing so rapidly that she cannot be safely controlled. All conning officers should be familiar with the tables of turning speeds and turning diameters for their ship. This information is contained in the ship's tactical data book.

4. After giving a rudder order, the conning officer should monitor its execution. He should do this by checking the rudder angle indicator to ensure there was no misinterpretation of the command.

5. In a turn without an ordered course, the helmsman should call out the ship's head for each ten degrees that the ship swings. If the conning officer does not wish the helmsman to do this, he should give the helmsman the order "Belay your headings." The helm should reply, "Belay my headings, aye, sir."

Engine-order commands to the lee helm
Basic format

Engine orders are always given in the following order:

1. Engine: Which engine is to be used. If both engines are to be used, the command is "All engines." On single-screw ships the command is always "Engine."

2. Direction: Ahead, back, or stop.

3. Amount: Ahead one-third, two-thirds, full, flank. Back one-third, two-thirds, full.

4. Shaft revolutions desired: Number of revolutions in three digits for the desired speed in knots. Shaft revolutions are not used for backing orders.

Examples

When it is desired to go ahead on both engines (twin-screw ship) to come to a speed of 6 knots:

Command: All engines ahead one-third. Indicate zero eight eight revolutions for 6 knots.

Reply: All engines ahead one-third. Indicate zero eight eight revolutions for 6 knots, aye, sir.

Report: Engine room answers all ahead one-third. Indicating zero eight eight revolutions for 6 knots, sir.

When different orders are given to port and starboard engines, revolutions should not be specified:

Command: Port engine ahead one-third, starboard engine back one-third.

Reply: Port engine ahead one-third, starboard engine back one-third, aye, sir.

Report: Engine room answers port ahead one-third, starboard back one-third, sir.

When the order is to only one engine, the report must include the status of both engines:

Command: Starboard engine ahead one-third, port engine back one-third.

Reply: Starboard engine ahead one-third, port engine back one-third, aye, sir.

Report: Engine room answers starboard engine ahead one-third, port engine back one-third, sir.

Command: Starboard engine stop.

Reply: Starboard engine stop, aye, sir.

Report: Engine room answers starboard engine stop. Port engine back one-third, sir.

When small changes of speed are desired, for example, when alongside for refueling or to keep station on the formation guide:

Command: Indicate one zero zero revolutions.
Reply: Indicate one zero zero revolutions, aye, sir.
Report: Engine room answers one zero zero revolutions for three revolutions over 11 knots, sir.

Note: When maneuvering in restricted waters, getting underway, docking or mooring, ships usually use what are known as "maneuvering bells." Under these circumstances, only engine, direction, and amount are given. Revolutions are not specified. Depending on the type of ship, each engine amount equates to a standard number of knots, e.g., $1/3 = 5$ knots, $2/3 = 10$ knots, etc. When "maneuvering bells" (or "maneuvering combination") are desired, the conning officer must so order the helmsman:

Command: Indicate maneuvering combination (bells). (By convention, this is usually an engine order for 999 revolutions.)
Reply: Indicate (999) revolutions for maneuvering combination (bells), sir.
Report: Engine room answers (999) revolutions for maneuvering combination (bells), sir.

Some commanding officers develop variation in the maneuvering bells to indicate one-half of the power increment, often by indicating 777 or 888. This tells the throttleman to cut his standard acceleration or deceleration and power levels in half to provide for more explicit shiphandling around the pier. The watch officer should consult his commanding officer's standing orders to see if this practice is acceptable on his ship.

Commands to line-handlers

Many a good approach to a landing is offset by improper use of mooring lines. Using them properly requires knowledge of the standard commands to line-handlers. The following examples and definitions are in common use in the fleet and form the basis of all orders to lines. Orders should state number of line, when appropriate, and telephone-talkers should be used for transmitting them.

Mooring lines are numbered from bow to stern in the order in which they are run out from the ship: 1, bow line; 2, after bow spring; 3, forward bow spring; 4, after quarter spring; 5, forward quarter spring; 6, stern line. The breast line amidships is not numbered.

Command	Meaning
"Stand by your lines"	Man the lines, ready to put them over, cast them off, or take them in.
"Let go" or "Let go all lines"	Slack off to permit people tending lines on the pier or on another ship to cast off.
"Send the lines over" or "Put over all lines"	Pass the lines to the pier, place the eye of each over the appropriate bollard, but take no strain.
"Take a strain on (line 3)"	Put the line under tension.
"Slack (line 3)"	Take tension off the line and let it hang slack.
"Ease (line 3)"	Let out enough of the line to lessen tension.
"Take (line 3) to the capstan" or to "power"	Lead the end of the line to the capstan, take the slack out of it, but put no strain on it.
"Heave around on (line 3)"	Apply tension on the line with the capstan.
"Avast heaving"	Stop the capstan.
"Hold what you've got on (line 3)"	Hold the line as it is.
"Hold (line 3)"	Do not allow any more line to go out. Note: "Hold" commands should be used with extreme caution, since they require the lines to be held even to parting.
"Check"	Hold heavy tension on line but let it slip as necessary to prevent it from parting.

Command	Meaning
"Surge"	Hold moderate tension on the line but let it slip enough to permit the ship to move.
"Double up"	Pass additional bights on all mooring lines so that there are three parts of each line to the pier.
"Single up"	Take in all bights and extra lines, leaving only a single part of each of the normal mooring lines.
"Take in all lines"	Have the ends of all lines cast off from the pier and brought on board.
"Cast off all lines"	Used when secured with *another* ship's lines in a nest. Cast off the ends of the lines and allow the other ship to retrieve her lines.
"Shift"	Used when moving a line along a pier. Followed by specification of the line and where it is to go: "Shift number 3 from the bollard to the cleat."

When a ship's auxiliary deck machinery is to be used to haul in on a line, the command given is "Take one (number one) to the winch (capstan or power)." This may be followed by "Heave around on one (number one)" and then "Avast heaving on one (number one)."

The proper naval term for the line-handling drum on the anchor windlass is *warping head*. Usage, however, has given authority to the synonyms *winch* and *capstan, winch* being the more common.

Commands to tugs

Tugs are handled more and more by two-way VHF radio. However, the following whistle and hand signals are still in use. They may be transmitted to tugs by flashing lights, but only when whistle or hand signals cannot be used.

Whistle signals

A blast lasts 2 to 3 seconds. A prolonged blast lasts 4 to 5 seconds. A short blast lasts about one second. Care must be exercised to ensure that whistle signals are directed to and received by the tug for which they are intended. Whistles of different tones have been used successfully to handle more than one tug.

Signal	*Meaning*
1 blast	From stop to half-speed ahead
1 blast	From half-speed ahead to stop
4 short blasts	From half-speed ahead to full speed ahead
1 blast	From full speed ahead to half-speed ahead
2 blasts	From stop to half-speed astern
4 short blasts	From half-speed astern to full speed astern
1 blast	From half-speed or full speed astern to stop
1 prolonged blast, 2 short blasts	Cast off, stand clear

Whistle signals are usually augmented by hand signals.

Hand signals

Signal	*Meaning*
Arm pointed in direction desired.	Half-speed (ahead or astern)
Fist describing arc	Full speed (ahead or astern)
Undulating movement of open hand, with palm down.	Dead slow (ahead or astern)
Open hand held aloft, with palm facing the tug.	Stop

Hand signals

Signal	Meaning
Closed fist with thumb extended, swung up and down.	Cast off, stand clear
Hand describing circle as if turning wheel to the right (clockwise), facing in the same direction as the tug.	Tug to use right rudder
Hand describing circle as if turning wheel to the left (counterclockwise), facing in the same direction as the tug.	Tug to use left rudder
Arm at side of body with hand extended, swung back and forth.	Tug to use rudder amidship

A tug must acknowledge all whistle and hand signals with one short toot (one second or less) from her whistle. The exceptions are the backing signal, which must be acknowledged with two short toots, and the cast-off signal, which must be acknowledged by one prolonged and two short toots.

Auxiliary power units

Auxiliary power units (APUs) on some newer classes of naval vessels have given an increased maneuvering capability in close-quarters situations. APUs are electrically driven, trainable motors positioned near the bow of the ship.

Command	Meaning
Train port APU 90 degrees	Position port APU to push the ship towards 090 degrees relative
Energize port (starboard) APU	Port (starboard) APU on
Stop port (starboard) APU	Port (starboard) APU off

Bow thrusters

Bow thrusters on amphibious ships are used to marry the ship's bow with a causeway for amphibious landings. Additionally, they improve maneuverability near the pier or in close-quarters situations. The bow thruster is an electrically driven, controllable-pitch propeller (CPP) located near the bow inside a transverse hull tube.

Command	*Meaning*
Bow thruster starboard one-half	Bow thruster will move the ship to starboard. CPP will slew to 50 per cent.
Bow thruster stop	Bow thruster CPP will slew to zero per cent pitch.

9 | THE WATCH OFFICER IN PORT

The command duty officer

The Command Duty Officer in port is that officer or authorized Petty Officer who has been designated for a particular watch by the Commanding Officer to carry out the routine of the unit in port and for supervising and directing the Officer of the Deck in matters concerning the safety and general duties of the unit. In the temporary absence of the Executive Officer, the duties of the Executive Officer will be carried out by the Command Duty Officer.

OpNavInst 3120.32 (Series).

The primary responsibility of the in-port duty section is the safety and security of the ship. The command duty officer (CDO), designated by the commanding officer, must lead his watch-standers in discharging this responsibility. He customarily stands his duty for a 24-hour period, and he sets the tone for the duty section's performance. He reports to the executive officer or, in his absence, the commanding officer on the performance of his duties. Routine reports made to the commanding officer by the OOD should also be made to the CDO. If the executive officer is temporarily absent, the heads of departments or their designated representatives report to the CDO concerning matters affecting the operation and administration of their departments. The CDO should conduct frequent inspections to ensure the safety and security of the ship. Additionally, he has the responsibility of drilling duty emergency parties.

Clearly, this is a critically important position that requires a great deal of forehandedness and preparation. Navy regulations state that the command duty officer will be an officer eligible for command. In fact, he may be required to get his ship underway on a moment's notice; although he rarely takes this action, the possibility shows how well prepared a CDO must be to accept the responsibilities of his watch. A good CDO does not attempt to execute his responsibilities from the confines of the wardroom; he makes frequent rounds of the ship and keeps himself informed as to the status of his vessel. Commanding officers and executive officers have specific guidelines for the CDO; the following general suggestions can help him maintan high standards for the duty section:

1. The CDO should conduct frequent and random inspections throughout the ship, keeping an eye out for safety hazards, fire hazards, cleanliness, crew appearance, work in progress, material condition, and ship-wide security.

2. He should always inform the quarterdeck of his whereabouts and how he may be contacted. If he is touring the ship, he should tell the quarterdeck where he expects to be.

3. He should attempt to be on the quarterdeck for the arrival and departure of the commanding officer and executive officer so that they can pass along information that they may want him to have.

4. He should pay close attention to drills by emergency response teams, and critique them. He should be creative, vary the scenario to cover common contingencies, and remember to exercise the rescue-and-assistance team.

5. He should inform the CO and XO if he is preparing to conduct a drill while they are on board. This is a courtesy that goes a long way to alleviate their anxiety when a drill is called away.

6. He should be on deck to observe special evolutions such as colors and sunrise. These evolutions are a sign of a ship's pride and professionalism, and the CDO's personal interest always helps to make them run smoothly and efficiently.

7. He should watch for sudden and unexpected changes in

weather (particularly a change in barometer pressure readings of .04 or more in any one hour). This is especially critical if he is conducting boat operations.

8. He should know the status of the ship's boats at all times.

9. He should frequently spot-check hazardous storage areas to ensure proper storage of volatile material.

10. He should always know the status of the engineering plant and frequently check it.

11. He should require the quarterdeck to inform him immediately of any changes in firemain pressure or any unusual readings observed by sounding-and-security or roving patrols.

12. He should mentally prepare to respond to emergencies and should have emergency service telephone numbers within easy access, such as those of the base fire department, ambulance, security, and chaplain.

13. He should ensure that preparations are made for upcoming events. For example, if the ship expects to get underway the following day, he should make sure that arrangements have been made to clear away paint floats, doughnuts, etc. He should think at least one day ahead of his duty day.

14. If in doubt, he should call the commanding officer or executive officer for assistance.

The CDO sets the standards for the duty section. Slovenly appearance, lack of interest in drills and exercises, or a lethargic attitude toward duty will be reflected by the watch team. On the other hand, an exuberant, visible, and concerned CDO will lead the way to a taut and safe watch.

The officer of the deck

The officer of the deck in port is that officer or petty officer on watch who has been designated by the commanding officer to be in charge of the unit. He is primarily responsible for the safety and proper operation of the unit.

OpNavInst 3120.32.

When a ship is in port, the OOD's responsibilities are considerably less complex than when he is standing a watch at sea. This does not mean, however, that the job is any less demanding. Even though he is not faced with tactical problems, maneuvering, or signals, the OOD in port is occupied with a seemingly endless series of things to supervise, inspect, and control. He is expected to make timely and sound decisions on matters that are, in their own way, as important as anything that happens at sea. If he is to stand his watch properly, he must be at least as well prepared as he would be at sea and must be ready to respond quickly to a variety of situations.

A chief petty officer or petty officer who is assigned as OOD in port has the same status as a commissioned or warrant officer so assigned, and his orders have the same force. He is designated in writing by the commanding officer and in most ships is required to complete the section of the surface-warfare officers' PQS that relates to the OOD in port.

Preparing for the watch

Considerable preparation in the form of reviewing ship's routine, instructions from local commanders and from the senior officer present afloat (SOPA), and policy concerning any special existing or possible situations is necessary before taking over a deck watch in port. The basic information that the OOD needs is usually kept in a folder on the quarterdeck, but every watch has its own special emphases, and the OOD should be aware of them. Some of the most important things that OODs in port must consider are listed below; experience or special circumstances will suggest others.

If the ship is at pierside:

1. Evolutions that may occur during the watch.
2. The status of visitors.
3. Quarterdeck search procedures that are in effect.
4. Local terrorist or antisecurity climate.
5. The last time the security watches reported.
6. The status of the ship's propulsion machinery.
7. Current material condition of readiness.
8. Who the SOPA is and what other commanders are present and their flagships.
9. What flags and pennants are flying.

10. The status of men aloft, men over the side, or divers in the water.

11. What guardships (military, medical, etc.) are present, what radio circuits are guarded, and whether visual guards are posted.

12. What services the ship is receiving from the pier.

13. The status of all boats in water, in skids, out of commission, away on trips, scheduled for trips, and so forth. The status of fuel in boats.

14. The status of the ship's vehicles—location, drivers, trips planned, fuel, and so forth.

15. The state of the weather, and changes anticipated.

16. The amount of rise and fall of the tide, the state of the tide, and the time of the next change in the tide.

17. The status of aircraft.

18. Who the CDO is and how he may be reached.

19. The status of ship's restricted men, prisoners, or medical cases.

20. What orders are currently in effect or unexecuted.

21. The location of the commanding officer and executive officer (aboard or ashore).

If the ship is at anchor:

In addition to the above, the OOD should also ascertain—

22. The anchorage bearings.

23. The nature of the holding ground, the depth of water, and the scope of chain on deck.

24. The position of the ship on the chart.

25. Anchor(s) in use.

26. Anchor(s) ready for letting go.

27. Steaming notice that would be required.

28. Other ships present and their location.

29. When the ship is moored to a buoy or buoys, the amount of chain or wire used.

Smart appearance

In port, more than at any other time, the initial impression a visitor receives is based almost solely on the appearance and smartness of the quarterdeck and the watch. This impression is all-encompassing: crew, officers, and captain. Thus the appearance of a ship, her boats, and her crew is a major responsibility of the OOD. He must not only know the proper standards of cleanliness and smartness, he must enforce them. It takes only a little practice to note such things as Irish pennants, slack halyards, and sloppy execution of the colors ceremony. But it takes energy, initiative, and patience to correct them. Junior officers vary in their powers of observation and in their attitude about taking action. The better an officer's reputation for standing a taut watch and for being intolerant of anything that downgrades his ship, the more readily will the crew respond. An officer with such a reputation is not likely to have men come on watch on the quarterdeck in frayed or soiled uniforms, or try to go ashore on liberty during his watch without being properly groomed. He will, in short, find his high standards easy to maintain. On the other hand, an officer who is slovenly and does not have the pride to stand a proper watch will find himself continually in hot water. His superiors will be constantly calling him on the appearance of the ship, and the crew will not be responsive to him. Every officer should resolve early in his career to run a taut and efficient watch. Men respect an officer who knows his job and performs it fairly and pleasantly, but in accordance with all directives and with the traditionally high standards of the navy.

Watch organization

The commanding officer will establish such watches as are necessary for the safety and proper operation of the command.

OpNavInst 3120.32.

Prior to taking over a watch, the OOD must find out what watches are being manned, who is manning them, and to whom each watch-stander reports. Since his watch team will probably not be centered in one place, as they are when the ship is underway, this information is very important in getting the watch started smoothly. The oncoming OOD should be informed of any changes to the watch bill that have been authorized, watches posted for special evolutions, and watch conditions that are in any way different from those promulgated in the plan of the day.

The petty officer of the watch

The petty officer of the watch is the primary enlisted assistant to the officer of the deck in port. When a boatswain's mate of the watch is assigned, he will carry out the duties of the petty officer of the watch. Those duties of the petty officer of the watch so indicated will be carried out by the quartermaster of the watch when one is assigned.

OpNavInst 3120.32.

The petty officer of the watch (POOW) is the OOD's right-hand man and should be given responsibility for overall supervision of the watch team. He usually is the person closest to the OOD in qualification and experience, and is specifically responsible for assisting him in training and inspecting the watch. If properly trained and briefed by the OOD, he can represent a second pair of eyes and be a means of double-checking the ship's routine. In addition to the duties required of him by naval and ship's policy, such as log-keeping, weather observations, and supervision of boats, he should be, under the OOD, the leader of the watch team.

Messenger of the watch

Normally a nonrated man, the messenger of the watch is detailed by the OOD and the petty officer of the watch to perform various routine duties, such as waking watch reliefs, escorting visitors, and periodically sprucing up the quarterdeck. Messengers should not be considered qualified until they have been aboard a ship long enough to know the location of all major working spaces, offices, officers' staterooms, and other frequently visited areas. A sure way to give the impression of a sloppy ship is to provide a visitor with a messenger escort who does not know his way around. When a watch is expected to be unusually active, two messengers should be assigned.

Sounding-and-security patrol

The sounding-and-security patrol is required to make his rounds in a random fashion and to report to the officer of the deck hourly. The small size of the average in-port duty section makes his duty particularly important. With the majority of the crew ashore on liberty, this watch-stander is likely to be the only person in a position to discover flooding, fire, or a breach of the ship's security. Therefore, his performance of duty should be closely monitored by the OOD and, whenever possible, double-checked by the POOW. It is a good practice for the OOD periodically to quiz the sounding-and-security watch when he makes his report, to ensure that he is actually getting to the spaces that he is assigned to check. Failure of this watch to make his report to the quarterdeck must be immediately investigated.

Master-at-arms

The duty master-at-arms is normally a petty officer, first class, who stands no other watches during his duty day. He is responsible for conducting periodic musters of restricted men, supervising the performance of extra duty, and conducting a number of routine inspections of various spaces to check for cleanliness and the completion of required cleanups. When a working party is called away, the duty master-at-arms should be placed in charge of mustering and supervising it.

One of his most important duties is to enforce required standards of good order and discipline. When a disciplinary problem is discovered or suspected, the duty master-at-arms should be called away at once, given instructions by the OOD, and charged with investigating the situation. In cases of drunkenness or disorderliness, the duty master-at-arms may be empowered to obtain assistance from other senior petty officers in the duty section and to assist in the required medical evaluations of drunk or incapacitated men.

Cold-iron watch

In ships whose main machinery is inactive or that have no auxiliary watch on duty below, a cold-iron watch is stationed. This watch consists of men of the engineer force who, at regular intervals, inspect all machinery spaces for violations of watertight integrity and for fire hazards.

External security

In port the security of the ship is one of the most important duties of the OOD. Threats to her security may be natural, in the form of fire, collision, and heavy weather, or they may arise from an almost infinite range of deliberate human actions. Tight security is a necessity at all times, and no matter how quiet and uneventful a watch may seem to be, the OOD should never allow it to be relaxed. Of growing concern is the terrorist threat to United States naval vessels. No ship is ever immune to this threat, which can be carried out in very unconventional ways. Fanatical America-haters are willing to die to further their cause. The quarterdeck watch team must always assume that the danger of terrorism is present and must not allow security procedures to become perfunctory.

If a breach in security is discovered, the OOD has a trained force ready to assist him. This is the self-defense force. The type of ship and its mission determine who constitute this force. Its members are specifically designated and trained in security procedures, and the OOD should know and fully understand these procedures. He should call away this security force if he thinks that the ship or crew is in any way threatened. This team will follow established procedures to ensure the security of the ship. The OOD should never hesitate to initiate a security alert; if there is any doubt, he should call it away. He should also periodically exercise this team in drill scenarios at the discretion of the CDO.

Control of visitors

Commanding officers are responsible for the control of visitors to their commands and shall comply with the relevant provisions of the

Department of the Navy Security Manual for Classified Information and other pertinent directives.

Navy Regulations.

Almost every naval vessel in commission is required to have provisions for the control, identification, and supervision of visitors. Depending on the security requirements in force, the OOD may be required to issue passes for visitors, check whether there is written authorization for them to come aboard, or provide them with escorts. No matter how busy the quarterdeck may get, the OOD must always maintain positive control over visitors. They should not be allowed to wander from the quarterdeck or to proceed without escort simply because they claim to know the way.

In general, dealers and tradesmen or their agents shall be admitted within a command only as authorized by the commanding officer for the following purposes:

1. To conduct public business.

2. To transact private business with individuals at the request of the latter.

3. To furnish necessary services and supplies that are not available to the personnel of the command or are not available in sufficient quantity.

Fleet and force regulations that restrict casual visiting and the approach of bumboats should be followed with great care. Persons with a legitimate reason to come on board must be received politely. Every person coming on board, even those in uniform or professing official or business connections, should present proper identification. The harder it may be for the OOD to screen visitors, the most important it is that he observe all precautions.

Inspection of packages and personal effects

As part of his responsibility for the security of the ship, the OOD is required to inspect all parcels, briefcases, and other items carried on board by both visitors and ship's company and, under some circumstances, those being carried off the ship. His authority is backed by federal regulation and there are no exceptions to it. Searches should include inspection for classified material, contraband, drugs, liquor, and weapons, as well as government property being removed from the ship without authorization. When circumstances so dictate, body searches of all or randomly chosen persons may be carried out. If a large number of persons are to be inspected at one time, the duty master-at-arms should be called away to assist and to prevent congestion on the quarterdeck.

Sentries and guards

When sentries and armed guards are needed, the OOD usually has only to implement existing directives covering the use of forecastle, fantail, and pier sentries. All sentries are guided by written instructions and must know the right way to challenge boats in order to identify their occupants before they come alongside. Forecastle and fantail sentries check mooring lines and make periodic reports to the OOD. Pier sentries control flow of personnel and traffic on the pier. All sentries may be armed when the situation demands. The OOD must be certain that armed sentries or guards are proficient in the use of their weapons. If doubt exists, he should send for gunner's mate with the duty and have the men properly instructed. An armed man who does not know his weapon is not only useless at his post but a danger to his ship and shipmates.

Sneak attack and sabotage

Particularly during hours of darkness, ships at anchor or moored are vulnerable to various forms of sneak attack and sabotage conducted by swimmers from shore or people in small boats, or by submarines. Limpet mines can be attached to the hull of the ship, explosive charges can be placed on the bottom below the ship, and mobile limpets can be used. Saboteurs may pose as bumboat crews or visitors, or they may mingle with a returning liberty party. Surreptitious boarding from the shore is possible when ships are moored to a pier. Attack may also consist of contamination of food and water supplies or destruction of vital equipment by explosives or other means.

Where such dangers exist, normal security measures must be increased. The OOD should maintain gangway security by considering all approaching boats, persons, and packages suspect until they have been identified and inspected. All unnecessary lines, fenders, and sea ladders should be taken in. Boats not in use should be hoisted in, and booms should be rigged out of reach of swimmers or boats. Guards should be posted at all topside openings and a party held in readiness to repel boarders. Automatic weapons should be manned, and all personnel armed. Unnecessary noise should be avoided. Swimmers and explosive-ordnance-disposal teams (EOD) may be assigned to inspect the ship's bottom, but only after the sonar has been secured and all sentries and boats have been advised, in order to ensure that no explosive charges will be dropped.

If an attack has started, the highest degree of material readiness should be set, the rail manned with armed personnel, the SOPA and all ships present notified, and the ship made ready for getting underway immediately if possible.

Internal security

The safety of a ship may be threatened by persons or forces within, particularly in times of international tension. The OOD should make sure that required patrols are carried out and reports are made to him in person and on time. In addition to making routine checks of watertight closures and other safety devices, the patrols should be alert to fire hazards, such as accumulations of trash, and to the presence of combustibles, such as paint, that have not been properly stowed.

Shipyard security

Except in matters coming within security and safety regulations of the ship, the commanding officer shall exercise no control over the officers or employees of a naval shipyard or station where his ship is moored, unless with the permission of the commander of the naval shipyard or station.

Navy Regulations.

A ship under repair and overhaul in a shipyard has particular security problems. All workmen coming on board must be identified. If their tools are stowed in racks on deck, they should be safeguarded by ship's sentries. Most shipyard workers are honest, but a small percentage might not be able to resist a souvenir or two, particularly if tools are left adrift. It must be the unpleasant duty of the watch on deck to see that theft, by both ship and shipyard personnel, is prevented or at least kept to a minimum.

Compartments containing classified matter must be secured, either by locks or by sentries. There are times when yard workmen have to enter locked spaces, and the OOD can anticipate such occasions if he keeps himself reasonably well informed of the nature and location of the work being done aboard ship. Fire watches are normally assigned to every welder and burner working on the ship. Another precaution that should be taken during shipyard work is the inspection of spaces after each shift for rubbish and other material that may constitute a fire hazard.

Inspections

In addition to seeing that the material inspections discussed above are made, the OOD should direct the JOOD, the petty officer of the watch, or the master-at-arms to make inspections throughout the ship, day and night. Particular vigilance must be exercised to prevent gambling, the smuggling of liquor, and the introduction of drugs. Only an alert watch and thorough inspection can prevent such practices. All these inspections should be made at irregular intervals and be as comprehensive as practicable. Their objective is the preservation of good order and discipline and the enforcement of such features of the daily routine as reveille and taps.

Custody of keys

Custody of a ship's keys is carefully organized and the OOD must fully understand this organization. Designated duty personnel will have custody of some of the keys to their spaces. *OpNavInst* 3120.32 states that department heads will maintain a key locker containing all the keys to their spaces. It also states that keys to the key locker will be available to the OOD at all times for use in an emergency. The OOD must know who his duty keyholders are and what procedures he must follow to access secured spaces.

Anchorage and moorings

When his ship is anchored, moored, or secured to a pier or wharf, the OOD's greatest responsibilities are in relation to the weather. At sea the commanding officer makes the big decisions; in port the OOD must often take action before the commanding officer can be advised of the situation.

Meterological forecasts are, in general, excellent, but they are not always available, nor can they be 100 per cent accurate. They may even lull inexperienced officers into a false sense of security. The *actual* weather at the ship's position is the important factor, not the weather that is *forecast* for that position. It is advisable for the OOD to know what sort of weather can be expected in a certain area at a certain time of year. Pilot charts are one source of this information. There may be very little possibility of winds over 40 knots in San Diego Bay at any time: but at Adak, in the Aleutians, the wind can whip up to 60 knots almost any afternoon. Thus the OOD should inspect the anchor chains or mooring lines as often as the weather and the nature of the mooring dictate and take appropriate action to avert potential problems.

Scope of chain

It is common practice to use a length of anchor chain equal to six times the depth of the water. The following table is a more accurate guide, but it applies only when moderately severe winds, perhaps up to force 7, are expected.

Depth of water	Recommended scope
Up to 10 fathoms	Depth multiplied by 7
10 to 15 fathoms	Depth multiplied by 6
15 to 20 fathoms	Depth multiplied by 5
20 to 30 fathoms	Depth multiplied by 4
More than 30 fathoms	Depth multiplied by 3

In extremely high winds, longer scope is necessary in order to provide the ground tackle with maximum holding power. *Knight's Modern Seamanship* contains a table giving maximum effective scope and an excellent discussion of ground tackle and its use in anchoring.

Dragging

When at anchor, the officer of the deck shall take proper precautions to detect and prevent dragging.

OpNavInst 3120.32.

The most certain indication of dragging is a change in anchorage bearings, particularly those near the beam. These bearings should be checked at regular intervals even in good weather. Ships sometimes part their chain when letting go the anchor. They then drag easily, because only the part of the anchor chain lying in the bottom is holding. A dragging anchor can be detected by watching the chain or by feeling it on deck. Anchor chain pulsates or jumps when the anchor is dragging, because the flukes are alternately taking hold and being pulled loose.

The major safeguards against collision or grounding caused by dragging are (1) having a second anchor ready to be let go and (2) having steam at the throttle, the steering gear ready for use, and the engine room ready to answer all bells. The latter course is expensive in man hours and fuel and should not be directed without good cause. However, the OOD should not hesitate to inform the commanding officer of the possibility of dragging. The commanding officer will then decide what precautionary measures shall be taken.

A ship secured to a well-anchored mooring buoy by her anchor chain is not likely to be in danger unless the wind is exceedingly high. However, in very severe weather, vessels as big as destroyers have been known to carry away from a mooring, generally because too little scope of chain to the buoy was used. When the scope of chain is not long enough to provide a catenary, the sudden strain as the bow of the ship pitches is sufficient to part the chain or the chain stopper on deck. To counter the yaw that results from a long scope to the buoy, an anchor dropped straight down (under foot) is often useful.

Heavy weather

A ship alongside a pier or wharf, with the standard mooring lines doubled up, is in little danger from high winds, except in extreme cases. When heavy seas and high winds are anticipated, the OOD should perform the following acts:

1. Request permission to hoist in all boats in the water, to trice up gangways, and to order boat-pool boats to return to their base or be secured astern on long painters.

2. Establish a special boat watch.

3. Call away the anchor detail and prepare to drop the anchor straight down (under foot) if directed.

4. Put over storm wires, spring lays, or anchor chain, as required, to augment mooring lines.

5. Try to get any camels that might be holding the ship off the pier removed.

6. Have all loose gear on deck secured and, if the ship is beginning to surge, be prepared to take in the brow.

7. Be prepared to disconnect shore power and shift to ship's power. Shore power cables that are placed under strain are liable to part, causing fires and explosions.

8. If extreme conditions are forecast, be prepared to light off one or more boilers to get underway when directed.

Hurricanes and typhoons

When warning is received that a hurricane or typhoon is moving into the area, it must be decided whether to put to sea to avoid the storm or remain in port and ride it out. If the decision is for putting to sea, the general procedures described in chapter 5, under *Hurricanes and Typhoons*, should be followed. If the ship is to remain in port, she may move to a sheltered anchorage, in which case all preparations for getting underway should be made and, in addition, the precautions listed above under *"Heavy weather"* should be carried out.

Preparations for riding out a storm are normally prescribed in the SOPA's instructions and include the following:

1. Double up the mooring lines and inspect them frequently.
2. Recall personnel to the ship and place the engineering plant and sea detail on stand-by.
3. Maintain radio and signal watches, man the radar, and keep a plot of the storm in CIC.
4. Police the dock area, secure topside gear, break out heavy-weather gear and flashlights, and inventory the rescue-assistance lockers.
5. Maintain a plot of the storm's movements and brief the crew on them.

The anchorage should allow room for the ship to swing with the longest scope of chain available. Main engines should be used to offset the wind, with rpm equivalent to from 3 to 5 knots.

Bearings on shore, radar, drift lead, continuous echo soundings, and a continuous watch on the chain should all be used to detect signs of a dragging anchor.

For complete details on procedures to be followed in hurricanes and typhoons, underway or in port, see William J. Kotsch's *Weather for the Mariner.*

Stores and fuel

When stores are to be loaded, the OOD must make certain that the right people have been notified and are in charge. The deck force is responsible for operating the gear and tackle needed, and the OOD should check to see that a competent boatswain's mate is on the job. The supply officer or his representative should check the stores aboard and direct their stowage.

When a ship is refueling in port, the OOD has clearly defined responsibilities both for safety and for the prevention of spills. In coordination with the engineer officer, he should ensure that the required stations are manned for the detection of spills and that oil-recovery materials are available for use on short notice should a spill occur. The reports required and the telephone numbers to call in case of a fuel spill should be at hand on the quarterdeck. The OOD is also responsible for displaying proper signals and passing the word restricting smoking while fueling is being conducted.

Liberty

Crews are granted liberty by sections. When a ship is in a foreign port, forward deployed, or in a high state of readiness, her crew is normally divided into three duty sections, two of which may be on liberty at a time. This practice is followed because experience has taught that the minimum number of men required to get a ship underway is about one-third of her crew. In home port and when no special conditions of readiness are in effect, most ships attempt to divide their crews into four or six duty sections, three or five of which may be on liberty at a time. Regardless of prevailing conditions, the duty section left on board should always be big enough to fight fires, deal with emergencies, and carry out the ship's routine. If the OOD feels that this condition is not being met, he should so inform the command duty officer immediately.

Inspection of liberty parties

The OOD and his watch team have the primary responsibility for enforcing the navy's and the ship's standards of dress and grooming. The OOD in port can expect to be continually required to inspect individuals going ashore and to judge, using his own common sense and knowledge of the rules, whether a man should be permitted to go ashore or be turned back.

Fashions and styles of dress change and, considering the range of age groups and interests represented in most ships, it is almost impossible to lay down definitive "do's and don'ts" for dress and grooming. However, it is reasonable to assume that the overwhelming majority of any crew will respect reasonable standards, especially if they are equitably enforced by all deck watch-standers.

In foreign ports the situation is slightly different. Because a sailor ashore represents his country, his navy, and his ship, the command has every right to expect that he will present an appearance that is a credit and not an embarrassment.

The return of liberty parties may be a routine matter or it may be quite a lively occasion. The OOD usually has only to identify the men. If the ship has just made port after a long voyage or is sailing the next day for an extended absence, there may be a few tipsy or noisy celebrants. A master-at-arms or corporal of the guard should be detailed to get them off the quarterdeck and persuade them to turn in below quietly. The OOD must remain apart from any confusion that may arise and let his experienced assistants handle such matters. However, persistent rowdies or troublemakers may require his special attention, and direct orders may be needed to control them. Physical contact should be avoided, and the enlisted men in the watch should be left to handle men who will not go below peacefully. The men most in need of attention are those who are brought aboard apparently drunk. They should be taken to sick bay and examined; they may have head injuries or be drugged instead of, or in addition to, being drunk. If necessary, the duty medical officer should be called to examine them. Matters of this sort must be recorded fully in the log, together with a written medical report.

Loading liberty boats

While juniors in the navy generally embark in boats and vehicles before their seniors, the procedure is sometimes reversed. When liberty parties are being loaded into boats or buses, the chief petty officers go first, followed by the other petty officers in descending order of rank. This practice enhances the prestige of the petty officers and provides them with a convenience that they well deserve. When many officers are waiting to go ashore, it may be necessary to have some of the junior officers wait for the next boat in order to ensure room for the senior officers.

Crew's mess

Each meal served in the general mess shall be sampled by an officer detailed by the commanding officer for that purpose. Should this officer find the quality or quantity of food unsatisfactory, or should any member of the mess object to the quality or quantity of the food, the commanding officer shall be immediately notified and he shall take appropriate action.

Navy Regulations.

It is normal procedure, when in port, for the command duty officer or the OOD to eat at least one meal in the crew's mess during his duty day. When underway, one of the watch officers should eat a meal with the crew daily. When an officer eats with the crew, he should note not only the quantity and quality of the food being served to the men but, equally important, the cleanliness and adequacy of mess gear, the manner in which food is served, and the cleanliness of food-handlers. It is not unusual for a commanding officer to make an unannounced visit to the crew's mess and eat there in order to check for himself on these important points.

Night rations

It is a custom of long standing to serve a night ration to the persons who have the midwatch. This helps them to stay awake and sustains them through the night tasks, which are often just as demanding as those of the day. In cold weather a warm ration is especially welcome to those going on or coming off watch topside, as well as to those standing watch in the engineering spaces.

Eight o'clock reports

Eight o'clock reports are an important part of a ship's routine. They serve two functions: they ensure that the necessary security and damage-control inspections have been made, and they furnish the executive officer with the information he needs to make his report on the condition of the ship at 20:00 to the commanding officer.

In accordance with time-honored usage, the reports made to the executive officer or command duty officer by the heads of departments at 20:00 are known as *eight o'clock reports*, not "twenty hundred reports."

Working parties

A ship's schedule often requires large working parties to complete without rest an important evolution, such as provisioning ship. These necessities are normally accepted by the men with reasonable understanding. Many times, when only small groups are involved, the OOD can contribute to the well-being of the crew by having consideration for their comfort. Leisure time and meal hours should be respected as much as possible. Men whose work is interrupted by a mealtime should not be required to change into another uniform just for the meal, and those who miss a regular meal should have a complete hot meal saved for them. Working parties leaving the ship should be provided with such comforts as rain gear and drinking water if circumstances warrant.

When men are required to do work that results in their losing sleep or missing regular meals, it is incumbent upon the responsible officer to see that they get compensatory rest and meals.

Apprehension and restraint

An OOD must know the difference between *apprehension* and the three degrees of restraint: *confinement, arrest,* and *restriction in lieu of arrest.* He will have occasion to take custody of men charged with misconduct. The men may be delivered by the shore patrol or by an officer or petty officer aboard ship. The men may even deliver themselves for such minor offenses as being out of uniform. It is important that the OOD know the legal meanings of the terms involved and also know what action to take. All officers, petty officers, and noncommissioned officers of any service have authority to apprehend offenders who are subject to the Uniform Code of Military Justice (UCMJ). Other enlisted men have the same authority when they are assigned such duties as shore patrol and military police.

Apprehension is accomplished by clearly informing the person that he is being taken into custody and of what he is accused. It should be noted here that in the armed services *ap-*

prehension means the same thing as *arrest* does in civilian life. A police officer informs a citizen that he is "under arrest," but a naval officer tells a man that he is being "apprehended," or taken into custody. *Custody* is control over the person apprehended until he is delivered to the proper authority, who, on board ship, is the OOD. In general, persons who have authority to apprehend may exercise only such force as is actually necessary. Petty officers should apprehend officers only in very unusual circumstances, such as to prevent disgrace to the service.

Restraint involves some deprivation of free movement. It is never imposed as a punishment, and the degree to which it is imposed should be no greater than is necessary to ensure the presence of the offender at further proceedings in his case. Thus, a man who is suspected of having committed an offense need not be restrained at all if his presence at future proceedings is assured.

Only the commanding officer may impose any degree of restraint on a commissioned officer or a warrant officer. If it is desired to restrain an officer, the commanding officer must be notified. Only officers may ordinarily impose any degree of restraint on enlisted men. However, the commanding officer may delegate this authority to warrant officers and enlisted men.

Confinement is physical restraint imposed in serious offenses to ensure the presence of the person at future proceedings.

Arrest is the moral restraint of a person, by oral or written order, to certain specified limits, pending disposition of charges against him. It is not imposed as punishment. It is imposed only for probable cause, based on known or reported facts concerning an alleged offense. It relieves a person of all military duties other than normal cleaning and policing. Arrest is imposed by telling the accused what are the limits of his arrest.

One of the disadvantages of placing an accused in arrest is that he may no longer be required to perform his military duties. Should he be required to do so, his arrest is automatically terminated. Consequently, a lesser form of restraint, called *restriction in lieu of arrest,* can be imposed.

Restriction is a restraint of the same nature as arrest. It is imposed under similar circumstances and by the same authorities, but it does not absolve the accused from performing his military duties.

A person apprehended on board ship is delivered, together with a misconduct report, into the custody of the OOD. The latter advises the executive officer (or command duty officer) of the situation and receives instructions regarding the nature of the restraint to be imposed, which depends on the gravity of the offense. If formal restraint, such as arrest, is ordered, the OOD notifies the offender, ensuring that the offender understands the nature of his restraint and the penalties for violating it. The OOD must get the offender's written acknowledgment that he has been so notified by having him sign the misconduct report slip. He then turns the offender over to the master-at-arms. The whole affair must, of course, be entered in the log with full details.

When the offense is relatively minor and it can be assumed that the accused will not attempt to leave the area to avoid trial, no restraint is necessary. Confinement before trial is used only when there is a risk of the accused's attempting to escape punishment. Arrest and restriction in lieu of arrest may be lifted only by the authority who ordered the restraint or his superior in the chain of command. Once a person has been confined, he can be released only by order of the commanding officer of the activity where the confinement takes place. On board ship, of course, the authority ordering the confinement is usually also the commanding officer of the confining activity.

For further discussion of this subject, see Edward M. Byrne's *Military Law,* chapter II.

Asylum and temporary refuge

Under the conventions of international law and as a matter of U. S. government policy, certain persons may, in certain circumstances, be granted asylum or temporary refuge on board a naval vessel. The terms and conditions under which asylum or temporary refuge may be granted are specified in the *Navy Regulations* cited below.

1. If an official of the Department of the Navy is requested to provide asylum or temporary refuge, the following procedures shall apply:
   a. On the high seas or in territories under exclusive United States jurisdiction (including territorial seas, the Commonwealth of Puerto Rico, territories under United States administration, and possessions):
      (1) At his request, an applicant for asylum will be received on board any naval aircraft or water-borne craft, Navy or Marine Corps activity or station.
      (2) Under no circumstances shall the person seeking asylum be surrendered to foreign jurisdiction or control, unless at the personal direction of the Secretary of the Navy or higher authority. Persons seeking political asylum should be afforded every reasonable care and protection permitted by the circumstances.
   b. In territories under foreign jurisdiction (including foreign territorial seas, territories, and possessions):
      (1) Temporary refuge shall be granted for humanitarian reasons on board a naval aircraft or water-borne craft, Navy or Marine Corps activity or station, only in extreme or exceptional circumstances wherein life or safety of a person is put in imminent danger, such as pursuit by a mob. When temporary refuge is granted, such protection shall be terminated only when directed by the Secretary of the Navy or higher authority.
      (2) A request by foreign authorities for return of custody of a person under the protection of temporary refuge will be reported to the CNO or Commandant of the Marine Corps. The requesting foreign authorities will be informed that the case has been referred to higher authorities for instructions.
      (3) Persons whose temporary refuge is terminated will be released to the protection of the authorities designated in the message authorizing release.
      (4) While temporary refuge can be granted in the circumstances set forth above, permanent asylum will not be granted.
      (5) Foreign nationals who request assistance in forwarding re-

quests for political asylum in the United States will be advised to apply in person at the nearest American Embassy or Consulate.

c. The Chief of Naval Operations or Commandant of the Marine Corps, as appropriate, will be informed by the most expeditious means of all action taken pursuant to subparagraphs 1a and 1b above, as well as the attendant circumstances. Telephone or voice communications will be used where possible, but must be confirmed as soon as possible with an immediate precedence message, information to the Secretary of State (for actions taken pursuant to subparagraphs 1b(1) and 1b(5) of this article, also make the appropriate American Embassy or Consular Office an information addressee). If communication by telephone or voice is not possible, notification will be effected by an immediate precedence message, as described above. The Chief of Naval Operations or Commandant of the Marine Corps will cause the Secretary of the Navy and the Deputy Director for Operations of the National Military Command Center to be notified without delay.

2. Personnel of the Department of the Navy shall neither directly nor indirectly invite persons to seek asylum or temporary refuge.

Operational commanders usually require, in addition to the above, a report of the circumstances surrounding a request for asylum or temporary refuge. The format for such reports is specific.

Reporting and detachment of personnel

An OOD should appreciate that the first impression made on newly reporting officers and men is important. When new people are being received, the provisions of the ship's organization manual should always be followed and every effort exerted to make a new officer or enlisted man feel immediately at ease. New men, especially those reporting to their first ship from boot camp or school, are likely to be overwhelmed by their new surroundings. If they can be made to feel welcome, their apprehension will be eased considerably by the knowledge that the ship is interested in their welfare. If a sponsor has not been assigned or is not on board, the OOD and the duty master-at-arms should see to it that a temporary escort is assigned to give the new man the help that he will need in finding his compartment, the mess decks, and the offices into which he will have to check.

People being detached should be processed on the quarter-deck as expeditiously as possible, since they may have transportation arrangements to make. If there is to be any sort of departure ceremony, those taking part in it should be standing by on the quarterdeck before the men arrive.

Receiving guests and visitors

The OOD is responsible for welcoming all guests and visitors to his ship. He usually has advance information as to who is expected, who will meet them on the quarterdeck, and what sort of assistance the watch is to provide. Exercise-observers and ship-riders are generally met by the cognizant department head or his representative, and VIPs by the commanding officer. When the ship is open to general visiting or to tours by special groups, arrangements prescribed by the ship's visiting bill should be checked in advance by the OOD, areas of the ship roped off as required, and tour guides mustered and inspected before the visitors arrive. When large numbers of visitors are expected, arrangements must be made in advance for the provision of local police or guard forces.

10 | SAFETY

The commanding officer shall require that all persons concerned are instructed and drilled in all applicable safety precautions and procedures, that these are complied with, and that applicable safety precautions, or extracts therefrom, are posted in appropriate places. In any instance where safety precautions have not been issued or are incomplete, he shall issue or augment such safety precautions as he deems necessary, notifying, when appropriate, higher authorities.

Navy Regulations.

Safety must be practiced twenty-four hours a day, because there is danger aboard every naval vessel and in every naval operation. Going to sea involves working with powerful machinery, high-speed equipment, steam under intensely high temperature and pressure, volatile and exotic fuels and propellants, heavy lifts, high explosives, stepped-up electrical voltages, and the elemental forces of wind and wave, which are unpredictable. Inexperienced sailors are inclined to be careless, if not downright reckless. It is a watch officer's responsibility to see that all precautions are observed, in order to protect the lives of his men and the safety of his ship.

Precautions are provided to ensure the safe operation of all equipment. The *Naval Ships Technical Manual* contains safety precautions, as do the manuals put out by the various bureaus and the *Standard Ship's Organization and Regulations Manual* (*OpNavInst* 3120.32). As new equipment is introduced into the fleet, new safety procedures and precautions are generated and old ones modified. Accidents and injuries also lead to a continual updating of safety precautions, the general trend being toward more detailed descriptions of procedures, checks, and inspections.

Every accident that occurs in a ship should be reported in standard form to the appropriate safety center, so that the defect or other condition that caused it can be investigated and corrective action taken. OODs should always be on the alert for dangerous conditions and violations of safety rules and should take quick and positive action to correct them.

The OOD, both in port and underway, should see that the following safety regulations and procedures, compiled from *OpNavInst* 3120.32A, are adhered to. Most ship, fleet, and type commanders supplement these regulations to fit specific situations or requirements. For example, specific and detailed procedures are issued for the guidance of qualified personnel who have to handle nuclear weapons. The watch officer is also directed to *Navy Safety Precautions for Forces Afloat* (*OpNavInst* 5100.19A) and the *Navy Occupational Safety and Health* (NAVOSH) *Program Manual* (*OpNavInst* 5100.23), NAVSHIPS technical manuals, and the planned maintenance system (PMS) maintenance requirement cards (MRCs) for detailed, specific guidelines and safety precautions applicable to their specific situation.

Ammunition. *See also* **Underway replenishment**

1. All personnel required to handle ammunition shall be carefully and frequently instructed in the safety regulations, methods of handling, storage, and uses of all kinds of ammunition and explosive ordnance with which the ship, aircraft unit, or station may be supplied.

2. No one shall be permitted to inspect, prepare, or adjust live ammunition and explosives until he thoroughly understands his duties, the precautions, and the hazards involved and has been properly certified.

3. Only careful, reliable, mentally sound, and physically fit persons shall be permitted to work with or use explosives or ammunition.

4. All persons who supervise the inspection, care, prepa-

ration, handling, use, or disposal of ammunition or explosives shall do the following:

  a. Exercise the utmost care that all regulations and instructions are observed, and remain vigilant throughout the operation.
  b. Carefully instruct and frequently warn those under them of the need for care and constant vigilance.
  c. Before beginning the operation, ensure that all subordinates are familiar with the characteristics of the explosive materials involved, the equipment to be used, safety regulations to be observed, and the hazards of fire, explosion, and other catastrophes that the safety regulations are intended to prevent.
  d. Be alert to detect any hazardous procedures or practices or symptoms of a deteriorating mental attitude, and take immediate corrective action when such are detected.

5. Smoking is not permitted in magazines or in the immediate vicinity of handling or loading operations involving explosives or ammunition. Matches, lighters, or spark- or flame-producing devices are not permitted in spaces in which ammunition or explosives are present.

6. Personnel engaged in working with explosives or ammunition shall be limited to the minimum number required to perform the operation properly. Unauthorized personnel shall not be permitted in magazines or in the immediate vicinity of handling or loading operations involving explosives or ammunition except for duly authorized inspections. Authorized visitors shall always be properly escorted.

7. When fused with firing mechanisms or assembled with them, mines, depth charges, rockets, projector charges, missiles, and aircraft bombs shall at all times be treated as if armed.

8. Live ammunition, rockets, or missiles shall be loaded into guns or on launchers only for firing purposes except where otherwise approved.

9. Supervisors shall require the maintenance of good housekeeping in explosives spaces. Nothing shall be stored in

such spaces except explosives, their containers, and authorized handling equipment.

10. No detonator shall be assembled in a warhead in or near a magazine containing explosives. Fusing shall be done at a designated fusing area.

Authorized operators. *See* **Hot work** and **Special equipment**

Boats

1. In motor launches, only the coxswain and the boat officer or the senior line officer may ride on the coxswain's flat. No more than two persons may be on the deck at one time.

2. Boat crews must keep their stations, especially when weather conditions are unpleasant, for it is usually during these times that vigilance is most needed.

3. Boats must always be properly loaded for the sea state. In heavy weather the boat is loaded slighty down by the stern and the passengers and crew kept in lifejackets. Boat passengers shall remain seated when a boat is underway and shall keep arms inboard of gunwales.

4. The coxswain, or boat officer when assigned, shall be responsible to the commanding officer for the enforcement of these regulations.

5. No boat shall be loaded beyond the capacities established by the commanding officer and published in the boat bill.

6. No person shall smoke in a boat.

7. No person other than those specifically designated by the engineer officer shall operate or attempt to operate a boat engine; test, remove, or charge a boat's battery, or tamper in any way with a boat's electrical system; or fuel a ship's boat.

8. No person shall be assigned as a member of a boat crew unless he is a qualified swimmer; has demonstrated a practical knowledge of boat seamanship, the Rules of the Road, and boat safety regulations; and has been duly qualified for his particular assignment.

9. All persons in boats being hoisted in or out, or hung in the davits, shall wear vest-type, inherently buoyant life preservers properly secured and safety helmets with chin straps unbuckled.

10. No person shall board a boat from a boat boom unless another is standing by on deck or in a boat at the same boom.

11. All members of a boat's crew shall wear rubber-soled canvas shoes when embarked in a ship's boat.

12. Fueling instructions must be posted in all power boats, and passengers must be kept clear of a boat that is being refueled.

13. Maximum operating speeds must be posted permanently upon the engine cover of all boats.

14. Standard equipment listed in the allowance list must be in boats at all times.

15. Prescribed lights must be displayed by all boats underway between sunset and daylight or in poor visibility.

16. Life buoys must be carried forward and aft in each boat, secured in such a manner that they can be easily broken out for use.

17. All boats leaving the ship shall have local charts with courses to and from their destination recorded thereon. Boat compasses and fog-signaling equipment must be carried.

18. All boats will have sufficient life preservers on board to accommodate all persons embarked, and the life preservers shall be readily available when rough seas, reduced visibility, or other hazards threaten.

19. No boat will be dispatched or permitted to proceed unless released by the OOD. Such release will not be given unless it has been determined that the boat crew and passengers are wearing life preservers, when advisable, and that weather and sea conditions are suitable for small-boat operations.

20. Recall and lifeboat signals must be posted in the boats where they can be easily read by the coxswains.

21. A set of standing orders to boat coxswains must be prepared and kept in each boat.

Bolos. *See* **Line-throwing gun**

Cargo

Special precautions observed in handling cargo include the following:

1. Open hatches in use should be cleared of any adjacent loose equipment that might fall into them and injure personnel below.

2. Traffic about the hatch is restricted to the off side from where cargo is being worked. The area over which the loads are traveling is roped off to traffic.

3. Hatch beams or other structures in the way of hatches where cargo is being worked are secured by bolts or removed. Personnel engaged in moving hatch beams shall wear a safety line, which shall be tended at all times.

4. Qualified personnel must always supervise the topping and lowering of booms. Before any repairs are made or any of the gear is replaced, booms should always be lowered on deck. When life lines are removed for any purpose, officers and petty officers concerned are required to ensure that emergency lines are rigged and that everyone is cautioned to keep clear.

Closed compartments

Danger of explosion, poisoning, and suffocation exists in closed compartments or poorly ventilated spaces, such as tanks, cofferdams, voids, and bilges. No person shall enter any such compartment or space until applicable safety regulations have been complied with and the space has been declared safe by a qualified gas-free engineer. The following precautions should be observed:

1. The seal around the manhole or other opening should be broken before all hold-down bolts or other fastenings are completely removed, to allow dissipation of any pressure that might have built up inside and to make it possible quickly to secure the cover again if gas or water is present.

2. No person shall enter any such space without permission from the responsible division officer, who shall obtain the approval of his department head and the gas-free engineer before granting permission.

3. No naked light or spark-producing electrical apparatus shall be carried into a closed space.

4. Safety lamps used in closed compartments must be in good operating condition. If the lamp fades or flares up, a dangerous condition exists and the space should not be entered.

5. No person shall work in such a compartment without a life line attached and a responsible man stationed outside the compartment to tend the line and maintain communications with him.

Compressed gases

Compressed gases used aboard ship include oxygen, acetylene, carbon dioxide (CO_2), and plain compressed air. Helium, nitrogen, ammonia, and certain insecticide fogs may also be used. All cylinders are identified in stenciled letters and by color, as follows:

Yellow. Flammable materials, such as acetylene, hydrogen, and petroleum gases.

Brown. Poisonous materials, such as chlorine, carbon monoxide, and sulphur dioxide.

Green. Oxidizing material, particularly pure oxygen.

Blue. Anesthetics and materials with similarly harmful fumes.

Gray. Physically dangerous materials: inert gas under high pressure or gas that would asphyxiate if breathed in confined areas, such as CO_2, nitrogen, and helium.

Red. Fire-protection materials, especially carbon dioxide and nitrogen.

Black with green striping. Compressed air and helium-oxygen and oxygen-carbon dioxide mixtures.

All flammable gases, such as acetylene, become highly explosive when mixed in certain proportions with air. Even an inert gas like CO_2 can cause an explosion if its cylinder becomes too hot or cracks because of rough handling. The following rules should be obeyed without exception:

1. Gas cylinders and air cylinders must be kept away from high-temperature areas. Oil should never be allowed to come

in contact with oxygen cylinder valves, since a violent explosion could result.

2. Gas cylinders must not be handled roughly, dropped, or clanked against each other. They should not be handled or transported without their valve caps in place.

3. Flames or sparks should not be permitted in any closed spaces where acetylene or oxygen tanks are stored, for seepage of gas from the tanks may have filled the compartment with a dangerous level of gas or pure oxygen.

4. Caution should be used around ammonia tanks and cylinders of similar poisonous gases. There is always the possibility that the gas is leaking from a loose valve or seeping through a defective connection.

5. In case of fire or other disaster, gas cylinders should quickly be moved from the danger area and, if necessary, thrown overboard.

Dangerous materials. *See* **Semisafe and dangerous materials**

Divers

Divers may go below the ship to perform necessary work, but only with the permission of the OOD. The OOD is responsible for seeing that the following safety precautions are observed before he grants permission:

1. When divers are working over the side, the location and status of all ship's machinery that might affect the diving area must be determined before operations begin. The status of this equipment must not be altered without prior notification by the engineering duty officer and the concurrence of the diving officer.

2. Divers shall not enter the water until permission is granted by the OOD and the international signal "CODE ALFA" is flying from the ship and the diving boat.

3. Without specific prior knowledge and concurrence in each instance by the diving officer,

    a. Main ballast tanks will not be flooded or blown.

    b. Sanitary tanks will not be blown.

c. The stern planes will not be moved.*

d. The rudder will not be moved.*

e. The screw will not be turned. With concurrence of the diving officer, screws may be turned at minimum jacking speed. In this case the OOD, via the engineering duty officer, shall ensure that screws are turning no faster than minimum jacking speed.

f. The mooring will not be adjusted.

g. The secondary propulsion motors will not be rigged out or trained, nor will the screw be turned except as noted above.*

h. The MSD system will not be operated.

i. The anchor and anchor chain will not be manipulated in any way.*

j. The torpedo tubes will not be exercised.*

k. Radioactive effluents will not be discharged.

4. All boats will stay at least 50 yards from the diving operations.

5. Except in extreme emergencies, no diving operation will commence unless four qualified divers are present.

6. Divers will always dive with one standby diver in a ready condition.

7. Divers will be checked for sickness and injury immediately upon leaving the water.

8. If in a nest, all ships in the nest shall be informed.

9. When divers are over the side, the word will be passed every 30 minutes, "Divers are over the side in the vicinity of _____."

10. The active sonar shall not be operated if divers are in the water anywhere in the nest.

11. When divers are working in the vicinity of adjacent ships, the regulations set forth in this article shall apply. The duty officer shall clear with the duty officer of the ship in which divers are working before undertaking any evolution prohibited by this article.

---

*Indicates system must be properly tagged out.

Electrical and electronic equipment

This includes generators, electrically powered machinery and mechanisms, power cables, controllers, transformers and associated equipment, radars, radios, power amplifiers, antennas, electronic warfare equipment, computers, and associated controls.

1. No person shall operate, repair, adjust, or otherwise tamper with any electrical or electronic equipment (unless it is within his functional assignment in the department organization manual to perform a specific function on certain equipment) except in emergencies, and then only when no qualified operator is available.

2. No person shall be assigned to operate, repair, or adjust electrical and electronic equipment unless he has demonstrated a practical knowledge of its operation and repair and of all applicable safety regulations, and then only when duly qualified by the head of department having cognizance over such equipment.

3. No person shall paint over or otherwise destroy or mutilate any markings, name plates, cable tags, or other identification on any electrical or electronic equipment.

4. No person shall hang anything on, or secure a line to, any power cable, antenna, wave guide, or other electrical or electronic equipment.

5. Only authorized portable electrical equipment that has been tested by the electric shop shall be used.

6. Electrical equipment shall be de-energized and, if possible, checked with a voltage tester or voltmeter to ensure it is de-energized before it is serviced or repaired. Circuit breakers and switches of de-energized circuits shall be locked or placed in the "off" position while work is in progress and a suitable warning tag shall be attached thereto.

7. If it is necessary to work on live circuits or equipment, every effort shall be made to insulate the person performing the work from the ground, and all other practical safety measures shall be used. If possible, rubber gloves shall be worn.

Another man shall be standing by to de-energize the circuit and to render first aid.

8. No personal electrical or electronic equipment shall be used aboard ship until it has been approved by the engineer officer and the executive officer.

9. Intentionally taking a shock from any voltage is always dangerous and shall not be done.

10. Bare lamps or fixtures with exposed lamps shall not be installed in machinery spaces. Only enclosed fixtures shall be installed in such spaces to minimize the hazard of fire caused by flammable fuels making contact with exposed lamps.

11. Personnel shall not be permitted to go aloft near energized antennas unless it has been determined that no danger exists. If any danger exists from rotating antennas, induced voltages in rigging and superstructure, or from high-power radiation that could cause direct biological injury, the equipment concerned shall be secured and a suitable warning tag shall be attached to the main supply switches. These precautions shall also be observed if any other antenna is in the vicinity, as on an adjacent ship.

12. Heads of departments shall ensure that electrical and electronic safety precautions are conspicuously posted in appropriate spaces and that personnel concerned are frequently and thoroughly instructed and drilled in their observance.

13. Appropriate heads of departments shall ensure that all electrical and electronics personnel are qualified in the administration of first-aid treatment for electrical shock and that emergency resuscitation procedures are posted in all spaces containing electronic equipment.

14. Appropriate heads of departments shall ensure that rubber matting is installed in operating areas in front and back of propulsion-control cubicles, power and lighting switchboards, IC switchboards, test switchboards, fire-control switchboards, ship announcing-system amplifiers and control panels; areas in and around radio, radar, sonar, and countermeasures equipment spaces that may be entered by personnel in servicing or tuning energized equipment; and around work

benches in electrical and electronics shops where equipment is tested or repaired.

Fire and explosion prevention

The reduction of fire and explosion hazards is the responsibility of every person on board, both individually and collectively. The gravity of these hazards is increased by the configuration of machinery spaces, the presence of fuel and heat, and the probable loss of systems that may contribute to the ship's fire-fighting capability. The following steps are essential:

1. Initiate action to ensure that all potential fire and explosion hazards, including nonessential combustibles, are eliminated.

2. Wherever possible, replace highly combustible materials with less flammable ones.

3. Limit to a minimum the amounts of essential combustibles carried.

4. Stow and protect all combustibles in designated storage lockers.

5. Avoid accumulation of oil and other flammable materials in bilges and inaccessible areas. Such accumulations must be flushed out or removed at the first opportunity after they are observed.

6. Stow oily rags in airtight metal containers.

7. Stow paint, paint brushes, rags, paint-thinners, and solvents in authorized locations.

8. Do not use compressed air to accelerate the flow from containers of oil, gasoline, or other combustible fluids.

9. Make regular and frequent inspections for fire hazards.

10. Train all personnel in fire-prevention and fire-fighting.

11. Enforce sound fire-prevention policies and practices.

12. Maintain damage-control equipment in a state of readiness for any emergency.

Fire watch. *See* **Hot work,** paragraph 2

Fuel oil. *See also* **Volatile fuels**

1. While oil is being received on board, no naked light, lighted cigarettes, or electrical apparatus that is likely to spark should be permitted within fifty feet of an oil hose, tank, or compartment containing the tank or the vent from a tank. No one may carry matches or cigarette-lighters on his person while at work loading or unloading (*see* **Underway replenishment,** paragraph 13).

2. No naked light, lighted cigarettes, or electrical fuses, switches (unless enclosed type), steel tools, or other apparatus that is liable to cause sparks should be permitted at any time in a compartment that contains the fuel-oil tank, fuel-oil pumps, or fuel-oil piping. Electric lamps used in such compartments must have gas-tight globes. However, the smoking of cigarettes may be permitted in the engine rooms and the fireroom. The term *naked light* includes oil lanterns as well as open lanterns, lighted candles, and lighted matches. Flashlights must not be turned on or off inside a fuel compartment lest a spark ignite vapors.

3. No person should be allowed to enter a fuel-oil tank until the tank has been freed of vapor, the person has obtained permission from the safety officer or CO, and the required precautions have been taken. No one should ever enter a fuel-oil tank without wearing a lifeline attended by someone outside the tank.

4. Compartments and tanks used for the storage of fuel oil should not be painted on the inside.

5. Whenever a fuel-oil tank is to be entered, work is to be done in it, or lights other than portable explosion-proof electric lights are to be used, and when work is to be done in the vicinity of an open tank or of pipes, all such tanks and pipes must be cleared of vapor after the fuel oil has been removed. No person should enter a fuel-oil tank for any purpose without obtaining permission from the safety officer or CO each time he wishes to enter.

6. Oil fires can be extinguished by smothering and cutting

off all oxygen. Carbon dioxide extinguishers and chemicals or water in the form of fog may be used.

Gasoline. *See* **Volatile fuels**

Hazardous material

OpNavInst 5100.19A, chapter 10, indicates that the following items are considered hazardous material aboard ships:

a. Acids, alkalies, and other chemicals.

b. Compressed gases and cylinders.

c. Solvents, plastics, metals (beryllium, cadmium, chromium, lead, mercury, zinc, and magnesium), and asbestos.

d. Paint.

e. Propellants, fuels, and oxidizers.

The labeling and hazard identification system on pages 185–87, taken from *OpNavInst* 5100.19A, is provided to help an observer determine the hazards of a material.

Heavy weather

Safety requires that the following precautions be taken in heavy weather:

1. Decks exposed to the seas should be kept clear of all personnel other than those who must be there for urgent duties. Word to this effect and concerning any other area to which entry is forbidden should be passed periodically.

2. Extra lifelines and snaking should be in place, particularly in areas where such evolutions as replenishment or recovery of a man overboard are being conducted.

Helicopters

Helicopters on ships are operated with permission from the OOD. The OOD is responsible for seeing that the following safety precautions are observed before he grants permission:

1. All helicopter safety crews (firefighting, pilot-rescue, etc.) shall be fully manned, on station and ready.

2. Only those actually involved shall be allowed in the vi-

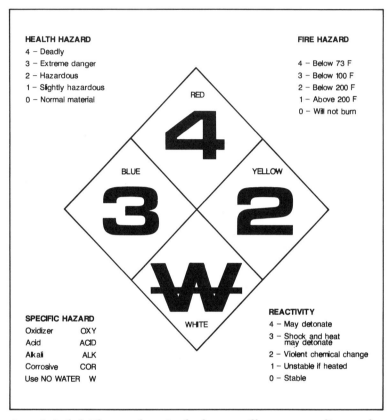

HEALTH HAZARD
4 – Deadly
3 – Extreme danger
2 – Hazardous
1 – Slightly hazardous
0 – Normal material

FIRE HAZARD
4 – Below 73 F
3 – Below 100 F
2 – Below 200 F
1 – Above 200 F
0 – Will not burn

RED

BLUE

YELLOW

WHITE

SPECIFIC HAZARD
Oxidizer   OXY
Acid   ACID
Alkali   ALK
Corrosive   COR
Use NO WATER   W

REACTIVITY
4 – May detonate
3 – Shock and heat may detonate
2 – Violent chemical change
1 – Unstable if heated
0 – Stable

Sample Label: The numbers in the boxes will vary according to the hazard presented by the material in the container.

cinity of helicopter operations, and they must wear appropriate safety helmets and vests.

3. A complete and thorough check shall be made of the helicopter area for loose gear or objects that might have blown free and could cause injury or damage.

4. All hands topside shall remain uncovered.

5. Passengers shall be led to and from a helicopter by a member of the handling crew or flight crew.

HAZARD IDENTIFICATION SYSTEM

Identification of Health Hazard *Color Code: BLUE* *Type of Possible Injury*	Signal	*Identification of Flammability* *Color Code: RED* *Susceptibility of Materials* *to Burning*	Signal	*Identification of Reactivity (Stability)* *Color Code: YELLOW* *Susceptibility to Release* *of Energy*	Signal
Materials which on very short exposure could cause death or major residual injury even though prompt medical treatment were given.	4	Materials which will rapidly or completely vaporize at atmospheric pressure and normal ambient temperature, or which are readily dispersed in air and which will burn readily.	4	Materials which are readily capable of detonation or of explosive decomposition or reaction at normal temperatures and pressures.	4
Materials which on short exposure could cause serious temporary or residual injury even though prompt medical treatment were given.	3	Liquids and solids that can be ignited under almost all ambient temperature conditions.	3	Materials which are capable of detonation or explosive reaction but require a strong initiating source or which must be heated under confinement before initiation or which react explosively with water.	3
Materials which on intense or continued exposure could cause temporary incapacitation or possible residual injury unless prompt medical treatment is given.	2	Materials that must be moderately heated or exposed to relatively high ambient temperatures before ignition can occur.	2	Materials which are normally unstable and readily undergo violent chemical change but do not detonate. Also materials which may react violently with water or which may form potentially explosive mixtures with water.	2
Materials which on exposure would cause irritation but only minor residual injury even if no treatment is given.	1	Materials that must be preheated before ignition can occur.	1	Materials which are normally stable, but which can become unstable at elevated temperatures and pressures or which may react with water with some release of energy but not violently.	1
Materials which on exposure under fire conditions would offer no hazard beyond that of ordinary combustible material.	0	Materials that will not burn.	0	Materials which are normally stable, even under fire exposure conditions, and which are not reactive with water.	0

Explanation of Label Designations.

Helm safety officer

The helm safety officer is a bridge watch-stander during special maneuvering evolutions when very precise ship handling and ship control is required. The helm safety officer is usually an OOD-qualified officer whose duty is to monitor the helmsman and lee helmsman, ensuring that all orders from the conning officer are carried out smartly and correctly.

Hot work

Hot work is work that involves welding, flame-cutting, the use of open-flame equipment, or the heating of metal to or above a red heat. There are numerous ways in which hot work near flammable or explosive materials can create a dangerous situation. No person shall undertake a job involving hot work until the gas-free engineer (or his authorized representative) has inspected the place where it is to be done and indicated that the applicable safety regulations have been complied with, that men can work in the area without danger of being poisoned or suffocated, and that there is no danger of fire or explosion.

1. No hot work shall be undertaken without the permission of the commanding officer underway or the duty officer in port.

2. When flammable or explosive materials are to be exposed to welding or cutting operations, a fire watch shall be posted in the vicinity. If fire hazards exist on both sides of a deck or bulkhead being worked on, a watch shall be posted on each side. Fire watches shall remain on their stations for at least thirty minutes after a job has been completed to ensure that no smoldering fires have been started. Suitable fire-extinguishing equipment shall be maintained near all welding and cutting operations.

3. No welding or burning shall be permitted in compartments where explosives are stored.

4. Various synthetic materials yield toxic gases when burned or heated. Suitable warning signs shall be placed in areas where dangerous vapors may accumulate.

5. Only qualified men may operate welding equipment.

Life jackets

Life jackets must be worn whenever there is a possibility of men's slipping, falling, or being carried into the water. The safest life jacket, when properly worn, is the navy's standard buoyant vest type. Life jackets must be worn by the following persons:

1. Men who are working over the side, in port and at sea, on stages and in boatswain's chairs, boats, or punts. *Over the side* means any part of the ship outside the lifelines or bulwarks.

2. Men going out on weather decks during heavy weather, even if they are to be exposed only long enough to go from one station to another.

3. Men who are handling lines or other deck equipment during such evolutions as transfers between ships, fueling underway, and towing.

4. Men in boats being raised or lowered, entering boats from a boom or Jacob's ladder, in boats underway, and in rough water or low visibility. Ring buoys with a line and light attached must be available for use when a sea ladder or a Jacob's ladder is being used.

5. Men being transferred by highline or helicopter. They must don life jackets before they get into the transfer seat or sling.

Life lines

No person shall lean on, sit on, stand on, or climb over any life line, either in port or when underway. Men working over the side in port may climb over life lines when necessary, but only if they are wearing life preservers.

No life line shall be dismantled or removed without the permission of the first lieutenant, and even then temporary life lines must be promptly rigged.

No person shall hang or secure any weight or line to any life line unless authorized to do so by the commanding officer.

Lights

When a ship is in port at night, weather decks shall be well lighted, as shall all accommodation ladders, gangways, and brows.

Lines and rigging. *See also* Synthetic lines

When work with lines and rigging is being done, the following precautions should be observed:

1. Lines or rigging under heavy strain should be eased to prevent overstress or parting. Men must keep clear of heavily stressed line or wire and under no circumstances stand in the bight of a line or on a taut fall.

2. The hoisting of heavy loads overhead shall be avoided, but if it is essential, the person responsible shall take steps to warn everyone away from the area directly beneath.

3. Boat falls and highlines should be replaced at the first indication of wear or overstress.

4. Lines not in use should be carefully made up and stowed clear of walkways and passages.

5. Lines must never be made fast to capstans or gipsy heads, but only to fittings provided for that purpose, such as cleats or bitts.

6. Steadying or frapping lines should be used on boat falls and on large lifts to prevent uncontrolled swinging or twisting.

Line-throwing gun

A line-throwing gun, or bolo, is used in the opening phase of replenishment operations, and the following safety precautions must always be observed:

1. Bolo-heavers and members of the line-throwing-gun crew must wear red helmets and highly visible red jackets so that they can be easily identified.

2. The bolo-heaver and line-throwing gunner must be thoroughly trained to place the line within easy reach of the receiving ship's crew, no matter what the conditions of range, wind, and relative motion may be.

3. Bolos and gun lines must be properly prepared for run-

ning. Even for the gun line, a loose coil in a bucket is preferable to a spindle.

4. When the receiving ship reaches the proper position, both ships pass the word over the bull horn and topside loudspeaker, "Stand by for shot line—all hands take cover."

5. The officer in charge at each replenishment station in the firing ship sounds a one-blast signal on a mouth whistle or passes the word "Stand by" on the electric megaphone. When he is in all respects ready to receive the shot line and all of his crew have taken cover, the officer in charge of the corresponding station in the receiving ship replies with a two-blast signal on a mouth whistle or passes the word "Ready" on the electric megaphone. After ascertaining that all hands in the vicinity of the target area are under cover, the officer in charge on the firing ship gives the order to fire. The bolo is thrown or the gun is fired only by order of the officer in charge.

6. Only those members of each replenishment station designated by the officer in charge may leave cover to retrieve the bolo or shot line. No one else in the receiving ship may leave cover until all bolos or shot lines are on board and the word has been passed on the topside loudspeaker: "Shot (bolo) lines secure."

7. The receiving ship, unless she is an aircraft carrier, does not fire her line-throwing guns unless ordered or requested to do so by the delivering ship.

8. All hands must be thoroughly indoctrinated to take cover immediately on receipt of the word to do so.

Machinery

The term *machinery* covers all engines, motors, generators, hydraulic systems, and other apparatus that supplies power or motive force.

1. Except in emergencies, and then only when no qualified operator is present, no person shall operate, repair, adjust, or otherwise tamper with any machinery or associated controls unless assigned by the head of his department to perform a specific function on machinery.

2. No person shall be assigned to operate, repair, or adjust

any machinery unless he has demonstrated a practical knowledge of its operation and repair and of all applicable safety regulations, and then only when certified by the head of the department having responsibility for such machinery.

3. The power or activation sources of machinery undergoing repair shall be tagged to that effect, in order to prevent the accidental application of power.

Painting

Poisonous effects from paint may be produced either by the vehicle or the pigment. The vehicle is a volatile solvent. Excessive exposure to a vaporized solvent produces irritation of the nose and throat, headache, dizziness, apparent drunkenness, loud or boisterous conversation, loss of memory, and a staggering gait. A man showing such symptoms must be quickly removed from exposure to paint fumes.

The pigment in most paints contains lead, which may be absorbed through the skin or inhaled as dust or atomized particles, particularly if a spray gun is used. The following precautions should be observed:

1. A man engaged in painting should wear a respirator and change its filter frequently. (Respirators offer no protection against paint fumes.)

2. After painting, men should wash their hands and clean under their fingernails to protect from pigment poisoning.

3. Soiled clothing should be changed as soon as possible.

4. Men exposed regularly to spray-gun work should be supplied with fresh air through a face mask.

Personnel protection

1. Men working on or near rotating machinery must not wear clothing with loose ends or loops that might be caught by moving equipment.

2. Men working on steam valves or other hot units must wear leather or other heavy gloves.

3. Men working in the vicinity of steam equipment must be careful to keep their bodies well covered to reduce the danger of steam burns, e.g., have their shirts buttoned and sleeves rolled down.

4. Men brazing, welding, or cutting must wear protective goggles or helmet and leather welding jackets.

5. Men must wear goggles whenever they are working with substances that are corrosive to the eyes.

6. Men must wear respirators when working in areas of excessive dust.

Personnel transfer

Personnel transfer at sea is performed under very strict requirements, to ensure the safety of persons being transferred.

1. Highline may be either 3-inch or 5-inch manila or 3-inch or 4-inch synthetic double-braided spun polyester (dacron). These are the only acceptable lines because of the requirement for hand tending a highline used in personnel transfers. The 3-inch synthetic and manila highlines have a 300-pound weight limit, and the 4-inch synthetic and 5-inch manila have a 600-pound weight limit.

2. The highline used for personnel transfer is tensioned by a minimum of 25 men. The highline is hand-tended to prevent parting of the line as a result of ship's movement.

3. A highline that has been tended by a capstan may not be used for personnel transfers.

4. Persons being transferred must wear orange-colored, inherently buoyant life preservers.

5. Bosun's chairs used in personnel transfers must have a quick-release seat belt. It is also suggested that the chair be fitted with a flotation device.

6. Stretchers used to transfer patients must be equipped with flotation gear.

Power tools. *See* Tools

Radiation

Radioactive material is present in a nuclear reactor core, in contaminants in the primary coolant, in nuclear warheads, in the sources used for calibration of radiation-monitoring equipment, and in certain electronic tubes.

1. Nuclear warheads shall not be disassembled or given any maintenance on board ship.

2. Radiation sources shall remain installed in the radiation-detection equipment or shall be stowed in their shipping containers in a locked storage.

3. Spare radioactive electronic tubes and fission chambers shall be stored in clearly marked containers and locked stowage.

4. All hands shall scrupulously obey radiation warning signs and shall remain clear of radiation barriers.

Safety devices

1. Mechanical, electrical, and electronic safety devices must be inspected at regular intervals and whenever unusual circumstances or conditions warrant. When practicable, such devices should be inspected while the equipment or unit to which they apply is in actual operation. Machinery or equipment must not be operated when it is known that their safety devices are not in proper working condition.

2. No person shall tamper with any safety device, interlock, ground strap, or similar device intended to protect the operators or the equipment.

Semisafe and dangerous materials

Semisafe materials are materials that are considered safe so long as they are in unopened containers that do not leak, it being understood that should leakage occur, any spilled material would be cleaned up promptly and the leaking containers disposed of. Some of the more common semisafe materials are diesel oil, grease, lubricating oil, metal polish, paint, safety matches, and wax.

Dangerous materials are materials that constitute considerable fire hazards or have other dangerous characteristics, whether or not they are in sealed containers. Some of the more common dangerous materials are acids, alcohol, anti-corrosive paint, bleaching powder (chlorinated lime), calcium hypochlorite, compressed gases, gasoline, kerosene, lacquer, paint-thinner, paint-stripping compound, paint-drier, rust-prevention compound, storage-battery electrolyte, turpentine, and varnish.

All semisafe and dangerous materials shall be stowed in storerooms specially designed for paint and flammable liquids, unless another designated stowage area is provided. Naked lights and spark-emitting devices must not be used in compartments that contain semisafe or dangerous materials.

Calcium hypochlorite and bleaching powder (chlorinated lime) must be stowed in a clean, cool, dry compartment or storeroom not adjacent to a magazine; they must be isolated from flammable materials, acids, and other chemicals. Their containers shall be inspected periodically to ensure that they are tightly sealed and that exteriors or cans are free of rust. The contents of defective containers must be used immediately or otherwise disposed of. Bleach in plastic containers must be stowed in a covered metal container.

Shoes

All persons must wear rubber-soled shoes, except that boat crews must wear rubber-soled canvas shoes when embarked in ship's boats. Only leather shoes may be worn in engineering spaces. Plastic (e.g., Corfam) shoes may not be worn. Safety shoes must be worn in areas designated as being foot-hazardous. Shoes with taps, cleats, or any other metal device on the heels or soles may not be worn on board ship or in ship's boats.

Sleeping topside

Sleeping topside when the ship is underway shall be carefully supervised to make sure that no cots are used and that there is no possibility of men rolling over the side.

Small arms

Small arms are hand-held pistols, rifles, machine guns, line-throwing guns, and flare guns of less than .50-caliber bore diameter.

1. No one may be issued a small arm unless he has demonstrated to his department head or division officer that he is fully acquainted with its operation and the safety regulations that pertain to it.

2. No one may insert a clip or otherwise load any small arm unless he intends and is required to use the weapon in the performance of his duty.

3. Only designated persons may clean, disassemble, adjust, or repair small arms.

4. A small arm must never be pointed at anyone unless its bearer intends to shoot him, or in any direction where accidental discharge could do harm.

Smoking

Smoking is prohibited in the following areas and during the following evolutions:

1. Holds, storerooms, gasoline-tank compartments, gasoline-pump rooms, voids, or trunks, any shop or space where flammable liquids are being handled, ship's boats, bunks or berths, magazines, handling rooms, ready-service rooms, gun mounts or turrets, gasoline-control stations, oil-relay tank rooms, battery and charging rooms, film-projection rooms and the vicinity of motion-picture stowage, photographic laboratories, and areas where vinyl or saran paint is being applied.

2. Any area of the ship where ammunition is being handled.

3. When ammunition is being either loaded or unloaded.

4. When fuel oil, diesel oil, aviation gasoline, or other volatile fuel is being received or transferred.

5. During general quarters, general drills, and emergencies, except as authorized by the commanding officer.

6. When the word is passed "The smoking lamp is out."

Special equipment

All personnel concerned with the operation of such equipment as davits, winches, and booms must be thoroughly familiar with the safety precautions peculiar to its use. Applicable safety precautions must be posted in the immediate vicinity of the equipment. Only personnel who have been instructed in their duties and have been authorized by the first lieutenant are permitted to operate cranes, capstans, winches, and windlasses. Except in an emergency, operation of the machinery must be supervised by a responsible officer.

Synthetic lines

Nylon, dacron, and other synthetic-fiber lines used for mooring and rigging have high elasticity and a low coefficient of friction. Therefore, persons working with them should take the following precautions:

1. Give an extra turn when securing synthetic-fiber line to bitts, cleats, capstans, and other holding devices.

2. Exercise extreme care when easing out synthetic-fiber lines from bitts, cleats, or other holding devices.

3. Ensure that no one is standing in the direct line of pull when heavy loads are applied to nylon line. Nylon line stretches to one and one-half times its original length and when it parts it snaps back.

Tagging

The proper tagging of equipment and instruments greatly enhances the safety of both crew and ship. Once a piece of equipment has been tagged, it cannot be untagged, operated, or used without specific directions from competent authority. General practice is as follows:

1. All tags must be filled out completely, dated, and signed.

2. A proper entry must be made in the tag-out log whenever machinery is tagged in or tagged out.

3. The individual who tagged the equipment must be notified before any change may be made to its status.

Tools

Danger from electric shock and flying particles accompanies the use of pneumatic or electrically powered tools. The rigorous use to which electrically powered tools are put and the metal construction of a ship make the possibility of electrical shorts a constant hazard to those who use them.

1. No person shall use an electric or pneumatic tool unless he has been specifically authorized to do so by his division officer, and then only after he has demonstrated that he knows how to use it and what safety measures to follow.

2. No electric tool shall be issued until it has been carefully inspected and checked for resistance to insulation.

3. No person shall use an electric or pneumatic tool for any purpose other than those specifically authorized by his department head.

4. No person shall use an electric tool unless its housing is grounded to the ship's metal structure, either through a grounded receptacle and plug or by direct connection to the hull.

5. All persons using pneumatic or electrically powered wire brushes, chippers, sanders, or grinders must wear goggles or eye shields and rubber gloves.

Toxic materials

The issue and use of materials that are potential health hazards must be strictly controlled by a medical officer or other designated person.

Methyl alcohol, commonly used in duplicator fluid, paint-thinners, cleaners, and antifreeze is hazardous if inhaled, absorbed through the skin, or swallowed. The swallowing of even small amounts can cause permanent blindness or death. Methyl alcohol and products containing methyl alcohol may be released only in the amount required and at the time needed to perform a specific job. It may be used only in well-ventilated spaces and in a manner that prevents it from coming into contact with the skin.

Halogenated hydrocarbons, normally used in gaseous or liquid form as solvents, refrigerants, fumigants, insecticides, paint-removers, dry-cleaning fluids, and propellants for pressurized containers, are also hazardous if inhaled, swallowed, or absorbed by the skin. They may be used only where there is adequate ventilation, by authorized personnel under close supervision, and in such a way that they do not come into contact with the eyes or skin.

Underway replenishment

In this operation speed is important but it must never be attained at the price of safety. It is impossible to anticipate all the hazardous situations that could arise, but the following general precautions, which should always be reviewed before an operation begins, provide an excellent start:

1. Only essential personnel should be allowed in the vicinity of any transfer station.

2. Life lines should be lowered only when absolutely necessary and if they are, temporary ones must be rigged.

3. When line-throwing guns or bolos are used, all hands on the receiving ship must take cover (see **Line-throwing gun**).

4. Topside personnel engaged in handling stores and lines must wear safety helmets and orange-colored, inherently buoyant, vest-type life preservers. If safety helmets have quick-acting breakaway devices, the chin strap must be fastened and worn under the chin. If helmets are not so equipped, the chin strap must be fastened behind the head or worn unbuckled. Between-ship telephone-talkers must not secure neckstraps around their necks, lest they be dragged over the side by their telephone lines.

5. Line-handlers must use the hand-over-hand method of hauling in a line. They must never hold a line and run with it to provide extra pull.

6. Cargo-handlers must wear safety shoes, and those handling wire-bound or banded cases must wear work gloves.

7. All hands must keep clear of bights, handle lines from the inboard side, and stay at least six feet away from any block through which lines pass. They must also keep clear of suspended loads and rig-attachment points until loads have been landed on deck.

8. Care must be taken to prevent the shifting of cargo. No one should get between any load and the rail.

9. Deck space in the vicinity of transfer stations must be covered with a slip-resistant deck material.

10. A life-buoy watch must be stationed well aft on the engaged side, and provisions made for rescuing anyone who

falls overboard. If a lifeguard ship is not available, a boat must be kept ready.

11. Suitable measures must be taken to avoid the hazards associated with high-energy radio transmissions. This is especially important when ammunition, gasoline, and other petroleum products are handled.

12. Dangerous materials, such as acids, compressed gases, and hypochlorites, must be transferred separately from one another and from other cargo. The delivery ship must notify the receiving ship of the type of dangerous material in each load before transferring it. The receiving ship must keep dangerous materials separated and stow them in designated storerooms as soon as possible.

13. When fuel oil is being received or transferred, naked lights or electrical or mechanical apparatus likely to spark may not be within fifty feet of an oil hose in use, an open fuel tank, the vent terminal from a fuel tank, or an area where fuel oil or fuel-oil vapors are or may be present. The term "naked light" includes all forms of oil and gas lanterns, lighted candles, matches, cigars, cigarettes, cigarette lighters, and apparatus for flame welding or arc welding and cutting; this is not a complete list. Portable electric lights for use during fueling must have explosion-proof protected globes, be thoroughly inspected for proper insulation, and be tested before they are used. When a ship is being fueled, portholes in the side of her structure on which she is being fueled must be closed and secured. Fuel-tank overboard discharges must be monitored by personnel who are in direct communication with the fuel-control station. All scuppers and deck drains around the fueling station should be blocked to prevent fuel spills.

14. When gasoline is being transferred, a ground wire must be connected between the two ships before the hose is brought aboard and left in place until the hose is clear. Gasoline hoses must be blown down by an inert gas after the completion of every transfer.

Voids and bilges. *See* **Closed compartments**

Volatile fuels

Aviation gasoline, motor gasoline, JP-4, and JP-5 are highly volatile liquids. They give off a vapor that, when combined with the proper proportion of air, forms an explosive mixture that can be set off by a slight spark or flame. Further, the vapor may travel along an air current for a considerable distance and then be ignited, the flash traveling back to the source of supply and causing an explosion or fire.

1. All spaces into which the vapors of volatile fuel issue must be constantly and thoroughly ventilated.

2. No smoking and no naked lights (see **Underway Replenishment,** paragraph 13) can be permitted in the vicinity of volatile-fuel tanks or filling connections, drums, cans, stowage, piping, or spaces through which such piping passes.

3. Care must be taken to prevent the striking of sparks in places where the vapors of volatile fuels may collect. Only spark-proof tools should be used.

4. When gasoline is carried in cans for a ship's own use, it must be stowed in the storeroom for paint and flammable liquids. If there is no such storeroom, it should be stowed on the weather deck so that the containers may be readily thrown overboard.

5. Gasoline may be issued only under the supervision of a reliable man, who must make sure that all containers are securely closed and all safety regulations are observed.

6. The metal nozzle at the end of a fuel hose must be properly grounded so as to prevent sparks from static electricity (see **Underway replenishment,** paragraph 14).

7. Gasoline may not be used for cleaning purposes under any circumstances.

8. Upon completion of loading or delivery, piping and hoses must be carefully drained back into the ship's tanks or into containers that can be closed and sealed.

Welding. *See* **Hot work**

Working aloft

Men may go aloft only to perform necessary work or duty, and then only with the permission of the OOD. The OOD is responsible for seeing that the following safety precautions are observed before he grants permission:

1. Power on all radio-transmitting antennas and radar antennas in the vicinity has been secured, and power switches have been tagged "Secured! Men aloft."

2. The engineer officer has been instructed to lift no safety valves and if men are to work in the vicinity of the whistle, to secure steam to the whistle.

3. The men, if they are to work in the vicinity of stack gases, have protective breathing masks and have been instructed to remain there for only a brief time.

4. The men have an approved safety harness, which they are to attach to the ship's structure at the level where they will be working.

5. All tools, buckets, paint pots, and brushes have lanyards with which they can be secured when used for work on masts, stacks, upper catwalks, weather decks, or sponsons that overhang areas where other men may be present.

6. An announcement has been made over the 1MC concerning the operation aloft and the applicable restrictions, to prevent any inadvertent changes in the status aloft.

7. The OODs of adjacent ships have been alerted to ensure that high-powered radio and radar equipments of their ships will not be energized or present a danger to the personnel going aloft.

8. If the ship is in port, the "kilo" flag has been hoisted to indicate men working aloft.

Working over the side. *See also* **Divers.**

Men who are to be assigned to work over the side must be instructed in all safety precautions by their division officers before they can be permitted on scaffolding or stages or in boatswain's chairs. The following precautions must be observed:

1. Men working over the side must be supervised by a competent petty officer, and qualified men must be assigned to tend safety lines.

2. All men working over the side of the ship on stages, in boatswain's chairs, or in boats along the side of the ship must wear inherently buoyant life preservers. With the exception of men in boats, they must also wear approved safety harnesses with shock-absorbing inertial attachment points and be equipped with safety lines tended from the deck above.

3. All tools, buckets, paint pots, and brushes used by men working over the side of the ship must be secured by lanyards to prevent their loss overboard and injury to personnel below.

4. Any person assigned to do work over the side of the ship while she is underway must have the permission of the commanding officer.

11 | BOATS AND VEHICLES

Small-boat operation requires particular attention by the watch officer. Today's sleek and powerful boats are valuable assets to their parent ships. They provide the means of immediate response to emergency situations when at sea and may serve as the primary connection with the beach, especially in some foreign ports. It is as true now as it was in the past—a ship is judged by the appearance and performance of her boats and crew. The watch officer should always remember that boat operation has the potential for catastrophe. Improper preparation and poor handling of boats have caused many accidents and much loss of life. Responsibility for the safety of a ship's boats and embarked passengers cannot be taken lightly. The complex coordination required to ensure safe, smart performance dictates that boat operation receive careful supervision and attention from both the CDO and the OOD.

Underway

During operations at sea, the OOD must be concerned with the readiness and security of the boats. *OpNavInst* 3120.32 requires that at least one motor whaleboat, if available, be prepared for lowering at all times and that at least one complete boat crew be assigned to rescue and assistance. The duty coxswain is required to conduct an inspection of his rescue boat at the beginning of each watch and report to the OOD on its readiness for service. The OOD should know the coxswain's qualifications and those of his crew, as well as where they are stationed and how long it would take to assemble them. He should also know which men would lower the boats in an emergency, who would be in charge of the operation, and how long it would take to lower the boats. The first lieutenant is responsible for providing qualified individuals for boat crews and ensuring that all personnel engaged in small-boat operations are adequately trained for this duty.

The readiness of boats' engines, the amount of fuel in the boats, and the rescue equipment carried are other matters of interest to the OOD. In cold weather, precautions must be taken to keep the engines warm, either by starting them frequently or by heaters. It goes without saying that, at sea, boats should be fueled to capacity. When lowering and recovering a boat, the OOD must be particularly concerned with safety. A boat should not be lowered in a trough or in waters too rough for recovery, and the ship should not exceed five knots speed even under the calmest of conditions, though a slight amount of headway is desirable during recovery for ease in hooking the boat to the falls. A course should be selected that gives the ship a minimum roll and provides a lee on the side of the ship where the evolution is taking place. The OOD should also try not to pick up a boat with sternway on the ship; if this is absolutely necessary, he should ensure that the falls are hooked or unhooked in reverse of normal order. A boat should not be lowered or hoisted with nonessential personnel on board. If practical, personnel other than the regular crew should enter or leave the boat only while it is waterborne. When not conducting boat operations, the OOD must be concerned with the security of the boat in its stowage. It is prudent to have a designated watch-stander check the boats once an hour, more often during heavy weather. When heavy weather is expected, the OOD should inform the first lieutenant so that he may take extra precautions to ensure the security of the boats. Any deficiencies in the condition of the boats, their readiness for operation, or the readiness of their crew should be brought to the attention of the first lieutenant and the commanding officer as soon as discovered.

All these matters are part of the routine of a well-run ship, but the OOD cannot afford to assume that all is well. For if a lifeboat is not ready when needed or is launched with a green crew, the OOD is certain to be held responsible.

In port

In port, the operation, appearance, and security of boats and vehicles are major responsibilities of the OOD. He exercises direct supervision of the ship's boats and ensures compliance with boat schedules promulgated by the executive officer. *OpNavInst* 3120.32, article 630.1.3, directs that the OOD shall perform the following duties:

1. Ensure that boats are operated safely and that all boat safety regulations are observed.

2. Ensure that boats are not overloaded and reduce the allowed loading capacity to a safe margin when weather conditions require unusual caution.

3. Use boat officers under such conditions as the following:
   a. Foul weather or reduced visibility, existing or expected.
   b. Unfamiliar harbors.
   c. Large liberty parties returning after sunset, especially just before sailing.
   d. Trips of long duration.
   e. Local regulations requiring such personnel.

4. Require all boat passengers and crew to wear life jackets when weather or sea conditions are hazardous.

5. Ensure that the boat coxswain understands the navigational information provided by the navigator.

6. Ensure that boats are fueled and inspected prior to 0800 daily, that they are clean and smart, and that the crew is in proper uniform.

7. Require one member of the boat crew to act as a bow lookout. This requirement is of major importance to boats such as LCMs, where the coxswain's vision ahead is severely limited.

8. Give the boat coxswains their trip orders and their orders to shove off.

9. Notify the CDO when weather conditions make the suspension or resumption of boating advisable.

10. Inspect boats secured alongside hourly. If weather or sea conditions threaten safety, take immediate action to hoist boats in or send them to a safe haven.

11. Require the coxswain of the lifeboat to inspect the lifeboat and report to him daily at sunset on its readiness for service.

Calling away, dispatching, fueling, and receiving boats and vehicles can be complicated and harassing for an OOD who has not organized his watch to handle them. Some sort of status sheet is almost mandatory to keep track of a number of boats and vehicles on a variety of missions. Even when an assistant is maintaining a record of missions and conditions of readiness, intelligent personal supervision by the OOD is still needed. Boats and vehicles should be inspected for appearance, and their equipment should be checked. If the instructions to be given a coxswain or driver are complicated, it is best to send for the man and discuss them. If there is any doubt about a man's memory, he should be given his instructions in writing, and they should be short, complete, and reasonable. The coxswain must be given a section of the harbor chart showing the ship's berth, other occupied anchorages, all commonly used landings and compass courses thereto, and a copy of the local traffic rules and navigational dangers and aids. Tracks to and from the boat's destination should also be clearly marked. A boat or vehicle should never be sent to wait for someone without a time limit on the trip, because if the passenger or passengers should fail to show up, the services of the boat or vehicle are lost until word can be gotten to the coxswain or driver, and that might take hours. The proper procedure for all boats and vehicles, except, of course, a gig, barge, or equivalent vehicle, is to direct them to wait for someone only for a certain length of time or until a specified hour.

Appearance

As stated, the appearance and smartness of a ship's boats and vehicles are important to officers and men who take pride in their ship and in their service. A smart boat reflects a smart ship and is often the criterion by which a ship and her crew are evaluated. Fresh, neat paintwork and fancy knotwork make a good impression, but the manner in which a boat is handled is even more significant. The OOD is responsible for ensuring that coxswains have good sea manners, which include rendering proper courtesies to passing boats and avoiding hot-rod landings and excessive wake.

The OOD can be a major factor in maintaining high standards for a ship's boats. His critical appraisal of a boat and her crew as she comes alongside is the first step. If he then corrects any deficiencies, he will have done much to ensure that his ship will be well represented by the boats that are used during his watch.

Boat Gongs

Although *OpNavInst* 3120.32 states that boat gongs will be sounded to indicate the departure of officers' boats (Article 520.2), many ships customarily use them to indicate that liberty boats will soon depart. Boat gongs are sounded over the ship's general announcing circuit, their meaning varying as follows:

Number of Gongs	Meaning
3	Boat departs in 10 minutes.
2	Boat departs in 5 minutes.
1	Boat departs in 1 minute.

Capacity

The capacity of a naval boat is indicated on a label plate affixed to her when she was built. The figure shown on the plate indicates maximum capacity under good conditions and should always be reduced in rough weather or when cargo is carried at the same time as passengers.

It is worth an OOD's while to learn the technique of loading a large liberty boat, because doing it properly is one of those small but significant signs that a ship is smartly run and has an efficient OOD. After the chief petty officers have been embarked, the other men should be required to go forward in the boat and load from fore to aft. A little supervision may be required to prevent men from filling up the center section first, but it will save people from having to climb over each other or engage in the dangerous practice of walking along the gunwales.

Crews

As previously stated, the first lieutenant is responsible for training the boat crew, but it is the OOD's responsibility to ensure that those who operate boats during his watch are qualified. The OOD must be especially diligent in this, because the potential for disaster is proportional to the crew's inexperience. The OOD's responsibility for safety dictates that he allow only fully qualified crew members to operate the boat. Inexperienced men may be allowed to go along for instruction if they wish but never as substitutes for fully qualified crewmen. There can be no compromise when safety is involved.

Equipment

Compasses, life jackets, and other items of boat equipment must be checked by the OOD as circumstances warrant. When a long boat passage is envisaged or visibility is likely to be low, a chart or compass-book entry showing heading and time on each course to be followed over the intended route should be prepared for guidance and reference. Life jackets, foul-weather clothing, harbor charts, and fire-fighting equipment are other items of boat equipment with which the OOD should be concerned. Life jackets should be checked and crews and passengers directed to wear them when weather or sea conditions so warrant. The number of people allowed in a boat should not exceed the number of life jackets in the boat. It should never be assumed that boats belonging to other units are properly equipped; the OOD should have them inspected if they are to be used by his ship.

Inspection

The engineer officer designates a qualified petty officer to make a daily check on the boats' engines, and the first lieutenant makes periodic checks on the condition of each boat and the equipment it carries. While these inspections can be assumed to be thorough, they do not guarantee that certain equipment will be in a certain boat at a particular time, nor do they relieve the OOD of exercising the prudence and foresight expected of a good seaman.

Orders

Orders to the coxswain of a boat should be given in a seamanlike and explicit manner. An unseamanlike order might be "All right, coxswain, shove off and get the navigator at the Dock Street Landing." Seamanlike and explicit orders would be "Coxswain! When told to shove off, go to the Dock Street Landing and bring off the navigator, Lieutenant Commander Jones. If he does not show up by _____ o'clock, return to the ship. Do you understand?" If the coxswain answers in the affirmative, the OOD would say, "Shove off and carry out your orders." It should be remembered that a boat "hauls out" to the boom, it does not "tie up" or "secure" to the boom. A ship "makes fast" to a pier, but a boat may "make fast" to the accommodation ladder (not to the gangway). A boat may be "secured," but this means a longer-lasting fastening than "made fast."

Safety

The safest way to secure boats is to hoist them in at night or in bad weather. When this procedure is not practicable, they should be hauled out to the boom and kept under surveillance. Boats usually ride well at the boom, but the practice of making fast astern is risky in bad weather. Boatkeepers or boat sentries are usually posted when the weather is bad enough for the safety of the ship's boats to be in doubt. Boats should never be permitted to lie unattended at the accommodation ladder.

If a boat is to be left in the water for a long time, the OOD should make a visual inspection of the boat at least once an hour and should direct all other available roving security patrols to check the boat. This is to prevent unauthorized use or theft or to discover a flooding problem quickly if it exists. (For detailed safety precautions governing boat operations, see chapter 10, **Safety**).

Schedules

The executive officer generally prescribes boat schedules, and they should be followed meticulously by the OOD. Only the most unusual circumstances should be allowed to cause cancellation of a scheduled boat, particularly at night when people ashore may be planning to return to the ship in that boat. If a scheduled boat trip must be canceled, permission for the cancellation must be obtained from the executive officer or CDO, and the word must be passed.

When, as often happens, officers and men waiting to leave the ship are going to the same destination as the senior officer, he usually allows them to embark in his gig or barge. The OOD should find out whether the senior officer concerned follows this practice and if so, embark the people before the captain or admiral comes onto the quarterdeck. If doubt exists, there is nothing wrong with asking the senior officer whether he desires to take any officers or men to his destination. If the answer is affirmative, as is invariably the case, every effort must be made to expedite the loading of the boat. Juniors always enter boats (and vehicles) *first* and leave them *last*. For an exception to this rule, see *Loading liberty boats* in chapter 9.

Security

One way to ensure the safe and efficient operation of boats is to provide a boat officer. This is true, of course, only if the officer assigned is qualified. For conditions calling for the assignment of a boat officer, see **In port** in this chapter.

A boat officer should wear a web belt and, except where prohibited by competent authority, a pistol, which is his badge of authority and distinguishes him from officer passengers. When there are not enough commissioned or warrant officers to act as boat officers, it is customary to assign chief petty officers of deck ratings.

For a more thorough study of small-boat operations, the reader is referred to "A Boat Officer's Handbook," published by the Naval Institute Press.

Vehicles

Ships in port are assigned vehicles to assist in carrying out daily business. The OOD is sometimes tasked with keeping track of the vehicles and ensuring that they are always ready for use. Losing track of the status of a ship's vehicles can significantly hamper a ship's in-port operation and is certain to ruin the OOD's day. The wise OOD will have direct control of the vehicles' keys. He will give them only to authorized users and require that they be turned back to him. Ship's vehicles should be parked within sight of the quarterdeck to prevent theft or damage. The OOD should keep notes on who is using the vehicles, who will require them, what the requirements are for, and how long the trips will take. Priorities must be established, and the OOD may find himself making unpopular decisions. Common sense is usually the rule. Often the consolidation of several trips can make for more efficient use of a vehicle. The name and whereabouts of the duty driver are also of concern to the OOD. The OOD must ensure that the duty driver is on station, in the correct uniform, and ready for an appointment ahead of schedule. Upon return of a vehicle's keys, the OOD should ascertain the fuel status of the vehicle and have it refueled if necessary.

Any number of things can go wrong with ship's vehicles, all of which spell trouble for the OOD. He can avoid most of this trouble by requiring a face-to-face turnover of keys before and after use. He should not lose track of a vehicle and should ensure that every vehicle is used for ship's business only.

Vehicle security

Marked government vehicles or vehicles carrying uniformed passengers are possible targets of terrorist activities. The OOD must always be alert to the possibility of a local terrorist threat and must take appropriate precautions. He must always consult the CDO for special precautions and instructions.

12 | HONORS AND CEREMONIES

Honors and ceremonies are based on a long-established code of customs, agreements, and regulations most of which are common to all navies. With some important exceptions, these honors and ceremonies take place in port, and the manner in which they are rendered or carried out under the supervision of the OOD does much to give his ship a reputation for smartness. Because so many honors and ceremonies are international in character, it is important that they be rendered and conducted in a manner that reflects credit on the U.S. Navy and the United States.

The governing source for appropriate honors is *U.S. Navy Regulations* (1973). However, the OOD need not commit *Navy Regulations* to memory. For convenience, he should memorize some honors, but most situations will allow time for preparation. To aid the OOD, some ships keep a "table of honors" posted on the quarterdeck for ready reference.

With honors and ceremonies, as with nearly all his activities, an OOD must look ahead. He should be able to estimate quite accurately the degree of readiness required at any given time. For example, if his ship is anchored at an advanced base, the weather is bad, and there is a possibility of air attack, he is not likely to need side boys standing by. On the other hand, the circumstances might be such that he should have the full guard ready at a moment's notice.

The following pages contain enough information from *Navy Regulations* to enable the OOD, under normal conditions, to discharge his duties. On special occasions, such as the death of an important person, he will have to refer to *Navy Regulations*.

The quarterdeck

The commanding officer of a ship shall establish the limits of the quarterdeck and the restrictions as to its use. The quarterdeck shall embrace so much of the main or other appropriate deck as may be necessary for the proper conduct of official and ceremonial functions.

Navy Regulations, Article 1056.

The quarterdeck functions as the command and control center for a ship's daily administrative activities and for the conduct of the ship's normal in-port routine. It is whatever part of the ship the commanding officer designates. It is normally on the main deck near the brow, making it the first line of security for the ship. It may be marked off by appropriate lines, deck markings, cartridge cases decoratively arranged, or fancy work. It is always kept particularly clean and shipshape. Men not on duty should not be allowed on or near the quarterdeck. The dignity and appearance of the quarterdeck are symbols of the professional and seamanlike attitude of a ship and her crew. The OOD should be zealous in upholding this dignity and appearance, together with the highest standards of smartness on the part of his personnel.

The brow should always be tended by the OOD or one of his assistants, for reasons of both security and courtesy. Every person who comes aboard should be greeted immediately by a member of the watch. His business should then be ascertained and his credentials examined. If all is in order, appropriate steps must be taken to have him escorted below or to send for the person he wishes to see. Officers' guests should be taken to the wardroom.

When an officer comes aboard, his boat usually lies alongside the accommodation ladder until it receives its orders. The OOD should ask the visitor or his aide what orders are desired for his boat, gig, or barge.

Side boys

Side boys, being the first members of the crew to come under the observation of an important visitor, should be particularly smart. Their shoes should be polished and their uniforms immaculate. They should be kept together under the eye of a petty officer and not employed in any activity that might spoil their good appearance or take them away from the quarterdeck. The OOD should see that they are properly instructed and can fall in without confusion. Similar care should be taken with the guard and band.

Piping the side

The call "alongside" is timed to finish just as the visitor's boat reaches the accommodation ladder. During this call, the side boys and the boatswain's mate stand at attention but do not salute.

For a visitor approaching by way of an accommodation ladder, the call "over the side" starts just as his head appears at quarterdeck level. For a visitor approaching over a brow, it starts when he arrives at a designated point at the outboard end of the brow. Side boys and boatswain's mate salute on the first note and drop their hands from salute on the last note. The boatswain's mate may salute with his left hand. Saluting and piping procedure is reversed when a visitor leaves.

Official visits

When the OOD is notified that an official visit is to be paid to the ship, he should take these steps:

1. Consult the table of honors in *Navy Regulations*.

2. Notify the admiral, chief of staff, commanding officer, executive officer, command duty officer, navigator, senior watch officer, flag lieutenant, and commanding officer of the Marine detachment.

3. Have on deck a qualified boatswain's mate and a quartermaster.

4. Inspect and rehearse the side boys.

5. Inspect the quarterdeck for appearance.

6. Station an alert lookout, notify the signal bridge to be prepared, and have the visitor's personal flag ready.

7. Notify the band.

8. If a salute is required, notify the weapons officer.

Salutes and honors

The following extracts from *Navy Regulations* provide a ready reference for the officer of the deck.

Morning and Evening Colors

1. The ceremonial hoisting and lowering of the national ensign at 0800 and sunset at a naval command ashore or aboard a ship of the Navy not underway shall be known as Morning Colors and Evening Colors, respectively, and shall be carried out as prescribed in this article.

2. The guard of the day and the band shall be paraded in the vicinity of the point of hoist of the ensign.

3. "Attention" shall be sounded, followed by the playing of the national anthem by the band.

4. At Morning Colors, the ensign shall be started up at the beginning of the music and hoisted smartly to the peak or truck. At Evening Colors, the ensign shall be started from the peak or truck at the beginning of the music and the lowering so regulated as to be completed at the last note.

5. At the completion of the music, "Carry On" shall be sounded.

6. In the absence of a band, an appropriate recording to be played over a public address system. "To the Colors" shall be played by the bugle at Morning Colors and "Retreat" at Evening Colors and the salute shall be rendered as prescribed for the National Anthem.

7. In the absence of music, "Attention" and "Carry On" shall be the signals for rendering and terminating the salute. "Carry On" shall be sounded as soon as the ensign is completely lowered.

8. During colors, a boat underway within sight or hearing of the ceremony shall lie to, or shall proceed at the slowest safe speed. The boat officer, or in his absence the coxswain, shall stand and salute except when dangerous to do so. Other persons in the boat shall remain seated or standing and shall not salute.

9. During colors, vehicles within sight or hearing of the ceremony shall be stopped. Persons riding in such vehicles shall remain seated at attention.

10. After Morning Colors, if foreign warships are present, the national anthem of each nation so represented shall be played in the order in which a gun salute would be fired to, or exchanged with, the senior official or officer present of each such nation; provided that, when in a foreign port, the national anthem of the port shall be played immediately after Morning Colors, followed by the national anthems of other foreign nations represented. Article 1006.

Salutes to the National Ensign

1. Each person in the naval service, upon coming on board a ship of the Navy, shall salute the national ensign if it is flying. He shall stop on reaching the upper platform of the accommodation ladder, or the shipboard end of the brow, face the national ensign, and render the salute, after which he shall salute the officer of the deck. On leaving the ship, he shall render the salutes in inverse order. The officer of the deck shall return both salutes in each case.

2. When passed by or passing the national ensign being carried, uncased, in a military formation, all persons in the naval service shall salute. Persons in vehicles or boats shall follow the procedure prescribed for such persons during colors.

3. The salutes prescribed in this article shall also be rendered to foreign national ensigns and aboard foreign men-of-war.   Article 2107.

Saluting Ships and Stations

Saluting ships and stations of the naval service are those designated as such by the Secretary of the Navy or his duly authorized representative. The gun salutes prescribed in these regulations shall be fired by such ships and stations. Other ships and stations shall not fire gun salutes, unless directed to do so by the senior officer present on exceptional occasions when courtesy requires.   Article 1012.

"Passing Honors" and "Close Aboard" Defined

"Passing honors" are those honors, other than gun salutes, rendered on occasions when ships of embarked officials or officers pass, or are passed, close aboard. "Close aboard" shall mean passing within six hundred yards for ships and four hundred yards for boats. These rules shall be interpreted liberally, to insure that appropriate honors are rendered.   Article 1027.

Passing Honors between Ships

1. Passing honors, consisting of sounding "Attention" and rendering the hand salute by all persons in view on deck and not in ranks, shall be exchanged between ships of the Navy, and between ships of the Navy and the Coast Guard, passing close aboard.

2. In addition, the honors prescribed in the following table shall be rendered by a ship of the Navy passing close aboard a ship or naval station displaying the flag of the official indicated therein; and by naval stations, insofar as practicable, when a ship displaying such flag passes close aboard. These honors shall be acknowledged by rendering the same honors in return.   Article 1028.

Passing Honors between Ships

Officer of the Deck of Junior Ship	Officer of the Deck of Senior Ship	Bugle Call	Battery Whistle
1. Sounds "attention" starboard (port)		"attention" starboard (port)	1 whistle starboard 2 whistles (port)
	2. Sounds "attention" starboard (port)		
3. Sounds "hand salute" (guard presents arms and band sounds off if required)		1 short note	1 short whistle
	4. Sounds "hand salute" (guard presents arms and band sounds off)		
	5. Sounds "TWO" (in 3 seconds or after band sounds off)	2 short notes	2 short whistles
6. Sounds "TWO"			
	7. Sounds "carry on"	"carry on"	3 short whistles
8. Sounds "carry on"			

Passing Honors to Officials and Officers Embarked in Boats

1. The honors prescribed in [the table of Passing Honors to Officials and Officers Embarked in Boats] shall be rendered by a ship of the Navy being passed close aboard by a boat displaying the flag or pennant of the . . . officials and officers listed [in the table].

2. Persons on the quarterdeck shall salute when a boat passes close aboard in which a flag officer, a unit commander, or a commanding officer is embarked under the following circumstances:

   a. When the officer in the boat is in uniform as indicated by the display of the national ensign in United States ports; or

   b. When a miniature of a flag or pennant is displayed in addition to the national ensign in foreign ports. Article 1029.

PASSING HONORS TO OFFICIALS EMBARKED IN SHIPS

Official	Uniform	Ruffles and flourishes	Music	Guard	Remarks
President	As prescribed by senior officer present	4	National anthem	Full	Man rail, unless otherwise directed by senior officer present.
Secretary of State when special foreign representative of the President	do	4	do	do	Crew at quarters.
Vice President	Of the day		do	do	do
Secretary of Defense, Deputy Secretary of Defense, or Secretary of the Navy	do		do	do	do
An Assistant Secretary of Defense, Under Secretary or an Assistant Secretary of the Navy	do		do	do	do

PASSING HONORS TO OFFICIALS AND OFFICERS EMBARKED IN BOATS

Official	Ruffles and flourishes	Music	Guard	Remarks
President	4	National anthem	Full	"Attention" sounded, and salute by all persons in view on deck. If directed by the senior officer present, man rail.[1]
Secretary of State when special foreign representative of President	4	do	do	"Attention" sounded, and salute by all persons in view on deck.
Vice President	4	Hail Columbia	do	do
Secretary of Defense, Deputy Secretary of Defense, Secretary of the Navy, an Assistant Secretary of Defense, Under Secretary or an Assistant Secretary of the Navy	4	Admiral's march	do	do
Other city official entitled to honors on official visit	—	—		do
Officer of an armed service	—	—		do

1. Those who man the rail will salute on signal.

Passing Honors to Foreign Dignitaries and Warships

1. The honors prescribed for the President of the United States shall be rendered by a ship of the Navy being passed close aboard by a ship or boat displaying the flag or standard of a foreign president, sovereign, or member of a reigning royal family, except that the foreign national anthem shall be played in lieu of the National Anthem of the United States.

2. Passing honors shall be exchanged with foreign warships passed close aboard and shall consist of parading the guard of the day, sounding "Attention," rendering the salute by all persons in view on deck, and playing the foreign national anthem.   Article 1030.

Sequence in Rendering Passing Honors

1. "Attention" shall be sounded by the junior when the bow of one ship passes the bow or stern of the other, or, if a senior be embarked in a boat, before the boat is abreast, or nearest to abreast, the quarterdeck.

2. The guard, if required, shall present arms, and all persons in view on deck shall salute.

3. The music, if required, shall sound off.

4. "Carry on" shall be sounded when the prescribed honors have been rendered and acknowledged.   Article 1031.

Dispensing with Passing Honors

1. Passing honors shall not be rendered after sunset or before 0800 except when international courtesy requires.

2. Passing honors shall not be exchanged between ships of the Navy engaged in tactical evolutions outside port.

3. The senior officer present may direct that passing honors be dispensed with in whole or in part.   Article 1032.

Crew at Quarters on Entering or Leaving Port

The crew shall be paraded at quarters during daylight on entering or leaving port on occasions of ceremony except when weather or other circumstances make it impracticable or undesirable to do so. Ordinarily occasions of ceremony shall be construed as visits that are not operational; at homeport when departing for or returning from a lengthy deployment; and visits to foreign ports not visited recently; and other special occasions so determined by a superior. In lieu of parading the entire crew at quarters, an honor guard may be paraded in a conspicuous place on weather decks.
                          Article 1033.

Side Honors

1. On the arrival and departure of civil officials and foreign officers, and of United States officers when so directed by the senior officer present, the side shall be piped and the appropriate number of side boys paraded.

2. Officers appropriate to the occasion shall attend the side on the arrival and departure of officials and officers.   Article 1049.

Dispensing with Side Boys, Guard, and Band

1. Side boys shall not be paraded on Sunday, or on other days between sunset and 0800, or during meal hours of the crew, general drills and evolutions, and period of regular overhaul; except in honor of civil officials or foreign officers, when they may be paraded at any time during daylight. Side boys shall be paraded only for scheduled visits.

2. Except for official visits and other formal occasions, side boys shall not be paraded in honor of officers of the armed services of the United States, unless otherwise directed by the senior officer present.

3. Side boys shall not be paraded in honor of an officer of the armed services in civilian clothes, unless such officer is at the time acting in an official civil capacity.

4. The side shall be piped when side boys are paraded, but not at other times.

5. The guard and band shall not be paraded in honor of the arrival or departure of an individual at times when side boys in his honor are dispensed with, except at naval shore installations.   Article 1050.

Honors at Official Inspection

1. When a flag officer or unit commander boards a ship of the Navy to make an official inspection, honors shall be rendered as for an official visit, except that the uniform shall be as prescribed by the inspection officer. His flag or command pennant shall be broken upon his arrival, unless otherwise prescribed in these regulations, and shall be hauled down on his departure.

2. The provisions of this article shall apply, insofar as practicable and appropriate, when a flag or general officer, in command ashore, makes an official inspection of a unit of his command.   Article 1054.

13 | FLAGS, PENNANTS, AND BOAT HAILS

The watch officer should be aware that the execution of honors and ceremonies, described in chapter 12, and the rules for displaying flags and pennants contained in this chapter, represent highly visible evolutions that will either enhance or detract from a ship's reputation for smartness or efficiency. Therefore, they are not an area to be given only cursory attention. Rather, the watch officer should ensure that each action is carried out in a precise, professional manner. Closely related to, and in fact overlapping, the subject of honors and ceremonies is the subject of flags and pennants. This chapter contains the most basic and commonly used information on the usage and customs related thereto. It is based on *Flags, Pennants, and Customs* (NTP-13) and *U.S. Navy Regulations*. The former publication should be studied by every officer on board ship who stands deck watches.

Many countries have variations of their national flag that are authorized for specific uses. The national flag used by men-of-war is the *ensign;* that used by merchant ships is the *merchant flag.* The United States of America has only one flag, the *colors,* which is used for all purposes. It may properly be called the *ensign* when used in the navy. A *union jack* is the *union,* or inner, upper corner of a national flag. The U.S. union is, of course, a blue field with fifty white stars on it.

General rules for display

The distinctive mark of a naval ship or craft in commission is an officer's personal flag, a command pennant, or a commission pennant. The distinctive mark of a naval hospital ship, in commission in time of war, is the Red Cross flag. Not more than one distinctive mark is displayed at the same time. Except as prescribed in *Navy Regulations* for certain occasions of ceremony and when civil officials are embarked, one of the distinctive marks mentioned above is displayed day and night at the after masthead or, in a mastless ship, from the most conspicuous hoist.

When a ship is not underway, the ensign and the union jack are displayed from 0800 until sunset from the flagstaff and the jackstaff, respectively. When a ship has entered port at night, at daylight she displays the ensign from the gaff, if appropriate, for a time sufficient to establish her nationality; it is customary for other ships of war to display their ensigns in return. When mooring or unmooring, the colors are shifted from the gaff to the flagstaff on the stern or the other way around. The union jack is raised or lowered simultaneously on the bow. The instant the last mooring line leaves the pier or the anchor is aweigh, the BMOW sounds a blast on a handheld whistle and passes the word over the 1MC "Underway, shift colors." This enables the lowering and raising of the respective flags to occur simultaneously. The jack on the jackstaff forward and the national ensign on the flagstaff aft, if flying, are hauled down smartly. At the same instant, the steaming ensign is hoisted on the gaff and the ship's international call sign and other pertinent signal flags are hoisted or broken. On mooring, the instant the anchor is let go or the first mooring line is made fast to the pier, the BMOW performs the same actions as for unmooring. At this signal the ship's call sign and steaming ensign are hauled down smartly and the jack and national ensign are run up.

Unless otherwise directed by the senior officer present, a ship displays the ensign during daylight from her gaff under the following circumstances:
1. Getting underway and coming to anchor.
2. Falling in with other ships.
3. Cruising near land.
4. In battle.

Rules for the U.S. ensign

During gun salutes

A ship of the U.S. Navy displays the ensign at a masthead while firing a salute in honor of a U.S. official or national anniversary, as follows:

1. At the main during the national salute prescribed for the third Monday in February and the 4th of July.

2. At the main during a 21-gun salute to a United States civil official, except by a ship displaying the personal flag of the official being saluted.

3. At the fore during a salute to any other United States civil official, except by a ship which is displaying the personal flag of the official being saluted.   *Navy Regulations,* Article 1001.

During a gun salute, the ensign must remain displayed from the gaff or the flagstaff, in addition to its display as prescribed above.

In boats

The national ensign is displayed from water-borne boats of the naval service:

1. When under way during daylight in a foreign port.

2. When ships are required to be dressed or full-dressed.

3. When going alongside a foreign vessel.

4. When an officer or official is embarked on an official occasion.

5. When a flag or general officer, a unit commander, a commanding officer, or a chief of staff, in uniform, is embarked in a boat of his command or in one assigned to his personal use.

6. At such other times as may be prescribed by the senior officer present.   *Naval Regulations,* Article 1062.

Dipping

When a vessel under U.S. registry, or under the registry of a nation formally recognized by the government of the United States, salutes a ship of the U.S. Navy by dipping her ensign, she is answered dip for dip. If the ensign is not already being displayed, it is hoisted, the dip is returned, and, after a suitable interval, it is hauled down. An ensign being displayed at half-mast is hoisted to the truck or peak for the purpose of answering a dip.

Ships of the U.S. Navy dip the ensign only in return for such compliment.

Half-masting

When an ensign that is not already being displayed is to be flown at half-mast, it must be hoisted to the truck or peak before being lowered to half-mast. Similarly, before the ensign is lowered from half-mast, it must be hoisted to the truck or peak.

When the ensign is half-masted, the union jack, if displayed from the jackstaff, must also be half-masted.

On Memorial Day, 30 May, every saluting ship must fire a twenty-one-gun salute at noon, and all ships display the ensign at half-mast from 0800 until the completion of the salute, or if no salute is fired, until 1220. Colors are half-masted when a ship is underway as well as when she is in port.

Since small boats are a part of a vessel, they follow the procedures of the parent vessel as regards the half-masting of colors.

Following motions of senior officer present

On board ship, whenever the ensign is to be hoisted, lowered, or half-masted, the motions of the senior officer present are followed, except as prescribed for answering a dip or firing a salute.

A ship displaying the flag of the president, secretary of defense, deputy secretary of defense, secretary of the navy, an assistant secretary of defense, under secretary of the navy, or an assistant secretary of the navy is regarded as the ship of the senior officer present.

Size of colors to be prescribed

When two or more vessels are in company in port, the senior officer present makes a preparatory signal at 0745, giving the size of colors to be hoisted at 0800. If a signal indicating the size of colors is made at any other time of day, the colors must be changed as soon as the signal is hauled down.

Display of foreign ensigns during gun salutes

When a ship is firing a salute to a foreign nation in one of that nation's ports, returning a salute fired by a foreign warship, or firing a salute on the occasion of a foreign national anniversary, celebration, or solemnity, she displays the ensign of the foreign nation at the main truck.

When a ship is firing a salute to a foreign dignitary or official entitled to twenty-one guns, she displays the national ensign of such dignitary or official at her main truck. When firing a salute to a foreign official entitled to less than twenty-one guns, or to a foreign officer, or when returning a salute fired by a foreign officer, she displays the national ensign of the foreign official or officer at her fore truck.

Display of the United Nations flag

The following policy concerning the display of the United Nations flag is quoted from Department of Defense Directive 1005.1:

1. The United Nations flag will be displayed at installations of the armed forces of the United States only upon occasion of visits of high dignitaries of the United Nations while in performance of their official duties with the United Nations, or on other special occasions in honor of the United Nations. When so displayed it will be displayed with the United States flag, both flags will be of the same approximate size and on the same level, the flag of the United States in the position of honor on the right (observer's left).

2. The United Nations flag will be carried by troops on occasions when the United Nations or high dignitaries thereof are to be honored. When so carried, the United Nations flag will be carried on the marching left of the United States flag and other United States colors or standards normally carried by such troops.

3. On occasions similar to those referred to in paragraph 2, above, U.S. Naval vessels will display the United Nations flag in the same manner as is prescribed for a foreign ensign during visits of a foreign President or Sovereign.

4. Except as indicated in paragraphs 1, 2, and 3, above, the United Nations flag will be displayed by United States Armed Forces only when so authorized by the President of the United States.

U.S. naval vessels authorized to display the United Nations flag display it in the same manner as is prescribed for a foreign ensign during visits of a foreign president or sovereign.

Personal flags and pennants

Afloat

Except as otherwise prescribed in *Navy Regulations,* a flag officer or a unit commander afloat displays his personal flag or his command pennant from his flagship. It should never be displayed from more than one ship.

When a flag officer eligible for command at sea is embarked for passage in a naval ship, that ship displays his personal flag, unless she is already displaying the flag of an officer who is his senior.

Flags or pennants of officers not eligible for command at sea are not displayed from ships of the U. S. Navy.

Broad and burgee command pennants

Broad command pennants and burgee command pennants are the personal pennants of officers, not flag officers, commanding units of ships or aircraft.

The broad command pennant indicates command of:

1. A division of aircraft carriers or cruisers.
2. A force, flotilla, or squadron of ships or craft of any type.
3. An aircraft wing.

The burgee command pennant indicates command of:

1. A division of ships or craft other than aircraft carriers or cruisers.
2. A major subdivision of an aircraft wing.

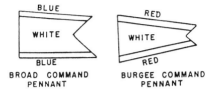

The broad and burgee command pennants are surcharged with numerals to indicate the organizational number within a ship type. When two commanders within a type are entitled to display the same command pennant and have the same organizational number in different echelons of command, the commander in the higher echelon uses Roman numerals in the surcharge. In all other cases, Arabic numerals are used. Blue numerals are used on board command pennants, and red numerals on burgee command pennants.

Bow and flagstaff insignia for boats

A boat regularly assigned to an officer for his personal use shall carry insignia on each bow as follows:

1. For a flag or general officer, the stars of his rank, as arranged on his flag.

2. For a unit commander not a flag officer, a replica of his command pennant.

3. For a commanding officer or a chief of staff not a flag officer, an arrow.

In a boat assigned to the personal use of a flag or general officer, unit commander, chief of staff, or commanding officer, or in which a civil official is embarked, flagstaffs for the ensign and for a personal flag or pennant must be fitted at the peak with devices as follows:

Spread Eagle: For an official entitled to a salute of nineteen or more guns.

Halberd: For a flag or general officer whose official salute is less than nineteen guns. For a civil official entitled to a salute of eleven or more guns but less than nineteen guns.

Ball: For an officer of the grade, or relative grade, of captain in the navy. For a career minister, a counselor or first secretary of embassy or legation, or a consul.

Star: For an officer of the grade, or relative grade, of commander in the navy.

Flat Truck: For an officer below the grade, or relative grade, of commander in the navy. For a civil official not listed above, and for whom honors are prescribed for an official visit.

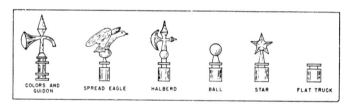

COLORS AND GUIDON   SPREAD EAGLE   HALBERD   BALL   STAR   FLAT TRUCK

Personal insignia at the masthead

When the president's flag is displayed at a masthead where an ensign is required to be displayed during an official visit or during periods of dressing or full-dressing ship, it shall remain at that masthead to port of the U. S. ensign and to starboard of a foreign ensign.

Except as provided above, a personal flag or command pennant is not displayed at the same masthead with a national ensign. When both are to be displayed, the personal flag or command pennant should be displayed as follows:

1. During a gun salute, it should be lowered clear of the ensign.

2. During an official visit, it should be shifted to the starboard yardarm in a single-masted ship and to the fore truck in a two-masted ship.

3. During periods of dressing or full-dressing ship:
   a. If displayed from the fore truck or from the masthead of a single-masted ship, it should be shifted to the starboard yardarm.
   b. If displayed from the main truck, it should be shifted to the fore truck in lieu of the ensign at that mast.
   c. If displayed from the after truck of a ship with more than two masts, it should remain at the after truck in lieu of the ensign at that mast.

Flags or pennants in boats and on automobiles

When embarked in a boat of the naval service on an official occasion, an officer in command, or a chief of staff acting for him, displays his personal flag or command pennant or, if not entitled to either, a commission pennant, from the bow.

When embarked in a boat of the naval service on other than official occasions, an officer entitled to display a personal flag or command pennant may display a miniature of such flag or pennant in the vicinity of the coxswain's station.

When riding in an automobile on an official occasion, an officer entitled to display a personal flag or command pennant may display such flag or pennant forward on the vehicle.

All flag officers are authorized to show the stars of their rank on automobiles assigned to them. Such stars may be displayed only on six-by-twelve-inch plates attached to or in the vicinity of the license plates. Stars or replicas of personal flags may not be painted on automobiles.

Half-masting

Personal flags, command pennants, and commission pennants should be half-masted for deceased officials or officers only as prescribed in *Navy Regulations.*

Civil officials in boats

When a U. S. civil official is embarked in a boat of the naval service on an official occasion, a flag should be displayed in the bow as follows:

A union jack for—

1. A diplomatic representative of or above the rank of chargé d'affaires, within the waters of the country to which he is accredited.

2. A governor general or governor commissioned as such by the president, within the area under his jurisdiction.

A consular flag for a consular representative.

A personal flag for other civil officials when they are entitled to the display of a personal flag during an official visit.

Officials of the United Nations and the North Atlantic Treaty Organization

When an official of the United Nations or the North Atlantic Treaty Organization is embarked in a U. S. naval vessel, he is not entitled to have his personal flag displayed unless he qualifies for displaying his personal flag by being a U. S. Navy flag officer eligible for command at sea.

Miscellaneous flags and pennants

Absence indicators

The absence from his ship of a flag officer, unit commander, chief of staff, or commanding officer is indicated from sunrise to sunset by the display of an absence indicator, as prescribed in the table below. Substitute pennants, as shown in the signal book, are used.

When a commanding officer who is acting as a temporary unit commander is absent from his ship, both absence pennants should be displayed.

Intention to depart

The hoisting of the speed pennant, where best seen (in port), indicates that the official or officer whose personal flag or command pennant is displayed will leave the ship officially in about five minutes. The hauling-down of the speed pennant means that the official or officer is departing.

The following procedure is used when a flag officer shifts his flag:

1. Five minutes before his departure, the flagship hoists the speed pennant at the main truck, below the personal flag.

USE OF SUBSTITUTE PENNANTS

Sub.	Indication	Where normally displayed	Absentee
1st	Absence of an official from his ship for a period of 72 hours or less	Starboard main yardarm (outboard)	Absence of a flag officer or unit commander whose personal flag or command pennant is flying in this ship.
2nd	Same as 1st substitute	Port main yard-arm (inboard)	Absence of chief of staff
3rd	Same as 1st substitute	Port main yard-arm (outboard)	Absence of captain (executive officer if captain is absent for a period exceeding 72 hours)
4th	Same as 1st substitute	Starboard main yardarm (inboard)	Absence of civil or military official whose flag is flying in this ship

2. As he departs, the flagship hauls down the speed pennant and hoists the appropriate absence pennant.

3. When he arrives in his new flagship, that ship breaks his flag at the main truck.

4. Simultaneously (or as nearly as possible) with the breaking of the personal flag in the new flagship, the former flagship hoists a commission pennant and hauls down the personal flag and the absentee pennant.

Church pennant

Public Law 829 authorizes the use of the church pennant above the ensign "during church services conducted by naval chaplains at sea." The words *at sea* are interpreted for U. S. Navy purposes as meaning "on board a naval vessel." Shore stations are not authorized to display the church pennant above the ensign, but they may display it separately, if desired.

If divine services are being conducted at the time of morning colors, or if they begin at that time, the ensign is hoisted to the peak at the time prescribed for it. The church pennant is then hoisted and the ensign dipped just clear of it.

Should the time of evening colors occur while divine services are being conducted, the church pennant is hauled down and the ensign hoisted to the peak just before the time for colors; the ensign is then hauled down at the prescribed time.

Should the ensign be displayed at half-mast, the church pennant should be hoisted just above it.

Union jack for general court-martial

The union jack is displayed at a yardarm to denote that a general court-martial or court of inquiry is in session. It is hoisted when the court meets and hauled down when the court adjourns.

Meal pennant (meal break)

When a ship is at anchor, the meal periods provided for the crew between sunrise and sunset are indicated by the hoisting of the meal pennant, also known as the meal break, on either yardarm.

Battle-efficiency pennant (meatball)

When a ship is at anchor, the battle-efficiency pennant, known familiarly as the meatball, is flown at the fore truck from sunrise to sunset, during the period provided in *Awards for Intra-Type Competition.*

When a guard flag, ready-duty flag, or Presidential Unit Citation pennant is displayed at the fore truck with the battle-efficiency pennant, the latter should be flown below the other flag.

Homeward-bound pennant

Use of the homeward-bound pennant is traditional. Specifications for its design and rules for its use have never been firmly established. The usage set forth in NTP-13 is believed to conform with tradition.

POW/MIA Flag

When prescribed by the senior officer present, the POW/ MIA flag shall be flown from 0800 until sunset. Ships underway shall not fly the POW/MIA flag. The point of display on board ships in port shall be the inboard halyard, port signal yardarm. The POW/MIA flag shall fly beneath the national ensign at shore activities. Additionally, shore activities may display the POW/MIA flag indoors to enhance commemoration ceremonies.

PUC, NUC, and MUC Pennants

At anchor, ships that have been awarded the Presidential Unit Citation, the Navy Unit Commendation or the Meritorious Unit Commendation should fly the appropriate pennant, described in NTP-13, at the fore truck from sunrise to sunset.

Special flag-hoist signals

The SOPA instructions may prescribe certain flag hoists for local use, such as request for the garbage or trash lighter or the water barge.

Dressing and full-dressing ship

Ships not underway are dressed or full-dressed from 0800 until sunset when prescribed or when directed. Ships underway are never dressed or full-dressed.

When full-dressing is prescribed, the senior officer present may direct that dressing be substituted for it if, in his opinion, the state of the weather makes such action advisable. He may also, under such circumstances, direct that the ensigns be hauled down from the mastheads after being hoisted. See NTP-13 for details of dressing and full-dressing, including the specified sequence of signal flags and pennants to be hoisted.

Boat hails

Night

All boats approaching a ship at night should be hailed as soon as they are within hearing distance. The watch on board ship should call out, "Boat ahoy!" and the coxswain should indicate the rank or rate of the senior person in the boat by replying as follows:

Rank or rate	Coxswain's reply
President or vice president of the united states	United States
Secretary of defense, deputy or assistant secretary of defense	Defense
Secretary, under secretary, or assistant secretary of the navy	Navy
Chief of naval operations, vice chief of naval operations	Naval operations
Fleet or force commander	Fleet, or abbreviation of administrative title
General officer	General officer
Chief of staff	Staff
Flotilla commander	_____Flot_____
Squadron commander	_____Ron_____
Division commander	_____Div_____
	The type and number abbreviation used is, for example, DesFlot-2, DesRon-6, DesDiv-22.
Marine officer commanding a brigade	Brigade commander
Commanding officer of a ship	(Name of ship)
Marine officer commanding a regiment	Regimental commander
Other commissioned officer	Aye, aye
Noncommissioned officer	No, no
Enlisted men	Hello
Boat not intending to come alongside, regardless of rank or rate of senior passenger	Passing

Day

During hours when honors are rendered, the officer of the deck should challenge an approaching boat as soon as possible by raising his arm with closed fist in the direction of the boat and should train a long glass or binoculars on the coxswain. The coxswain should reply by holding up the number of fingers corresponding to the number, if any, of side boys who should be standing by to honor the officer in his boat. A wave-off from the coxswain indicates that no side boys are required.

APPENDIXES

A | SAMPLE ORDERS

Standing orders

The following is a set of standing orders such as might be promulgated by the commanding officer of a destroyer. Standing orders vary from ship to ship, depending on mission and operational situation, but in most cases contain the information and guidance shown below.

Relieving the watch

1. Report in sufficient time to visit CIC and sonar control, thoroughly acquaint yourself with the tactical and navigational situation, and relieve the watch on time. Do not relieve the watch when you are in doubt about any conditions relating to your responsibilities as officer of the deck. Notify me immediately if you have any such doubts.

2. Consistent with the execution of your primary duties, you are required, upon taking the watch, to be rested and alert, with your eyes adapted to darkness. Full night adaptation normally takes about thirty minutes.

Safe navigation

1. Know at all times whether you are in international or inland waters, and comply with the applicable Rules of the Road.

2. Have all navigational sightings taken and their bearings recorded. Verify navigational lights with a stop watch. Notify me and the navigator if any lights are not sighted within fifteen minutes of the time expected. Report to the navigator and me sightings of land, shoals, rocks, beacons, buoys, dis-

colored water, and any other unusual atmospheric or environmental condition.

3. When underway, ensure that the ship's position is plotted on the chart periodically, the intervals between fixes being in accordance with safe navigational practices. Verify your course frequently. Make use of all aids such as radar, fathometer, loran, omega, and sonar, as appropriate, to supplement your navigation, but do not blindly depend upon any of them. On the high seas, plot a DR position hourly, and maintain at least a six-hour advance DR track. Unless otherwise directed, advise the navigator and me of deviations from the DR of more than three miles and, of course, of changes intended to return to the track.

4. Have the steering and standard compasses compared every half-hour and whenever the course is changed, and the results entered in the compass record book. Notify the navigator and me of unaccountable discrepancies.

5. When visibility is low or a questionable situation develops ahead, reduce speed. If you are ever in doubt as to the navigational safety of the ship, stop her (and by this is meant get all way off), taking into account any danger of collision or drift on the lee shore, and call me and the navigator.

6. Notify me immediately of any marked changes in the barometer (for example, a drop of 00.04 inches in one hour), in the direction of the wind, in the state of the sea, in visibility, and of any other indications or warnings of storms or bad weather. In the event visibility closes to two miles or less, sound fog signals, post a lookout in the eyes of the ship with a second man to handle sound-powered communications to the bridge, and notify me. Comply promptly and meticulously with the Rules of the Road requiring you to sound fog signals and to stop your engines when another vessel is heard forward of the beam. Should we be part of a formation, the sounding of fog signals will be as directed by the OTC or, where the possibility of collision exists, in strict accordance with the Rules of the Road.

7. When necessary to change course to avoid a stand-on vessel, do so early and with a clearly recognizable change in course. *Do not cross ahead of such a vessel.*

8. In peacetime, ensure that navigational lights are operating or operable as appropriate, and require the BMOW to make an oral report of this every thirty minutes. When, in your opinion, the use of running lights is essential to safety, in spite of "darken ship" having been signaled, use them, and notify me.

Tactical matters

1. You are required to understand and comply with applicable portions of *U. S. Navy Regulations, 1973, OpNavInst* 3120.32, International and Inland Rules of the Road, and fleet regulations for the pertinent ship type. Be thoroughly familiar with current operation orders and directives before coming on watch. Be sure the required tactical publications are at hand and that you know how to use them.

2. Notify me and the navigator of all changes of disposition, course, or speed, except minor changes necessary to maintain station in formation. Except in the case of patrolling an area or conforming to a signaled zig-zag or sinuous course, course changes of 5° or more and speed changes of 1 knot or more required to maintain station are *not* minor changes.

3. In the event of a tactical maneuver, such as a change of screen join-up or departure, or column formation from a screen, call me early enough to allow me to reach the bridge in time to adjust to the situation. Call me, for example, when the signal is "in the air" pending execution or ten minutes before a planned order's scheduled execution in an Op Order. You should train yourself to anticipate tactical maneuvers.

4. Apprise me of sightings and radar and sonar contacts, including bearing movements, when possible. When a contact that is extraneous to the disposition of which we are part is within five miles or less of the ship, or whose closest point of approach (CPA) will be within five miles of the ship, notify me promptly, giving the following information:

a. General location with respect to dead ahead, i.e., "on starboard bow," "on port beam," etc.

b. Bearings

c. Range
d. General bearing drift, i.e., drawing right or drawing left
e. Target angle, if possible
f. CPA
g. Time of CPA
h. Right of way, in accordance with the Rules of the Road
i. Recommended action, if any.

5. CIC is required to track and report to you all contacts within twenty miles, unless directed to report them at greater distances, providing course, speed, CPA, and time of CPA, until you authorize them to cease reporting. Ensure that this information is provided to you promptly and that your talkers relay it to you accurately and completely.

6. Advise me when any ship in company is seriously off station.

7. *When time permits,* double-check with CIC the address and text of any operational signal received by voice radio before complying with it. When a question concerning a signal arises, be sure that CIC records electrically messages received over the primary tactical circuits.

8. Have recognition signals ready whenever applicable, and when operational requirements permit, have the signalman ascertain the identity of passing ships.

Emergency procedures

Rehearse in your mind the action to be taken in an emergency such as the presence of a vessel or light close aboard, man overboard, fire, collision, main or steering engine casualty, or dragging anchor on this or a ship in close proximity. In addition, rehearse in your mind the action to be taken in the event of a tactical maneuver being signaled unexpectedly.

Watch performance

1. *Eternal vigilance is the price of safety at sea.* Keep a good lookout. Do not permit minor matters to divert you from your primary responsibility, the safety of the ship and its personnel.

2. You are responsible for the conduct and training of the watch. Ensure that:

a. The ship's deck log is accurately and fully maintained.
b. Damage Control Central reports ship's security to you hourly.
c. The roving patrol reports to you every half-hour.
d. The bridge is quiet and darkened at night.
3. The helmsman and lee helmsman are on station, quiet, alert, and not smoking.
f. All watch personnel are in the required uniform and making all reports and replies in a seamanlike manner, using standard phraseology.
g. All lookouts are alert and conducting a systematic search of their areas.
h. Members of the watch, including the after steersman (if one is posted) and the after lookout, are rotated for training in all watch stations to help keep them alert.
i. When practicable, each watch is exercised in casualty steering.

3. When heavy weather is forecast, ensure that everything about the ship is properly secured and the appropriate material condition is set. Prohibit all but essential movement of personnel on the weather decks. Ensure that lookouts are provided with appropriate clothing during inclement weather.

4. When relieved, verify and sign the deck log for the period of your watch. You are responsible for its completeness and accuracy.

The conn

1. The following basic principles have been accepted by experienced seagoing officers for years and shall be considered doctrine on this ship:
a. One and only one officer, and that is the officer who "has the conn," may give orders to the helmsman.
b. The identity of the officer giving such orders must be known to the personnel on the bridge and in the pilot house. On this ship we normally make this known by the conning officer's announcing loudly to the helmsman, "This is (name and rank). I have the conn."
c. The OOD may be relieved of the conn by another officer, but he retains responsibility for the ship's safety.

d. As captain I may take over the deck, or I may take over the conn. When I do the former, the OOD has no legal responsibility for the safety of the ship, except as I specifically detail. But, when I take the conn, the OOD is required to carry out all the duties assigned by *OpNavInst* 3120, article 433. Normally, I will not take over the deck, but I will take the conn if I consider it prudent to do so in certain situations.

e. When I take the conn from the OOD, I will do so in the manner specified above, unless emergency action is required. In the latter case, my issuing an order direct to the helmsman will constitute my assumption of responsibility for directing the ship's movement, i.e., I shall have taken the conn but not the deck. Furthermore, when I take the conn in this manner, I shall retain it until I turn it over formally to another officer.

f. I have authorized the executive officer and the senior watch officer to take the conn from the OOD if, in their opinion, such action is necessary and I am not available.

g. The only officers authorized to take the conn away from the OOD are the executive officer, the senior watch officer, and I.

2. Although "control" in the sense of positive recommendations may be passed to CIC or other operational stations under certain circumstances, "conn" in the accepted sense and the responsibility it entails never leave the bridge.

Reports to the captain

1. You are authorized to take immediate action when and how your best judgment dictates, without waiting for my arrival on the bridge. You are responsible for keeping me promptly and completely informed of any action you do take.

2. I am always on duty. When in doubt as to the navigational or tactical situation or any other matter affecting the ship or ship's company, *never hesitate to call me.* If I have to be awakened, make sure that I understand the reports that are made to me; do not hesitate to be forthright, positive, even in-

sistent. *You will never be reprimanded for awakening me.* When the circumstances dictate or when, in your opinion, the ship is standing into danger, call me to the bridge by the most expeditious means at hand, including passing the word on the 1MC "Captain to the bridge."

Remember:

Common sense and good judgment must always be exercised. You are responsible to me for the safety of the ship and her crew; a taut watch is the only watch that will ensure that safety. Forehandedness on your part will keep emergencies to a minimum; rehearsal in your mind of the steps to be taken in emergencies will enable you to cope with them when they do arise.

Supplementary watch procedures at anchor

1. A rated quartermaster or operations specialist, PQS qualified in visual piloting and assigned by the watch bill, will take bearings to navigational points designated by the navigator and plot them on the chart in the pilot house at least every fifteen minutes. See that the points are carefully and correctly noted in the bearing book, so that there cannot be any misidentification. The fix interval will be decreased to every ten minutes when the wind velocity exceeds 15 knots.

2. The OOD will personally take and plot bearings before he relieves the watch, and he and the CDO will spot-check them at least once per watch.

3. When two successive fixes plot outside of the drag circle previously laid down on the anchorage chart, the ship is dragging anchor. In all but the most unusual circumstances, this condition is very serious and requires that the special sea detail be stationed preparatory to getting underway to reposition the anchor.

4. Except when the commanding officer authorizes it to "steam auxiliary," in order to permit repairs, the engineering department is required to keep steam to the guarding valve.

5. The sea detail for each section must be drilled on its first duty day at anchor in each port.

Captain's night orders (Part I)

Ship .... Time Zone .... Date ....

En route from .... to ....

Operating with .... Area ....

OTC .... Flagship ....

Standard Tactical Data

Formation ....

Base Course ...... °T ...... ° pstgc Speed ...... Kts ...... RPM

Axix .... °T Guide .... Bears .... °T Dist .... Yds

Screen Data

Type of screen .... Screen axis .... Circle ....

No. stations .... No. ships .... Unassigned sta.'s ....

Screen cdr. .... Screen cdr. ship ....

Own ship station .... Patrolling station   Yes ( )   No ( )

Sta. ship .... Sta. ship .... Sta. ship .... Sta. ship

....

....

....

Own Ship Data

Engines on the line .... Generators on the line ....

Plant .... Ship darkened   Yes ( )   No ( )

Equipment casualties .... ETR .... ETR ....

....

....

....

Captain's night orders (Part II)

Weather Data

Sunrise .... Sunset .... Moonrise .... Moonset ....

Navigation and weather remarks ....

....

....

....

Night intentions ....

....

....

....

1. Carry out standing night orders. Check them over to refresh your memory.

2. Eternal vigilance is the price of safety.

3. Call me when in doubt and in any event at ....

Signature (Commanding Officer) ....

Signature .... Signature ....
            (Navigator)   (Executive Officer)

Watch	OOD	JOOD
20–24		
00–04		
04–08 *		

Watch remarks ....

....

....

....

* Return to captain by 0800

6. In addition to watch-relief procedures outlined previously in this book, a relieving officer of the deck must identify ranges ashore, e.g., two buildings, a tree and a building, a jetty and a signboard, against which radical movement of the ship can be detected from the quarterdeck.

7. An OOD must go to the forecastle to detect a dragging anchor, because it is only from there that shocks transmitted up the chain as the anchor alternately pulls out of the bottom and catches again, or bounces over rocks, can be felt.

8. Weather and weather forecasts must be monitored closely. The OOD must be able to recognize the impending passage of fronts and of thunderstorm activity. Consult sailing directions or the coast pilot for weather and climate in the area where the ship is anchored. When weather deteriorates and winds rise as shown below, take the relevant precautionary actions:

Wind 15 knots: Notify CO and CDO. Commence fixing ship's position every ten minutes.

Wind 20 knots: Notify CO and CDO. Post qualified anchor watch and be sure he has a means of communicating rapidly with the bridge. Post a watch officer on the bridge and assign an officer or chief petty officer as OOD. If on auxiliary get the main plant lighted off.

Wind 25 knots: Notify CO and CDO. Complete any action not yet completed for 20 knots.

Wind 30 knots: Notify CO and CDO. Complete any action not yet completed for 25 knots. Ship may begin to yaw with some vigor at this wind speed. Shift your watch to the bridge. Light off steering gear.

Wind 35 knots or more: Station the sea detail. Disengage jacking gear and begin spinning the engine with rudder over full to spoil the yaw. Be ready to get underway on a moment's notice. Check that the unshackling kit is on the forecastle.

If space permits, veer chain by walking it out to 100 fathoms or more.

Other considerations

1. Severe yawing, heaving of the ship due to swells, and heavy gusts of wind all put sudden loads on the anchor, the chain, and the forecastle equipment, and may precipitate dragging when the average wind speed is as low as 25 to 30 knots. Sudden changes of 60 degrees or more in wind direction tend to make an anchor "flip over," which reduces its holding capacity until it digs in again. Anchoring where there is a current with a crosswise wind may allow surprisingly heavy strains to be put on the anchor chain. The existence of any of these conditions may warrant precautionary action earlier than indicated in paragraph 8 above. If the wind velocity begins to increase rapidly, don't wait to see where it steadies out before taking action. I will not criticize bold action.

2. Do not forget to watch boating carefully and to consult coxswains about boat-handling conditions. You should consider restricting boating (limit trips, limit boat capacity, require life jackets, assign boat officers, etc.) when winds are above 20 knots, and canceling all but emergency trips when winds are above 30 knots. Obviously, the sea state is the controlling factor and boating might well be possible in a protected anchorage when wind velocities would make it impossible in an open area.

3. If it appears that some engineering problem will make it impossible for the ship to get underway, then it will be necessary to anchor securely and hope for the best.

4. If you have been forehanded, you will be ready for dragging when it occurs. If there is room to drag without fouling other ships or getting in shoal water, it may be prudent to allow the ship to drag. If, however, it appears to you to be wise to get underway and stand out, proceed to do so. It may be necessary to move in order to avoid ships that are blowing down on us. If you have time to do so, retrieve the anchor in

the usual fashion. If you have been blown into a tightly restricted area and the ship is not headed fair, you may want to leave the anchor at short stay to steady the bow as you get turned around. If you must get out fast, slip the chain and go, marking its position with a buoy if possible.

5. If you are taken by surprise by weather, collision, or freakish accident and find that you are adrift, the safety of the ship and crew will depend upon your action. Get engine power as soon as you can, but in the meantime drop the other anchor (if equipped with a second), tow the ship with boats, pass a line to an adjacent ship, or take any other step that will stop the ship or slow her drifting long enough to get the engines going. Don't forget to make use of the steering gear. Seek assistance from SOPA or OTC as quickly as possible.

6. The ship will be safe if you and your watch are alert. Dragging anchor can be easily handled if it is promptly detected. Supervise your watch closely enough to be certain they understand their duties and are performing reliably. Do not be reluctant to assign additional personnel, officer or enlisted, duty section or other, to any function that is not being performed adequately by the watch.

B | BEAUFORT SCALE

Beau-fort No.	Sea miles per hour (knots)	Seaman's description	Effect at sea
0	Less than 1	Calm	Sea like a mirror.
1	1–3	Light air	Ripples that look like fish scales are formed but without foam crests.
2	4–6	Light breeze	Small wavelets, short but pronounced; crests look glassy and do not break.
3	7–10	Gentle breeze	Large wavelets. Crests begin to break. Glassy-looking foam. Perhaps scattered white horses.
4	11–16	Moderate breeze	Small waves, becoming longer; fairly frequent white horses.
5	17–21	Fresh breeze	Moderate waves, taking a pronounced long form; many white horses. Chance of some spray.
6	22–27	Strong breeze	Large waves begin to form; extensive white foam crests everywhere. Probably some spray.
7	28–33	Moderate gale (high wind)	Sea heaps up and white foam from breaking waves begins to be blown in streaks along

Beaufort No.	Sea miles per hour (knots)	Seaman's description	Effect at sea
			the direction of the wind. Spindrift begins.
8	34–40	Fresh gale	Moderately high, long waves; edges of crests break into spindrift. Foam is blown in well-marked streaks along the direction of the wind.
9	41–47	Strong gale	High waves. Dense streaks of foam along the direction of the wind. Sea begins to roll. Spray may affect visibility.
10	48–55	Whole gale	Very high waves with long overhanging crests. The resulting foam in great patches is blown in dense white streaks along the direction of the wind. The surface of the sea looks white, and its rolling becomes heavy. Visibility is affected.
11	56–63	Storm	Waves so high that even medium-sized ships might be lost to view behind them for a long time. The sea is completely covered with long, white patches of foam lying along the direction of the wind. Everywhere the edges of the wave crests are blown into froth. Visibility seriously affected.
12 to 17	Above 64	Hurricane	The air is filled with foam and spray. Sea completely white with driving spray. Visibility very seriously affected.

C | MATERIAL CONDITIONS OF READINESS

The three standard conditions of material readiness that apply to U.S. Navy surface ships are the following:

XRAY Set only in secure harbors and naval facilities. All fittings marked XRAY (X) are closed at all times except when in use.

YOKE Normal peacetime in port and underway cruising condition. All fittings marked XRAY (X) and YOKE (Y) are closed at all times except when in use. When open, the fittings should be so logged in the D.C. closure log.

ZEBRA Set during peacetime emergency evolutions and wartime battle situations. All fittings marked XRAY (X), YOKE (Y), and ZEBRA (Z) are closed and may be opened only on receipt of permission from D.C. Central.

The following classifications of fittings are found on board U.S. Navy surface ships:

XRAY
X Closed at all times when not in use.

YOKE Fittings for which alternate ZEBRA accesses exist.
Y Normally closed when not in use, the only exception being when condition XRAY is set.

ZEBRA Normally open for operation of the ship, habitability, and access. Closed during battle or emergency evolutions and conditions.
Z

WILLIAM Ventilation and plumbing fittings normally open during all conditions of readiness.
W

CIRCLE
XRAY
(X)   Fittings that may be opened without special au-
CIRCLE   thority to allow the transfer of ammunition and
YOKE   the operation of vital systems.
(Y)
CIRCLE   May be opened during condition ZEBRA on au-
ZEBRA   thority of the commanding officer to allow the dis-
(Z)   tribution of food, access to sanitary facilities, or
                  ventilation of battle stations and other vital areas.
                  When open, must be guarded for immediate clo-
                  sure if necessary.
BLACK D   Closed for darkening ship at night.
ZEBRA
(Z)
CIRCLE   Nonvital ventilation and plumbing fittings nor-
WILLIAM   mally open during condition ZEBRA but may be
(W)   closed in the event of an NBC attack.

D | TYPICAL TIME SCHEDULE FOR GETTING UNDERWAY

Time	Event	Responsibility
48 to 6 hours	Verify schedule for lighting off boilers (steam ships)	Engineer officer/ EOOW
8 hours	Start gyros	Engineer/EOOW
2 hours	1. Ascertain from the executive officer the following: a. Any variation in standard time of setting special sea detail. b. Time of heaving in to short stay. c. Disposition of boats. d. Instructions concerning U.S. and guard mail. e. Number of passengers, if any, and expected time of arrival.	OOD or CDO
	2. After obtaining permission from the executive officer, start hoisting in boats and vehicles no longer required.	OOD or CDO
	3. After obtaining permission from the executive officer, rig in booms and accommodation ladders not in use and secure them for sea.	OOD or CDO

Time	Event	Responsibility
	4. Have the word passed giving the time the ship will get underway.	OOD or CDO
	5. Energize and check all CIC equipment.	CIC officer
	6. Conduct radio checks.	Communications officer
1 hour	1. Set material condition *YOKE* (material condition *ZEBRA* in low visibility).	Division officers
	2. Clear ship of visitors and make inspection for stowaways.	CMAA
45 minutes	1. Pass the word "All hands shift into uniform of the day."	OOD
	2. Muster crew on station.	Division officers
	3. "OC" and "R" divisions man after steering and pilot house; test steering engine, controls, communications, and emergency steering alarm.	Navigator
	4. Test engine-order telegraph and revolution indicator.	Engineer officer
	5. Test anchor windlass.	Engineer officer
	6. Test running lights.	Engineer officer
30 minutes	1. Pass the word "Station the special sea detail."	OOD
	2. Test fathometer and sonar equipment.	Navigator/ASW officer
	3. Adjust bridge PPI radarscope.	CIC officer
	4. Check navigation equipment on bridge. Check gyro repeaters against master gyro.	Navigator
	5. Test sound-powered communication circuits.	OOD

Time	Event	Responsibility
	6. Receive departmental reports of readiness to get underway, including material condition *YOKE/ZEBRA* set.	OOD
	7. Make report of inspection for stowaways.	CMAA
	8. Record fore and aft draft of ship.	DCA
	9. Direct engineering control to report when main engines are ready for testing. Upon receiving this report, obtain from the commanding officer permission to test main engines and direct engineering control accordingly. A qualified OOD must be on the bridge when engines are tested.	OOD
	10. Disconnect utility lines to pier and stow.	Engineer officer
	11. Pass the word "The officer of the deck is shifting his watch to the bridge."	OOD
	12. Light off gas turbine (if applicable).	
15 minutes	1. Report ready for getting underway to the executive officer, who will report to the commanding officer.	OOD
	2. If moored to a buoy, take in chain or wire, and ride to manila lines when ordered.	OOD
	3. When directed, test the ship's whistle.	OOD
	4. When directed, rig in brow.	First lieutenant

Time	Event	Responsibility
	5. As boats are hoisted or cleared away, rig in booms and davits.	First lieutenant
	6. Check ship for smart appearance.	OOD
	7. Obtain permission to get underway from SOPA or whoever is designated.	OOD
10 minutes	Pass the word "All hands not on watch, fall in at quarters for leaving port."	OOD
Immediately before getting underway	Warn engineering control to stand by to answer all bells.	OOD

E | TYPICAL TIME SCHEDULE FOR ENTERING PORT

Time	Event	Responsibility
Before entering restricted waters	1. Deballast as required.	Engineer officer
	2. Pump bilges when conditions permit (Oil Pollution Act of 1972).	Engineer officer
	3. Dump trash and garbage when conditions permit.	First lieutenant
1 hour	1. Ascertain time of anchoring (mooring) from the navigator, and notify engineer officer, weapons officer, first lieutenant, and engineering control.	OOD
	2. Pass the word "Make all preparations for entering port. Ship will anchor (moor _____ side to) at about _____."	OOD
	3. Ascertain time for quarters for entering port from the executive officer.	OOD
	4. Check smartness of ship for entering port.	OOD
	5. Obtain information concerning boating from executive officer, and inform the first lieutenant.	OOD
	6. Lay out mooring lines if they are required.	First lieutenant

Time	Event	Responsibility
	7. Prepare anchors for letting go.	First lieutenant
	8. Pass the word "All hands shift into the uniform of the day."	OOD
30 minutes	1. Blow tubes on all steaming boilers. Set material condition *YOKE* (material condition *ZEBRA* in restricted visibility).	OOD
	2. Station the special sea and anchor details.	OOD
	3. Obtain from the navigator information on depth of water at anchorage, and from the commanding officer what anchor and scope of chain are to be used, and inform the first lieutenant. When mooring to a pier, inform the first lieutenant as to range of tide and time of high water.	OOD
20 minutes	1. Complete setting of special sea detail.	OOD
	2. Recheck appearance of ship.	OOD
	3. Direct the chief master-at-arms to inspect upper decks to see that crew is in proper uniform.	OOD
	4. Swing lifeboat in or out as necessary.	First lieutenant
	5. Request permission to enter port from proper authority before anchoring or mooring.	OOD
	6. Pass the word "All hands to quarters for entering port."	OOD

Time	Event	Responsibility
15 minutes before mooring or anchoring	1. Station quarterdeck watch.	SWO
	2. Assemble on the quarterdeck the guard mail petty officer, mail clerk, movie operator, shore patrol, or other details leaving the ship in the first boat.	Oncoming OOD
	3. If mooring to a buoy, lower boat with buoy detail as directed.	First lieutenant
	4. Stand by to receive tugs if requested and if required in going alongside.	First lieutenant
Upon anchoring or mooring	1. Rig out boat booms and lower accommodation ladders.	First lieutenant
	2. Lower boat as directed.	First lieutenant
	3. Record draft of ship fore and aft.	DCA
	4. Secure main engines as directed by the commanding officer.	Engineer officer
	5. Secure the special sea detail. Set in-port watches.	OOD
	6. Secure gyros only if permission is obtained from the commanding officer.	Executive officer/navigator
	7. Pass the word "The officer of the deck is shifting his watch to the quarterdeck."	OOD

SUGGESTED READING AND REFERENCES

Department of the Navy

Allied Maritime Tactical Instructions and Procedures (ATP-1, Vol. I)

Allied Maritime Tactical Signal Book (ATP-1, Vol. II)

Bureau of Naval Personnel Manual

Flags, Pennants, and Customs (NTP-13)

Excellence in the Surface Navy (unpublished paper by CDR Greg G. Gullickson, USN, and LCDR Richard D. Chenette, USN, Dept. of Administrative Sciences, NPGS, Monterey, Ca., 1984)

Manual for Ship's Surface Weather Observations (NAVWEA-SERVCOMINST 3144.1)

Manual of the Judge Advocate General (JAGMAN)

National Search and Rescue Manual (NWP-37)

Naval Arctic Manual (ATP-17)

Naval Ships Technical Manual

Naval Terminology (NWP-3)

Navy Occupational Safety and Health Program (NAVOSH) (*OpNavInst* 5100.23)

Navy Safety Precautions for Forces Afloat (*OpNavInst* 5100.9A)

Replenishment at Sea (ATP-16)

Replenishment at Sea (NWP-14)

Shipboard Damage Control (NWP-50-3)

Shipboard Helicopter Operating Procedures (NWP-42)

Standard Organization and Regulation of the U.S. Navy (*OpNavInst* 3120.32)

Tactical Action Officer's Handbook (NWP-12-5)
Uniform Code of Military Justice (UCMJ)
U.S. Navy Regulations
U.S. Navy Shore Patrol Manual

Coast Guard

Navigation Rules, International-Inland (CG-169)
Rules of the Road, Great Lakes (CG-172)
Rules of the Road, Western Rivers (CG-184)

Other

The Boat Officer's Handbook, Lt. David D. Winters, USN. Annapolis: Naval Institute Press, 1981.

Knight's Modern Seamanship, 16th ed., Capt. John V. Noel, Jr., USN (Ret.). New York: Van Nostrand Reinhold Company, 1977.

Naval Shiphandling, 4th ed., Capt. R. S. Crenshaw, Jr., USN (Ret.). Annapolis: Naval Institute Press, 1975.

INDEX

Absentee pennant, 232
Absentees, log entry for, 42
Acceleration, 100
Accountability, 4–5
Aircraft carriers: flight operations, 82; OOD in, 82–83; right of way of, 103–4
Air operations, log entries for, 31
Alarms, 24, 112
Ammunition: log entry for expenditures, 34; log entry for loading of, 32; safe handling of, 173–75
Anchorage and moorings, 159
Anchorage, log entry for bearings, 30
Anchors: dragging, 160–61; scope of chain, 159–60
Anderson turn, 114
Apprehension, 166–67
Arrest, 167–68
Asylum, 168–70
Authority of OOD, 4
Auxiliary power units, 144

Battle-efficiency pennant, 236
Beaufort Scale, 253–54
Bell book, engineer's, 27–28
Bilges, 177–78
Binoculars, care of, 94
Boat gongs, 60–61
Boat hails: day, 237; night, 235–36
Boats: appearance, 207–8; at sea, 204–5; boat gongs, 208; bow and flag staff insignia, 229; capacity, 208; crews, 209; equipment, 209;

flags or pennants, 225, 231; fueling, 176; in port, 206–7; inspections, 209; lights, 176; loading of, 175; orders to coxswain, 210; as responsibility of OOD, 176; safety, 175–76, 210; schedules, 210–11; security, 211
Boatswain's mate of the watch, 19, 22, 74, 205
Bolos, 190–91
Bow thrusters, 145
Broad command pennants, 228–29
Burgee command pennants, 228–29

Captain's night orders, sample entries, 248–49
Cargo, safe handling of, 177
Casualties: log entries for personnel, 43; material, 93
Ceremonies. See Honors and Ceremonies
Church pennant, 233–34
Civil officials, passing honors for, 234
"Close aboard" defined, 217
Closed compartments, safety in, 177–78
Close station-keeping, 104–8
Cold-iron watch, 154
Collisions: frequent causes and safeguards against, 122–24
Colors, morning and evening, 216
Combat information center (CIC), 8, 15, 68–69, 79–81
Command duty officer (CDO), 9, 146–48

Commanding officer: assumption of conn, 77–79; navigation responsibilities, 121; reports to, 95–96
Commands: manner of giving, 132–34; auxiliary power units, 144; bow thrusters, 145; to engine-order telegraph, 138–40; to helmsman, 134–40; to line-handlers, 140–42; to tugs, 142–44
Communications: external, 61–65; internal, 48–61; record, 65; visual, 64–65; use of boat gongs, 60–61; MC circuits, 49–59; ships' alarms, 60; sound-powered telephone, 59; voice, 62–64
Compressed gases, safety in handling of, 178–79
Conditions of readiness for storms, 90–92
Conduct on watch, 22–23
Confinement, 167
Conn: OOD's responsibility for, 77–79; sample orders concerning, 245–46
Courts and boards, log entry for, 42–43
Crew's mess, 164–65

Damage: log entry for, 32–33; control of, 92–93
Dangerous materials, 194–95
Darkness, adaptation to, 69–71
Dead-reckoning, 126–27
Death, log entry for, 43
Deceleration, 100
Deck-log entries: abbreviations, 29; accuracy, 26–27; erasures, 27–28; format, 26; general, 26–28; official record, 26; samples, 29–47
Definitions of terms used in shiphandling, 97–98
Delayed turns, 107
Desertion, log entry for, 43
Detachment of personnel, 170–71
Divers, precautions for, 179–80
Dragging anchor, 160–61

Dressing ship, 235
Drills and exercises, log entries for, 33–34
Dry-docking, log entry for, 38–39
Duty officer, staff, 23

Eight o'clock reports, 165
Electrical and electronic equipment, safe handling of, 181–83
Emergency procedures, familiarity with, 244
Engineering log, 27–28
Engineering officer of the watch (EOOW), 7, 15
Engineer's bell book, 27–28
Enlisted men: performance of duty, 5–6; relations with, 12; training, 80–81
Enlisted watch-standers: duties of boatswain's mate of the watch, 19, 22, 74, 205; bridge talker, 79–81; bridge watch, 69–70; cold-iron watch, 154; coxswains, 175–76; engine-order telegraph operator, 79–81; helmsman, 74; line-handlers, 140–42; lookouts, 129–30; master-at-arms, 153; messenger of the watch, 152; petty officer of the watch, 152–53; quartermaster of the watch, 9, 75; sounding and security patrol, 153; telephone talkers, 79–81, 129–30
Entering port, sample time schedule, 261–63
Executive officer (XO), 12, 165, 168
Explosions, prevention of, 183
External communications, 61–65
External security, 154–57

Fire prevention, 183
Fire watch, 188
Fire work, 188
Flag lieutenant, 23
Flags and pennants: absence indicators, 232; battle-efficiency pennants, 236; boat hails, 235–37; in

boats and automobiles, 225, 231; broad and burgee pennants, 228–29; church pennant, 233–34; for civil officials in boats, 234; display rules, 223–24; dressing ship, 235; foreign ensigns, 227; during gun salutes, 225; half-masting, 226, 231; homeward-bound pennant, 234; intention to depart, 232–33; meal pennant, 234; miscellaneous flags, 232–35; national ensign, 225–26; personal, 229–31; POW/MIA flag, 235; PUC, NUC, and MUC pennants, 235; special flag hoists, 235; substitute pennants, 233; union jack for general court-martial, 234; UN flag, 227–28; for UN and NATO officials, 232

Flight operations from aircraft carriers, 82

Fog: navigation in, 128–29; safety in, 128–29

Formations, 102–8

Fueling at sea, 89–90

Fueling, log entry for, 35–36, 117–19

Fuel oil, 184–88

Gasoline, safety in handling, 201

General announcing system, 20–21

Getting underway, time schedule for, 257–60

Groundings, 124–25

Gun salute, 215–16, 225

Gyro compasses, 125

Half-masting, 226, 231

Hazardous identification system, 187

Hazardous material, precautions for, 185

Heavy weather, 90–92, 161, 185

Helicopters: log entries for, 32; operations, 83–84; emergencies, 86; readiness, 85–86; safe handling of, 185–86; shipboard procedures, 84–85

Helmsman, steering commands to, 134–40

Honors. *See* Salutes and Honors

Honors and ceremonies: 213; colors, morning and evening, 216; crew at quarters, 221; gun salutes, 215–16; inspections, 222; national anthems and ensigns, 216–17; official visits, 215, 218–20; "passing honors" and "close aboard" defined, 217; passing honors prescribed, 217–21; quarterdeck, 214; salutes to national ensign, 217; salutes to ships and stations, 217; side boys, 214–15, 222; side honors, 222

Hot work, precautions for, 188

Hurricanes, 90–92, 161–62

Injuries, log entries for, 43–44

In port: liberty, 163–64; reporting and detachment of personnel, 170–71; stores and fuel, 162–63

Inspections: of boats, 209; of liberty parties, 163–64; log entries for, 37; honors for inspection party, 222

Internal communications, 48–61

Internal security, 157

Junior officer of the deck (JOOD), 76–77

Keys, custody of, 158–59

Knowing the ship, 24–25

Leadership, 12, 18–19

Leave, log entry for, 45

Letters of instruction (LOI), 14

Liberty: organization, 163; inspection of parties, 163–64; loading boats for, 164

Life jackets, 189

Lifelines, use of, 189

Lights, 190
Line-handlers, commands to, 140–42
Lines of bearing, 108–9
Lines and rigging, 190
Lines, synthetic, 197
Line-throwing gun, 190–91
Logs, general, 26–28
Lookouts, 129–30
Low visibility, 128–29

Machinery, 191–92
Magnetic compass record book, 27
Maneuvering board, 102–3
Maneuvers, log entries for, 29
Man overboard: 112–17; alarm, 112; Anderson turn, 114; helicopter recovery, 112–13; in formation, 103–4; racetrack turn, 115; Williamson turn, 113–14; Y-backing turn, 115
Master-at-arms, 153
Material casualties, 93
Material conditions of readiness, 255–56
MC circuits: control of, 20–21; purposes of, 49–59
Mean pennant, 234
"Meat ball," 234
Merchant ships, communications with, 64–65
Mess, crew's, 164–65
Messenger of the watch, 152
Midwatch, log entry, 29–30
Moorings, 159

National anthems, 216
National ensigns: dipping, 225–26; display from boats, 225; during gun salutes, 225; following motions of SOP, 226
Navigation: checking the gyro, 125; collisions, 122–24; course and speed changes, 128; dead-reckoning plot, 126–27; emergency actions, 123–24; in fog and low visibility, 128–29; groundings, 124–25; log entries, 37–41; lookouts, 129; by radar, 125–26; safety in, 241–42
Navigator: responsibilities for log, 28; and OOD, 127–28
Night-order book, 71
Night rations, 165
Night vision, 69–71
Nimitz, Chester W., quoted, 130–31
Nuclear weapon security, 173–74

Observers, 171
Officer in tactical command (OTC), 16, 34–35
Officer of the deck (OOD): accountability, 4–5; in an aircraft carrier, 82–83; boats, responsibility for, 176; characteristics of, 10–12; command relationships, 6–10; conning the ship, 77–79; deck log, responsibility for, 26–29; duties in port, 146–71; in a flagship, 23; navigational information, 127–28; organizing the watch, 74–79; preparation, 13–15, 149–50; priorities, 5–6; readiness information, 73; relations with CIC, 68–69; relations with navigator, 9; relations with TAO, 8–9; relieving the watch, 15–17; representative of the captain, 3; responsibility and authority, 3–4; security, 154–59; in a submarine, 86–88; tactical information, 72–73; training of watch, 3
Official inspections, honors at, 222
Official visits, 215, 218–20
Oil and waste discharge, 94–95

Painting, precautions for, 192
Passengers, log entry for, 44
Passing honors: between ships, 217–18; defined, 217; dispensing with, 221; sequence in rendering, 221; to those embarked in ships and boats, 219–30
Passing the word, 20–21

Patients, log entry for, 44
Pennants. *See* Flags and pennants
Personnel, protection of, 192–93
Personnel transfers, 193
Petty officer of the watch (POOW), 152–53
Pilots, 119–20
Piping the side, 215
Plan of the day, 19–20
Pollution control, 94–95
Power tools, 197–98
PQS, 18
Preparation to relieve watch, 13–15
Psychological factors, 130–31

Quarterdeck, appearance of, 214
Quartermaster of the watch (QMOW), 9, 75
Quartermaster's notebook, 27

Racetrack turn, 113, 115
Radar: in fog and low visibility, 128–29; navigation by, 125–26
Radiation, protection from, 193–94
Range to the guide, 111
Rations, 164–65
Readiness information, 73
Readiness, material conditions of, 255–56
Receiving guests, 171
Refuse disposal, 94–95
Relations between OOD and staff, 6–10, 23
Relieving the watch: adaptation to darkness, 69–71; declining to relieve, 17; sample standing orders, 241; tactical information and readiness, 250; turnover period, 15–17, 23, 69–73
Replenishment at sea, 89–90; log entry for, 35–36, 117–19
Reporting of new personnel, 170–71
Reports to commanding officer, 95–96, 246–47
Restraint, 167
Restriction, 168
Routine, daily, 19–20

Sabotage, 156–57
Safe navigation: 121–31; in sample orders, 241–43
Safety devices; 194
Safety precautions: ammunition, 173–75; boats, 175–76; cargo, 177; closed compartments, 177–78; compressed gases, 178–79; divers, 179–80; electrical and electronic equipment, 181–83; fire and explosion prevention, 183; fuel oil, 184–85; hazardous material, 185; heavy weather, 185; helicopter operations, 185–86; helm safety officer, 188; hot work, 188; life jackets, 189; lifelines, 189; lights, 190; lines and rigging, 190; line-throwing gun, 190–91; machinery, 191–92; painting, 192; personnel protection, 192–93; personnel transfers, 193; radiation, 193–94; safety devices, 194; semisafe and dangerous materials, 194–95; shoes, 195; sleeping topside, 195; small arms, 195; smoking, 196; special equipment, 196–97; synthetic lines, 197; tagging, 197; tools, 197–98; toxic materials, 198; underway replenishment, 199–200; volatile fuels, 201; working aloft, 202; working over the side, 202–3
Salutes and honors, 219–20
Saluting ships and stations, 217
Sample deck-log entries: air operations, 31; ceremonies and official visits, 36; damage, 32–33; drills and exercises, 33–34; environmental conditions, 47; formations, 34–35; fueling, 35–36; inspections, 37; loading and transferring operations, 32; midwatch, 29; navigation, 37–41; personnel, 41–45; ship's movements, 45; ship's operational control, 46–47
Sample orders: captain's night orders, 248–49; the conn, 245–46;

Sample orders (*continued*) emergency procedures, 244; relieving the watch, 241, 250; reports to the captain, 246–47; safe navigation, 241–43; tactical matters, 243–44; watch performance, 244–45; watch procedures at anchor, 247–52

Search and rescue, 88

Security: external, 154–57; internal, 157–59; patrols, 153; sabotage, 156–57; sentries and guards, 156; shipyard inspections, 157; sneak attack, 156–57

Semisafe and dangerous materials, precautions for, 194–95

Sentries and guards, 156

Shiphandling: acceleration and deceleration, 100; backing power, 100; change of course, 106–8; definitions, 97–98; formations, 102–3; formations with aircraft carriers, 103–4; formations, station-keeping, 109–10; general principles, 98; guide ship, 105–6; line of bearing, 108–9; man overboard, 112–17; pilots, 119–20; range to guide, 111; replenishment at sea, 117–19; screening, 110–11; shallow water, 99; stadimeter, 104; station-keeping, 104–6; time lag, 99; turbulence or "kick," 104; turning, 100–1; effect of wind and speed on turns, 98–99

Ship's deck log, 26–47

Ship's regulations, 7

Ship's watch organization, 11–13

Ship's *Weather Observation Sheet*, 27

Shipyard security, 157–58

Shoes, safe, 195

Side boys, 61, 214–15, 222

Signals, hand and whistle, 143–44

Sleeping topside, supervision of, 195

Small arms, 195

Smoking, prohibitions against, 196

Sounding-and-security patrol, 153

Staff duty officer, 23

Staff, OOD's relationship with, 6–10, 23

Standard commands, 132–45

Standard Ship's Organization and Regulations Manual (SORM), 13–14, 21

Standing orders: 14–15; sample, 241–52

Station-keeping, 104–6

Stores and fuel, in port, 162–63

Submarine operations, 86–88

Substitute pennants, 233

Surface warfare personnel qualifications standards (PQS), 18

Synthetic lines, precautions in using, 197

Tactical action officer (TAO), 8–9, 14, 68

Tactical information, 72–73

Tactical matters, in sample orders, 243–44

Tagging, 197

Technical knowledge needed by OOD, 12, 24–25

Telephone circuits, 48–49

Temporary additional duty (TAD), log entry for, 44

Temporary refuge, 168–70

Tides, log entries for, 40

Time schedules: for entering port, 261–63; for getting underway, 257–60

Time zones, log entries for, 40

Tools, care in use of, 197–98

Toxic materials, safety precautions for, 198

Training on watch, 80–81

Turning over the watch, 23–24

Turns, effects of wind and speed on, 97

Typhoons, 90–92, 161–62

Underway, log entry for, 29

Underway replenishment, 199–200

Union jack for general court-martial (GCM), 234
United Nations flag, 227–28

Vehicles, ships', 211–12
Vigilance, 10–11
Visitors: control of, 154–55; hospitality, 171
Visits, official, 215, 218–20
Visual communications, 64–65
Voice telephone procedures, 62–64
Voids, 177–78
Volatile fuels, precautions for, 201

Waste discharge, 94–95
Watch: general, 13; appearance of, 22, 150–51; cold-iron, 154; conduct on, 22–23; declining to assume, 17; leadership responsibilities, 18–19; organization of, 74–76, 151–54; passing the word, 20–21; preparation, 13–15; relieving, 15–17, 23, 69–73; routine, 19
Watch organization, in port, 151–54

Watch performance, in sample orders, 244–45
Watch procedure, at anchor, in sample orders, 247–52
Watch underway: 66–96; CIC, 67–68, 79–81; damage-control settings, 92–93; heavy weather, 90–92; pollution control, 94–95; preparation for, 66–67; refuse disposal, 94–95; relieving, 73–74; replenishment at sea, 89–90
Weather: fog and low visibility, 128–29; hurricanes and typhoons, 90–92, 161–62; log entries for, 47; *Weather Observation Sheet*, 27
Welding, 188
Wheeling, 106–7
Whistle signals, 143
Williamson turn, 113–14
Wind: in port, 161; sail area, 98
Working aloft, precautions for, 202
Working over the side, precautions for, 202–3
Working parties, handling of, 166

Y-backing turn, 113, 115

The Naval Institute Press is the book-publishing arm of the U.S. Naval Institute, a private, nonprofit professional society for members of the sea services and civilians who share an interest in naval and maritime affairs. Established in 1873 at the U.S. Naval Academy in Annapolis, Maryland, where its offices remain today, the Naval Institute has more than 100,000 members worldwide.

Members of the Naval Institute receive the influential monthly naval magazine *Proceedings* and substantial discounts on fine nautical prints, ship and aircraft photos, and subscriptions to the Institute's recently inaugurated quarterly, *Naval History*. They also have access to the transcripts of the Institute's Oral History Program and may attend any of the Institute-sponsored seminars regularly offered around the country.

The book-publishing program, begun in 1898 with basic guides to naval practices, has broadened its scope in recent years to include books of more general interest. Now the Naval Institute Press publishes more than forty new titles each year, ranging from how-to books on boating and navigation to battle histories, biographies, ship guides, and novels. Institute members receive discounts on the Press's more than 300 books.

For a free catalog describing books currently available and for further information about U.S. Naval Institute membership, please write to:

Membership Department
U.S. Naval Institute
Annapolis, Maryland 21402

or call, toll-free, 800-233-USNI.